Alfred Noyes -

COLLECTED POEMS

BY
ALFRED NOYES

VOLUME ONE

NEW YORK
FREDERICK A. STOKES COMPANY
PUBLISHERS

CONTENTS

	Page
The Loom of Years	1
In the Heart of the Woods	2
Art	5
Triolet	8
A Triple Ballad of Old Japan	8
The Symbolist	10
Haunted in Old Japan	11
Necromancy	12
The Mystic	15
The Flower of Old Japan	17
Apes and Ivory	48
A Song of Sherwood	49
The World's May-Queen	50
Pirates	53
A Song of England	55
The Old Sceptic	57
The Death of Chopin	59
Song	62
Butterflies	62
Song of the Wooden-Legged Fiddler	66
The Fisher-Girl	67
A Song of Two Burdens	71
Earth-Bound	72
Art, The Herald	74
The Optimist	74
A Post-Impression	76
The Barrel-Organ	80
The Litany of War	85
The Origin of Life	86
The Last Battle	88
The Paradox	89

PAGE

THE PROGRESS OF LOVE 94
THE FOREST OF WILD THYME 123
FORTY SINGING SEAMEN 171
THE EMPIRE BUILDERS 175
NELSON'S YEAR 177
IN TIME OF WAR 180
ODE FOR THE SEVENTIETH BIRTHDAY OF SWINBURNE . . 186
IN CLOAK OF GREY 188
A RIDE FOR THE QUEEN 189
SONG 191
THE HIGHWAYMAN 192
THE HAUNTED PALACE 196
THE SCULPTOR 200
SUMMER 201
AT DAWN 204
THE SWIMMER'S RACE 206
THE VENUS OF MILO 208
THE NET OF VULCAN 209
NIOBE 209
ORPHEUS AND EURYDICE 211
FROM THE SHORE 220
THE RETURN 222
REMEMBRANCE 223
A PRAYER 224
LOVE'S GHOST 224
ON A RAILWAY PLATFORM 225
OXFORD REVISITED 226
THE THREE SHIPS 228
SLUMBER-SONGS OF THE MADONNA 230
ENCELADUS 235
IN THE COOL OF THE EVENING 241
A ROUNDHEAD'S RALLYING SONG 242
VICISTI, GALILÆE 243
DRAKE 246

COLLECTED POEMS

EARLY POEMS

DEDICATED TO THE MEMORY OF JAMES PAYN

THE LOOM OF YEARS

In the light of the silent stars that shine on the struggling sea,
In the weary cry of the wind and the whisper of flower and
      tree,
Under the breath of laughter, deep in the tide of tears,
I hear the Loom of the Weaver that weaves the Web of Years.

The leaves of the winter wither and sink in the forest mould
To colour the flowers of April with purple and white and gold:
Light and scent and music die and are born again
In the heart of a grey-haired woman who wakes in a world
      of pain.

The hound, the fawn and the hawk, and the doves that croon
      and coo,
We are all one woof of the weaving and the one warp threads
      us through,
One flying cloud on the shuttle that carries our hopes and fears
As it goes thro' the Loom of the Weaver that weaves the Web
      of Years.

The crosiers of the fern, and the crown, the crown of the
      rose,
Pass with our hearts to the Silence where the wings of music
      close,
Pass and pass to the Timeless that never a moment mars,
Pass and pass to the Darkness that made the suns and stars.

Has the soul gone out in the Darkness? Is the dust sealed
        from sight?
Ah, hush, for the woof of the ages returns thro' the warp of
        the night!
Never that shuttle loses one thread of our hopes and fears,
As it comes thro' the Loom of the Weaver that weaves the
        Web of Years.

O, woven in one wide Loom thro' the throbbing weft of the
        whole,
One in spirit and flesh, one in body and soul,
The leaf on the winds of autumn, the bird in its hour to
        die,
The heart in its muffled anguish, the sea in its mournful cry,

One with the flower of a day, one with the withered moon,
One with the granite mountains that melt into the noon,
One with the dream that triumphs beyond the light of the
        spheres,
We come from the Loom of the Weaver that weaves the
        Web of Years.

IN THE HEART OF THE WOODS

I

THE Heart of the woods, I hear it, beating, beating afar,
In the glamour and gloom of the night, in the light of the
        rosy star,
In the cold sweet voice of the bird, in the throb of the flower-
        soft sea! . . .
For the Heart of the woods is the Heart of the world and the
        Heart of Eternity,
Ay, and the burning passionate Heart of the heart in you
        and me.

Love of my heart, love of the world, linking the golden moon
With the flowery moths that flutter thro' the scented leaves of
        June,

And the mind of man with beauty, and youth with the dreaming night
Of stars and flowers and waters and breasts of glimmering
  white,
And streaming hair of fragrant dusk and flying limbs of lovely
  light;

Life of me, life of me, shining in sun and cloud and wind,
In the dark eyes of the fawn and the eyes of the hound behind,
In the leaves that lie in the seed unsown, and the dream
  of the babe unborn,
O, flaming tides of my blood, as you flow thro' flower and
  root and thorn,
I feel you burning the boughs of night to kindle the fires of
  morn.

Soul of me, soul of me, yearning wherever a lavrock sings,
Or the crimson gloom is winnowed by the whirr of wood-
  doves' wings,
Or the spray of the foam-bow rustles in the white dawn of
  the moon,
And mournful billows moan aloud, *Come soon, soon, soon,
Come soon, O Death with the Heart of love and the secret of the
  rune.*

Heart of me, heart of me, heart of me, beating, beating afar,
In the green gloom of the night, in the light of the rosy star,
In the cold sweet voice of the bird, in the throb of the flower-
  soft sea! . . .
O, the Heart of the woods is the Heart of the world and the
  Heart of Eternity,
Ay, and the burning passionate Heart of the heart in you and
  me.

II

O, Death will never find us in the heart of the wood,
  The song is in my blood, night and day:
We will pluck a scented petal from the Rose upon the Rood
  Where Love lies bleeding on the way.

We will listen to the linnet and watch the waters leap,
  When the clouds go dreaming by,
And under the wild roses and the stars we will sleep,
  And wander on together, you and I.

We shall understand the mystery that none has understood,
  We shall know why the leafy gloom is green.
O, Death will never find us in the heart of the wood
  When we see what the stars have seen!
We have heard the hidden song of the soft dews falling
  At the end of the last dark sky,
Where all the sorrows of the world are calling,
  We must wander on together, you and I.

They are calling, calling, *Away, come away!*
  And we know not whence they call;
For the song is in our hearts, we hear it night and day,
  As the deep tides rise and fall:
O, Death will never find us in the heart of the wood,
  While the hours and the years roll by!
We have heard it, we have heard it, but we have not understood,
      derstood,
  We must wander on together, you and I.

The wind may beat upon us, the rain may blind our eyes,
  The leaves may fall beneath the winter's wing;
But we shall hear the music of the dream that never dies,
  And we shall know the secret of the Spring.
We shall know how all the blossoms of evil and of good
  Are mingled in the meadows of the sky;
And then—if Death can find us in the heart of the wood—
  We shall wander on together, you and I.

ART

(IMITATED FROM DE BANVILLE AND GAUTIER)

I

Yes! Beauty still rebels!
Our dreams like clouds disperse:
      She dwells
In agate, marble, verse.

No false constraint be thine!
But, for right walking, choose
      The fine,
The strict cothurnus, Muse.

Vainly ye seek to escape
The toil!   The yielding phrase
      Ye shape
Is clay, not chrysoprase.

And all in vain ye scorn
That seeming ease which ne'er
      Was born
Of aught but love and care.

Take up the sculptor's tool!
Recall the gods that die
      To rule
In Parian o'er the sky.

For Beauty still rebels!
Our dreams like clouds disperse:
      She dwells
In agate, marble, verse.

II

When Beauty from the sea,
With breasts of whiter rose
      Than we
Behold on earth, arose.

Naked thro' Time returned
The Bliss of Heaven that day,
     And burned
The dross of earth away.

Kings at her splendour quailed.
For all his triple steel
     She haled
War at her chariot-wheel.

The rose and lily bowed
To cast, of odour sweet
     A cloud
Before her wandering feet.

And from her radiant eyes
There shone on soul and sense
     The skies'
Divine indifference.

O, mortal memory fond!
Slowly she passed away
     Beyond
The curling clouds of day.

Return, we cry, *return*,
Till in the sadder light
     We learn
That she was infinite.

The Dream that from the sea
With breasts of whiter rose
     Than we
Behold on earth, arose.

III

Take up the sculptor's tool!
Recall the dreams that die
     To rule
In Parian o'er the sky;

And kings that not endure
In bronze to re-ascend
      Secure
Until the world shall end.

Poet, let passion sleep
Till with the cosmic rhyme
      You keep
Eternal tone and time,

By rule of hour and flower,
By strength of stern restraint
      And power
To fail and not to faint.

The task is hard to learn
While all the songs of Spring
      Return
Along the blood and sing.

Yet hear—from her deep skies,
How Art, for all your pain,
      Still cries
Ye must be born again!

Reject the wreath of rose,
Take up the crown of thorn
      That shows
To-night a child is born.

The far immortal face
In chosen onyx fine
      Enchase,
Delicate line by line.

Strive with Carrara, fight
With Parian, till there steal
      To light
Apollo's pure profile.

Set the great lucid form
Free from its marble tomb
    To storm
The heights of death and doom.

Take up the sculptor's tool!
Recall the gods that die
    To rule
In Parian o'er the sky.

TRIOLET

LOVE, awake!   Ah, let thine eyes
  Open, clouded with thy dreams.
Now the shy sweet rosy skies,
  Love, awake.   Ah, let thine eyes
Dawn before the last star dies.
  O'er thy breast the rose-light gleams:
Love, awake!   Ah, let thine eyes
  Open, clouded with thy dreams.

A TRIPLE BALLAD OF OLD JAPAN

IN old Japan, by creek and bay,
  The blue plum-blossoms blow,
Where birds with sea-blue plumage gay
  Thro' sea-blue branches go:
Dragons are coiling down below
  Like dragons on a fan;
And pig-tailed sailors lurching slow
  Thro' streets of old Japan.

There, in the dim blue death of day
  Where white tea-roses grow,
Petals and scents are strewn astray
  Till night be sweet enow,
Then lovers wander whispering low
  As lovers only can,
Where rosy paper lanterns glow
  Thro' streets of old Japan.

From Wonderland to Yea-or-Nay
 The junks of Weal-and-Woe
Dream on the purple water-way
 Nor ever meet a foe;
Though still, with stiff mustachio
 And crookéd ataghan,
Their pirates guard with pomp and show
 The ships of old Japan.

That land is very far away,
 We lost it long ago!
No fairies ride the cherry spray,
 No witches mop and mow,
The violet wells have ceased to flow;
 And O, how faint and wan
The dawn on Fusiyama's snow,
 The peak of old Japan.

Half smilingly our hearts delay,
 Half mournfully forego
The blue fantastic twisted day
 When faithful Konojo,
For small white Lily Hasu-ko
 Knelt in the Butsudan,
And her tomb opened to bestrow
 Lilies thro' old Japan.

There was a game they used to play
 I' the San-ju-san-jen Dō,
They filled a little lacquer tray
 With powders in a row,
Dry dust of flowers from Tashiro
 To Mount Daimugenzan,
Dry little heaps of dust, but O
 They breathed of old Japan.

Then knights in blue and gold array
 Would on their thumbs bestow
A pinch from every heap and say,
 With many a *hum* and *ho*,

What blossoms, nodding to and fro
    For joy of maid or man,
Conceived the scents that puzzled so
    The brains of old Japan.

The hundred ghosts have ceased to affray
    The dust of Kyotó,
Ah yet, what phantom blooms a-sway
    Murmur, a-loft, a-low,
In dells no scythe of death can mow,
    No power of reason scan,
O, what Samúrai singers know
    The Flower of old Japan?

Dry dust of blossoms, dim and gray,
    Lost on the wind?   Ah, no,
Hark, from yon clump of English may,
    A cherub's mocking crow,
A sudden twang, a sweet, swift throe,
    As Daisy trips by Dan,
And careless Cupid drops his bow
    And laughs—from old Japan.

There, in the dim blue death of day
    Where white tea-roses grow,
Petals and scents are strewn astray
    Till night be sweet enow,
Then lovers wander, whispering low,
    As lovers only can,
Where rosy paper lanterns glow
    Thro' streets of old Japan.

THE SYMBOLIST

HELP me to seek that unknown land!
    I kneel before the shrine.
Help me to feel the hidden hand
    That ever holdeth mine.

I kneel before the Word, I kneel
　　Before the Cross of flame
I cry, as thro' the gloom I steal,
　　The glory of the Name.

Help me to mourn, and I shall love;
　　What grief is like to mine?
Crown me with thorn, the stars above
　　Shall in the circlet shine!

The Temple opens wide: none sees
　　The love, the dream, the light!
O, blind and finite, are not these
　　Blinding and infinite?

The veil, the veil is rent: the skies
　　Are white with wings of fire,
Where victim souls triumphant rise
　　In torment of desire.

Help me to seek: I would not find,
　　For when I find I know
I shall have clasped the hollow wind
　　And built a house of snow.

HAUNTED IN OLD JAPAN

Music of the star-shine shimmering o'er the sea
Mirror me no longer in the dusk of memory:
Dim and white the rose-leaves drift along the shore.
Wind among the roses, blow no more!

All along the purple creek, lit with silver foam,
Silent, silent voices, cry no more of home!
Soft beyond the cherry-trees, o'er the dim lagoon,
Dawns the crimson lantern of the large low moon.

We that loved in April, we that turned away
Laughing ere the wood-dove crooned across the May,
Watch the withered rose-leaves drift along the shore.
Wind among the roses, blow no more!

We the Sons of Reason, we that chose to bride
Knowledge, and rejected the Dream that we denied,
We that chose the Wisdom that triumphs for an hour,
We that let the young love perish like a flower. . . .

We that hurt the kind heart, we that went astray,
We that in the darkness idly dreamed of day. . . .
. . . Ah! The dreary rose-leaves drift along the shore.
Wind among the roses, blow no more!

Lonely starry faces, wonderful and white,
Yearning with a cry across the dim sweet night,
All our dreams are blown a-drift as flowers before a fan,
All our hearts are haunted in the heart of old Japan.

Haunted, haunted, haunted—we that mocked and sinned
Hear the vanished voices wailing down the wind,
Watch the ruined rose-leaves drift along the shore.
Wind among the roses, blow no more!

All along the purple creek, lit with silver foam,
Sobbing, sobbing voices, cry no more of home!
Soft beyond the cherry-trees, o'er the dim lagoon,
Dawns the crimson lantern of the large low moon.

NECROMANCY

(AFTER THE PROSE OF BAUDELAIRE)

THIS necromantic palace, dim and rich,
    Dim as a dream, rich as a reverie,
I knew it all of old, surely I knew
This floating twilight tinged with rose and blue,
    This moon-soft carven niche
Whence the calm marble, wan as memory,
Slopes to the wine-brimmed bath of cold dark fire
Perfumed with old regret and dead desire.

There the soul, slumbering in the purple waves
  Of indolence, dreams of the phantom years,
Dreams of the wild sweet flower of red young lips
Meeting and murmuring in the dark eclipse
      Of joy, where pain still craves
  One tear of love to mingle with their tears,
One passionate welcome ere the wild farewell,
One flash of heaven across the fires of hell.

.   .   .   .

Queen of my dreams, queen of my pitiless dreams,
  Dim idol, moulded of the wild white rose,
Coiled like a panther in that silken gloom
Of scented cushions, where the rich hushed room
      Breaks into soft warm gleams,
As from her slumbrous clouds Queen Venus glows,
Slowly thine arms up-lift to me, thine eyes
Meet mine, without communion or surmise.

Here, at thy feet, I watched, I watched all day
  Night floating in thine eyes, then with my hands
Covered my face from that dumb cry of pain:
And when at last I dared to look again
      My heart was far away,
Wrapt in the fragrant gloom of Eastern lands,
Under the flower-white stars of tropic skies
Where soft black floating flowers turned to . . . thine
      eyes.

I breathe, I breathe the perfume of thine hair:
  Bury in thy deep hair my fevered face,
Till as to men athirst in desert dreams
The savour and colour and sound of cool dark streams
      Float round me everywhere,
  And memories float from some forgotten place,
Fulfilling hopeless eyes with hopeless tears
And fleeting light of unforgotten years.

Dim clouds of music in the dim rich hours
  Float to me thro' the twilight of thine hair,
And sails like blossoms float o'er purple seas,
And under dark green skies the soft warm breeze
      Washes dark fruit, dark flowers,
  Dark tropic maidens in some island lair
Couched on the warm sand nigh the creaming foam
To dream and sing their tawny lovers home.

Lost in the magic ocean of thine hair
  I find the haven of the heart of song:
There tired ships rest against the pale red sky!
And yet again there comes a thin sad cry
      And all the shining air
  Fades, where the tall dark singing seamen throng
From many generations, many climes,
Fades, fades, as it has faded many times.

I hear the sweet cool whisper of the waves!
  Drowned in the slumbrous billows of thine hair,
I dream as one that sinks thro' passionate hours
In a strange ship's wild fraughtage of dark flowers
      Culled for pale poets' graves;
  And opiate odours load the empurpled air
That flows and droops, a dark resplendent pall
Under the floating wreaths funereal.

Under the heavy midnight of thine hair
  An altar flames with spices of the south
Burning my flesh and spirit in the flame;
Till, looking tow'rds the land from whence I came
      I find no comfort there,
  And all the darkness to my thirsty mouth
Is fire, but always and in every place
Blossoms the secret wonder of thy face.

The walls, the very walls are woven of dreams,
  All undefined by blasphemies of art!
Here, pure from finite hues the very night
Conceives the mystic harmonies of light,
     Delicious glooms and gleams;
  And sorrow falls in rose-leaves on the heart,
And pain that yearns upon the passing hour
Is but a perfume haunting a dead flower.

Hark, as a hammer on a coffin falls
  A knock upon the door!   The colours wane,
The dreams vanish!   And leave that foul white scar,
Tattoo'd with dreadful marks, the old calendar
     Blotching the blistered walls!
  The winter whistles thro' a shivered pane,
And scatters on the bare boards at my feet
These poor soiled manuscripts, torn, incomplete. . .

The scent of opium floats about my breath;
  But Time resumes his dark and hideous reign;
And, with him, hideous memories troop, I know.
Hark, how the battered clock ticks, to and fro,—
     Life, Death—Life, Death—Life, Death—
  O fool to cry!   O slave to bow to pain,.
Coward to live thus tortured with desire
By demon nerves in hells of sensual fire.

THE MYSTIC

WITH wounds out-reddening every moon-washed rose
King Love went thro' earth's garden-close!
  From that first gate of birth in the golden gloom,
I traced Him.   Thorns had frayed His garment's hem,
Ay, and His flesh!   I marked, I followed them
  Down to that threshold of—the tomb?

And there Love vanished, yet I entered!   Night
And Doubt mocked at the dwindling light:
  Strange claw-like hands flung me their shadowy hate.
I clomb the dreadful stairways of desire
Between a thousand eyes and wings of fire
  And knocked upon the second Gate.

The second Gate!   When, like a warrior helmed,
In battle on battle overwhelmed,
   My soul lay stabbed by all the swords of sense,
Blinded and stunned by stars and flowers and trees,
Did I not struggle to my bended knees
   And wrestle with Omnipotence?

Did earth not flee before me, when the breath
Of worship smote her with strange death,
   Withered her gilded garment, broke her sword,
Shattered her graven images and smote
All her light sorrows thro' the breast and throat
   Whose death-cry crowned me God and Lord?

Yea, God and Lord!   Had tears not purged my sight?
I saw the myriad gates of Light
   Opening and shutting in each way-side flower,
And like a warder in the gleam of each,
Death, whispering in some strange eternal speech
   To every passing hour.

The second Gate?   Was I not born to pass
A million?   Though the skies be brass
   And the earth iron, shall I not win thro' all?
Shall I who made the infinite heavens my mark
Shrink from this first wild horror of the dark,
   These formless gulfs, these glooms that crawl?

Never was mine that easy faithless hope
Which makes all life one flowery slope
   To heaven!   Mine be the vast assaults of doom,
Trumpets, defeats, red anguish, age-long strife,
Ten million deaths, ten million gates to life,
   The insurgent heart that bursts the tomb.

Vain, vain, unutterably vain are all
The sights and sounds that sink and fall,
   The words and symbols of this fleeting breath:
Shall I not drown the finite in the Whole,
Cast off this body and complete my soul
   Thro' deaths beyond this gate of death?

It will not open!   Through the bars I see
The glory and the mystery
     Wind upward ever!   The earth-dawn breaks!   I bleed
With beating here for entrance.   Hark, O hark,
Love, Love, return and give me the great Dark,
     Which is the Light of Life indeed.

THE FLOWER OF OLD JAPAN

DEDICATED TO
CAROL, A LITTLE MAIDEN OF MYAKO.

PERSONS OF THE TALE

OURSELVES
THE TALL THIN MAN
THE DWARF BEHIND THE TWISTED
     PEAR-TREE

CREEPING SIN
THE MAD MOONSHEE
THE NAMELESS ONE

Pirates, Mandarins, Bonzes, Priests, Jugglers, Merchants,
Ghastroi, Weirdrians, etc.

PRELUDE

You that have known the wonder zone
     Of islands far away;
You that have heard the dinky bird
And roamed in rich Cathay;
You that have sailed o'er unknown seas
To woods of Amfalula trees
Where craggy dragons play:
Oh, girl or woman, boy or man,
You've plucked the Flower of Old Japan!

Do you remember the blue stream;
The bridge of pale bamboo;
The path that seemed a twisted dream
Where everything came true;
The purple cherry-trees; the house
With jutting eaves below the boughs;
The mandarins in blue,
With tiny, tapping, tilted toes,
And curious curved mustachios?

The road to Old Japan! you cry,
  And is it far or near?
Some never find it till they die;
  Some find it everywhere;
The road where restful Time forgets
His weary thoughts and wild regrets
  And calls the golden year
Back in a fairy dream to smile
On young and old a little while.

Some seek it with a blazing sword,
  And some with old blue plates;
Some with a miser's golden hoard;
  Some with a book of dates;
Some with a box of paints; a few
Whose loads of truth would ne'er pass through
  The first, white, fairy gates;
And, oh, how shocked they are to find
That truths are false when left behind!

Do you remember all the tales
  That Tusitala told,
When first we plunged thro' purple vales
  In quest of buried gold?
Do you remember how he said
That if we fell and hurt our head
  Our hearts must still be bold,
And we must never mind the pain
But rise up and go on again?

Do you remember?   Yes; I know
  You must remember still:
He left us, not so long ago,
  Carolling with a will,
Because he knew that he should lie
Under the comfortable sky
  Upon a lonely hill,
In Old Japan, when day was done;
"Dear Robert Louis Stevenson."

And there he knew that he should find
   The hills that haunt us now;
The whaups that cried upon the wind
   His heart remembered how;
And friends he loved and left, to roam
Far from the pleasant hearth of home,
   Should touch his dreaming brow;
Where fishes fly and birds have fins,
And children teach the mandarins.

Ah, let us follow, follow far
   Beyond the purple seas;
Beyond the rosy foaming bar,
   The coral reef, the trees,
The land of parrots, and the wild
That rolls before the fearless child
   Its ancient mysteries:
Onward and onward, if we can,
To Old Japan—to Old Japan.

PART I

EMBARKATION

WHEN the firelight, red and clear,
   Flutters in the black wet pane,
It is very good to hear
   Howling winds and trotting rain:
It is very good indeed,
   When the nights are dark and cold,
Near the friendly hearth to read
   Tales of ghosts and buried gold.

So with cozy toes and hands
   We were dreaming, just like you;
Till we thought of palmy lands
   Coloured like a cockatoo;
All in drowsy nursery nooks
   Near the clutching fire we sat,
Searching quaint old story-books
   Piled upon the furry mat,

Something haunted us that night
  Like a half-remembered name;
Worn old pages in that light
  Seemed the same, yet not the same:
Curling in the pleasant heat
  Smoothly as a shell-shaped fan,
O, they breathed and smelt so sweet
  When we turned to Old Japan!

Suddenly we thought we heard
  Someone tapping on the wall,
Tapping, tapping like a bird.
  Then a panel seemed to fall
Quietly; and a tall thin man
  Stepped into the glimmering room,
And he held a little fan,
  And he waved it in the gloom.

Curious red, and golds, and greens
  Danced before our startled eyes,
Birds from painted Indian screens,
  Beads, and shells, and dragon-flies;
Wings, and flowers, and scent, and flam.
  Fans and fish and heliotrope;
Till the magic air became
  Like a dream kaleidoscope.

Then he told us of a land
  Far across a fairy sea;
And he waved his thin white hand
  Like a flower, melodiously;
While a red and blue macaw
  Perched upon his pointed head,
And as in a dream, we saw
  All the curious things he said.

Tucked in tiny palanquins,
  Magically swinging there,
Flowery-kirtled mandarins
  Floated through the scented air;

Wandering dogs and prowling cats
   Grinned at fish in painted lakes;
Cross-legged conjurers on mats
   Fluted low to listening snakes.

Fat black bonzes on the shore
   Watched where singing, faint and far,
Boys in long blue garments bore
   Roses in a golden jar.
While at carven dragon ships
   Floating o'er that silent sea,
Squat-limbed gods with dreadful lips
   Leered and smiled mysteriously.

Like an idol, shrined alone,
   Watched by secret oval eyes,
Where the ruby wishing-stone
   Smouldering in the darkness lies,
Anyone that wanted things
   Touched the jewel and they came;
We were wealthier than kings
   Coüld we only do the same.

Yes; we knew a hundred ways
   We might use it if we could;
To be happy all our days
   As an Indian in a wood;
No more daily lesson task,
   No more sorrow, no more care;
So we thought that we would ask
   If he'd kindly lead us there.

Ah, but then he waved his fan,
   Laughed and vanished through the wall;
Yet as in a dream, we ran
   Tumbling after, one and all;
Never pausing once to think,
   Panting after him we sped;
Far away his robe of pink
   Floated backward as he fled.

Down a secret passage deep,
  Under roofs of spidery stairs,
Where the bat-winged nightmares creep,
  And a sheeted phantom glares
Rushed we; ah, how strange it was
  Where no human watcher stood;
Till we reached a gate of glass
  Opening on a flowery wood.

Where the rose-pink robe had flown,
  Borne by swifter feet than ours,
On to Wonder-Wander town,
  Through the wood of monstrous flowers;
Mailed in monstrous gold and blue
  Dragon-flies like peacocks fled;
Butterflies like carpets, too,
  Softly fluttered overhead.

Down the valley, tip-a-toe,
  Where the broad-limbed giants lie
Snoring, as when long ago
  Jack on a bean-stalk scaled the sky;
On to Wonder-Wander town
  Stole we past old dreams again,
Castles long since battered down,
  Dungeons of forgotten pain.

Noonday brooded on the wood,
  Evening caught us ere we crept
Where a twisted pear-tree stood,
  And a dwarf behind it slept;
Round his scraggy throat he wore,
  Knotted tight, a scarlet scarf;
Timidly we watched him snore,
  For he seemed a surly dwarf.

Yet, he looked so very small,
  He could hardly hurt us much;
We were nearly twice as tall,
  So we woke him with a touch

Gently, and in tones polite,
  Asked him to direct our path;
O, his wrinkled eyes grew bright
  Green with ugly gnomish wrath.

      He seemed to choke,
      And gruffly spoke,
"You're lost: deny it, if you can!
      You want to know
      The way to go?
There's no such place as Old Japan.

      "You want to seek—
      No, no, don't speak!
You mean you want to steal a fan.
      You want to see
      The fields of tea?
They don't grow tea in Old Japan.

      "In China, well
      Perhaps you'd smell
The cherry bloom: that's if you ran
      A million miles
      And jumped the stiles,
And never dreamed of Old Japan.

      "What, palanquins,
      And mandarins?
And, what d'you say, a blue divan?
      And what?   Hee! hee!
      You'll never see
A pig-tailed head in Old Japan.

      "You'd take away
      The ruby, hey?
I never heard of such a plan!
      Upon my word
      It's quite absurd
There's not a gem in Old Japan!

"Oh, dear me, no!
 You'd better go
Straight home again, my little man:
 Ah, well, you'll see
 But don't blame me;
I don't believe in Old Japan."

Then, before we could obey,
 O'er our startled heads he cast,
Spider-like, a webby grey
 Net that held us prisoned fast;
How we screamed, he only grinned,
 It was such a lonely place;
And he said we should be pinned
 Safely in his beetle-case.

Out he dragged a monstrous box
 From a cave behind the tree!
It had four-and-twenty locks,
 But he could not find the key,
And his face grew very pale
 When a sudden voice began
Drawing nearer through the vale,
 Singing songs of Old Japan.

SONG

Satin sails in a crimson dawn
 Over the silky silver sea;
Purple veils of the dark withdrawn;
 Heavens of pearl and porphyry;
Purple and white in the morning light
 Over the water the town we knew,
In tiny state, like a willow-plate,
 Shone, and behind it the hills were blue.

There, we remembered, the shadows pass
 All day long like dreams in the night;
There, in the meadows of dim blue grass,
 Crimson daisies are ringed with white.

There the roses flutter their petals,
  Over the meadows they take their flight,
There the moth that sleepily settles
  Turns to a flower in the warm soft light.

There when the sunset colours the streets
  Everyone buys at wonderful stalls
Toys and chocolates, guns and sweets,
  Ivory pistols, and Persian shawls:
Everyone's pockets are crammed with gold;
  Nobody's heart is worn with care,
Nobody ever grows tired and old,
  And nobody calls you "Baby" there.

There with a hat like a round white dish
  Upside down on each pig-tailed head,
Jugglers offer you snakes and fish,
  Dreams and dragons and gingerbread;
Beautiful books with marvellous pictures,
  Painted pirates and streaming gore,
And everyone reads, without any strictures,
  Tales he remembers for evermore.

There when the dim blue daylight lingers
  Listening, and the West grows holy,
Singers crouch with their long white fingers
  Floating over the zithern slowly:
Paper lamps with a peachy bloom
  Burn above on the dim blue bough,
While the zitherns gild the gloom
  With curious music!   I hear it now!

Now: and at that mighty word
  Holding out his magic fan,
Through the waving flowers appeared,
  Suddenly, the tall thin man:
And we saw the crumpled dwarf
  Trying to hide behind the tree,
But his knotted scarlet scarf
  Made him very plain to see.

Like a soft and smoky cloud
   Passed the webby net away;
While its owner squealing loud
   Down behind the pear-tree lay;
For the tall thin man came near,
   And his words were dark and gruff,
And he swung the dwarf in the air
   By his long and scraggy scruff.

There he kickled whimpering.
   But our rescuer touched the box,
Open with a sudden spring
   Clashed the four-and-twenty locks;
Then he crammed the dwarf inside,
   And the locks all clattered tight:
Four-and-twenty times he tried
   Whether they were fastened right.

Ah, he led us on our road,
   Showed us Wonder-Wander town;
Then he fled: behind him flowed
   Once again the rose-pink gown:
Down the long deserted street,
   All the windows winked like eyes,
And our little trotting feet
   Echoed to the starry skies.

Low and long for evermore
   Where the Wonder-Wander sea
Whispers to the wistful shore
   Purple songs of mystery,
Down the shadowy quay we came—
   Though it hides behind the hill
You will find it just the same
   And the seamen singing still.

There we chose a ship of pearl,
   And her milky silken sail
Seemed by magic to unfurl,
   Puffed before a fairy gale;

Shimmering o'er the purple deep,
  Out across the silvery bar,
Softly as the wings of sleep
  Sailed we towards the morning star.

Over us the skies were dark,
  Yet we never needed light;
Softly shone our tiny bark
  Gliding through the solemn night;
Softly bright our moony gleam,
  Glimmered o'er the glistening waves,
Like a cold sea-maiden's dream
  Globed in twilit ocean caves.

So all night our shallop passed
  Many a haunt of old desire,
Blurs of savage blossom massed
  Red above a pirate-fire;
Huts that gloomed and glanced among
  Fruitage dipping in the blue;
Songs the sirens never sung,
  Shores Ulysses never knew.

All our fairy rigging shone
  Richly as a rainbow seen
Where the moonlight floats upon
  Gossamers of gold and green:
All the tiny spars were bright;
  Beaten gold the bowsprit was;
But our pilot was the night,
  And our chart a looking-glass.

PART II

THE ARRIVAL

WITH rosy finger-tips the Dawn
  Drew back the silver veils,
Till lilac shimmered into lawn
  Above the satin sails;

And o'er the waters, white and wan,
  In tiny patterned state,
We saw the streets of Old Japan
  Shine, like a willow plate.

O, many a milk-white pigeon roams
  The purple cherry crops,
The mottled miles of pearly domes,
  And blue pagoda tops,
The river with its golden canes
  And dark piratic dhows,
To where beyond the twisting vanes
  The burning mountain glows.

A snow-peak in the silver skies
  Beyond that magic world,
We saw the great volcano rise
  With incense o'er it curled,
Whose tiny thread of rose and blue
  Has risen since time began,
Before the first enchanter knew
  The peak of Old Japan.

Nobody watched us quietly steer
The pinnace to the painted pier,
  Except one pig-tailed mandarin,
Who sat upon a chest of tea
Pretending not to hear or see! . . .
  His hands were very long and thin,
His face was very broad and white;
And O, it was a fearful sight
  To see him sit alone and grin!

His grin was very sleek and sly:
Timidly we passed him by.
  He did not seem at all to care:
So, thinking we were safely past,
We ventured to look back at last.
  O, dreadful blank!—*He was not there!*
He must have hid behind his chest:
We did not stay to see the rest.

But, as in reckless haste we ran,
We came upon the tall thin man,
Who called to us and waved his fan,
    And offered us his palanquin:
He said we must not go alone
To seek the ruby wishing-stone,
    Because the white-faced mandarin
Would dog our steps for many a mile,
And sit upon each purple stile
Before we came to it, and smile
    And smile; his name was Creeping Sin.

He played with children's beating hearts,
And stuck them full of poisoned darts
    And long green thorns that stabbed and stung:
He'd watch until we tried to speak,
Then thrust inside his pasty cheek
    His long, white, slimy tongue:
And smile at everything we said;
And sometimes pat us on the head,
    And say that we were very young:
He was a cousin of the man
Who said that there was no Japan.

And night and day this Creeping Sin
Would follow the path of the palanquin;
    Yet if we still were fain to touch
The ruby, we must have no fear,
Whatever we might see or hear,
And the tall thin man would take us there;
    He did not fear that Sly One much,
Except perhaps on a moonless night,
Nor even then if the stars were bright.

So, in the yellow palankeen
We swung along in state between
Twinkling domes of gold and green
    Through the rich bazaar,

Where the cross-legged merchants sat,
Old and almond-eyed and fat,
Each upon a gorgeous mat,
    Each in a cymar;
Each in crimson samite breeches,
Watching his barbaric riches.

Cherry blossom breathing sweet
Whispered o'er the dim blue street
Where with fierce uncertain feet
    Tawny pirates walk:
All in belts and baggy blouses,
Out of dreadful opium houses,
Out of dens where Death carouses,
    Horribly they stalk;
Girt with ataghan and dagger,
Right across the road they swagger.

And where the cherry orchards blow,
We saw the maids of Miyako,
Swaying softly to and fro
    Through the dimness of the dance:
Like sweet thoughts that shine through dreams
They glided, wreathing rosy gleams,
With stately sounds of silken streams,
    And many a slim kohl-lidded glance;
Then fluttered with tiny rose-bud feet
To a soft *frou-frou* and a rhythmic beat
As the music shimmered, pursuit, retreat,
    "Hands across, retire, advance!"
And again it changed and the glimmering throng
Faded into a distant song.

SONG

The maidens of Miyako
    Dance in the sunset hours,
Deep in the sunset glow,
    Under the cherry flowers.

With dreamy hands of pearl
  Floating like butterflies,
Dimly the dancers whirl
  As the rose-light dies;

And their floating gowns, their hair
  Upbound with curious pins,
Fade thro' the darkening air
  With the dancing mandarins.

And then, as we went, the tall thin man
Explained the manners of Old Japan;
  If you pitied a thing, you pretended to sneer;
Yet if you were glad you ran to buy
A captive pigeon and let it fly;
  And, if you were sad, you took a spear
To wound yourself, for fear your pain
Should quietly grow less again.

And, again he said, if we wished to find
The mystic City that enshrined
  The stone so few on earth had found,
We must be very brave; it lay
A hundred haunted leagues away,
  Past many a griffon-guarded ground,
In depths of dark and curious art,
Where passion-flowers enfold apart
The Temple of the Flaming Heart,
  The City of the Secret Wound.

About the fragrant fall of day
We saw beside the twisted way
  A blue-domed tea-house, bossed with gold;
Hungry and thirsty we entered in,
How should we know what Creeping Sin
  Had breathed in that Emperor's ear who sold
His own dumb soul for an evil jewel
To the earth-gods, blind and ugly and cruel?
  We drank sweet tea as his tale was told,
In a garden of blue chrysanthemums,
While a drowsy swarming of gongs and drums
  Out of the sunset dreamily rolled.

But, as the murmur nearer drew,
A fat black bonze, in a robe of blue,
    Suddenly at the gate appeared;
And close behind, with that evil grin,
Was it Creeping Sin, was it Creeping Sin?
    The bonze looked quietly down and sneered.
Our guide! Was he sleeping?   We could not
            wake him,
However we tried to pinch and shake him!

Nearer, nearer the tumult came,
Till, as a glare of sound and flame,
    Blind from a terrible furnace door
Blares, or the mouth of a dragon, blazed
The seething gateway: deaf and dazed
    With the clanging and the wild uproar
We stood; while a thousand oval eyes
Gapped our fear with a sick surmise.

Then, as the dead sea parted asunder,
The clamour clove with a sound of thunder
    In two great billows; and all was quiet.
Gaunt and black was the palankeen
That came in dreadful state between
    The frozen waves of the wild-eyed riot
Curling back from the breathless track
Of the Nameless One who is never seen:
    The close drawn curtains were thick and black;
But wizen and white was the tall thin man
    As he rose in his sleep:
His eyes were closed, his lips were wan,
    He crouched like a leopard that dares not
            leap.

The bearers halted: the tall thin man,
Fearfully dreaming, waved his fan,
    With wizard fingers, to and fro;
While, with a whimper of evil glee,
The Nameless Emperor's mad Moonshee
    Stepped in front of us: dark and slow

Were the words of the doom that he dared not
        name;
But, over the ground, as he spoke there came
Tiny circles of soft blue flame;
    Like ghosts of flowers they began to glow,
And flow like a moonlit brook between
Our feet and the terrible palankeen.

But the Moonshee wrinkled his long thin eyes,
And sneered, "Have you stolen the strength of
        the skies?
    Then pour before us a stream of pearl!
Give us the pearl and the gold we know,
And our hearts will be softened and let you go;
    But these are toys for a foolish girl—
These vanishing blossoms—what are they worth?
They are not so heavy as dust and earth:
    Pour before us a stream of pearl!"

Then, with a wild strange laugh, our guide
Stretched his arms to the West and cried
    Once, and a song came over the sea;
And all the blossoms of moon-soft fire
Woke and breathed as a wind-swept lyre,
    And the garden surged into harmony;
Till it seemed that the soul of the whole world
        sung,
And every petal became a tongue
    To tell the thoughts of Eternity.

But the Moonshee lifted his painted brows
And stared at the gold on the blue tea-house:
    "Can you clothe your body with dreams?"
        he sneered;
"If you taught us the truths that we alway
        know
Our heart might be softened and let you go:
    Can you tell us the length of a monkey
        beard,
Or the weight of the gems on the Emperor's fan,
Or the number of parrots in Old Japan?"

3

And again, with a wild strange laugh, our guide
Looked at him; and he shrunk aside,
    Shrivelling like a flame-touched leaf;
For the red-cross blossoms of soft blue fire
Were growing and fluttering higher and higher,
    Shaking their petals out, sheaf by sheaf,
Till with disks like shields and stems like towers
Burned the host of the passion-flowers
        . . . Had the Moonshee flown like a midnight
            thief?
    . . . Yet a thing like a monkey, shrivelled and
            black,
Chattered and danced as they forced him back.

As the coward chatters for empty pride,
    In the face of a foe that he cannot but fear,
It chattered and leapt from side to side,
    And its voice rang strangely upon the ear.
As the cry of a wizard that dares not own
Another's brighter and mightier throne;
As the wrath of a fool that rails aloud
    On the fire that burnt him; the brazen bray
Clamoured and sang o'er the gaping crowd,
    And flapped like a gabbling goose away.

THE CRY OF THE MAD MOONSHEE

If the blossoms were beans,
    I should know what it means—
This blaze, which I certainly cannot endure;
    It is evil, too,
    For its colour is blue,
And the sense of the matter is quite obscure.
    Celestial truth
    Is the food of youth;
But the music was dark as a moonless night.
    The facts in the song
    Were all of them wrong,

And there was not a single sum done right;
Tho' a metaphysician amongst the crowd,
In a voice that was notably deep and loud,
Repeated, as fast as he was able,
The whole of the multiplication table.

So the cry flapped off as a wild goose flies,
And the stars came out in the trembling skies,
   And ever the mystic glory grew
In the garden of blue chrysanthemums,
Till there came a rumble of distant drums;
   And the multitude suddenly turned and flew.
. . . A dead ape lay where their feet had
        been . . .
And we called for the yellow palankeen,
   And the flowers divided and let us through.

The black-barred moon was large and low
When we came to the Forest of Ancient Woe;
   And over our heads the stars were bright.
But through the forest the path we travelled
Its phosphorescent aisle unravelled
   In one thin ribbon of dwindling light:
And twice and thrice on the fainting track
We paused to listen. The moon grew black,
   But the coolies' faces glimmered white,
As the wild woods echoed in dreadful chorus
A laugh that came horribly hopping o'er us
   Like monstrous frogs thro' the murky night.

Then the tall thin man as we swung along
Sang us an old enchanted song
   That lightened our hearts of their fearful load.
But, e'en as the moonlit air grew sweet,
We heard the pad of stealthy feet
   Dogging us down the thin white road;
And the song grew weary again and harsh,
And the black trees dripped like the fringe of a
        marsh,
   And a laugh crept out like a shadowy toad;
And we knew it was neither ghoul nor djinn:
It was Creeping Sin!   It was Creeping Sin!

But we came to a bend, and the white moon
    glowed
Like a gate at the end of the narrowing road
    Far away; and on either hand,
As guards of a path to the heart's desire,
The strange tall blossoms of soft blue fire
    Stretched away thro' that unknown land,
League on league with their dwindling lane
Down to the large low moon; and again
There shimmered around us that mystical strain,
    In a tongue that it seemed we could under-
        stand.

SONG

Hold by right and rule by fear
Till the slowly broadening sphere
Melting through the skies above
Merge into the sphere of love.

Hold by might until you find
Might is powerless o'er the mind:
Hold by Truth until you see,
Though they bow before the wind,
Its towers can mock at liberty.

Time, the seneschal, is blind;
Time is blind: and what are we?
Captives of Infinity,
Claiming through Truth's prison bars
Kinship with the wandering stars.

O, who could tell the wild weird sights
We saw in all the days and nights
    We travelled through those forests old.
We saw the griffons on white cliffs,
Among fantastic hieroglyphs,
    Guarding enormous heaps of gold:

We saw the Ghastroi—curious men
Who dwell, like tigers, in a den,
    And howl whene'er the moon is cold;
They stripe themselves with red and black
And ride upon the yellow Yak.

Their dens are always ankle-deep
With twisted knives, and in their sleep
    They often cut themselves; they say
That if you wish to live in peace
The surest way is not to cease
    Collecting knives; and never a day
Can pass, unless they buy a few;
And as their enemies buy them too
    They all avert the impending fray,
And starve their children and their wives
To buy the necessary knives.

*   *   *   *   *

The forest leapt with shadowy shapes
As we came to the great black Tower of
                    Apes:
But we gave them purple figs and grapes
    In alabaster amphoras:
We gave them curious kinds of fruit
With betel nuts and orris-root,
    And then they let us pass:
And when we reached the Tower of Snakes
We gave them soft white honey-cakes,
    And warm sweet milk in bowls of brass:
And on the hundredth eve we found
The City of the Secret Wound.

We saw the mystic blossoms blow
Round the City, far below;
Faintly in the sunset glow
We saw the soft blue glory flow

O'er many a golden garden gate:
And o'er the tiny dark green seas
Of tamarisks and tulip-trees,
Domes like golden oranges
    Dream aloft elate.

And clearer, clearer as we went,
We heard from tower and battlement
A whisper, like a warning, sent
    From watchers out of sight;
And clearer, brighter, as we drew
Close to the walls, we saw the blue
Flashing of plumes where peacocks flew
    Thro' zones of pearly light.

On either side, a fat black bonze
Guarded the gates of red-wrought bronze,
Blazoned with blue sea-dragons
    And mouths of yawning flame;
Down the road of dusty red,
Though their brown feet ached and bled,
Our coolies went with joyful tread:
Like living fans the gates outspread
    And opened as we came.

PART III

THE MYSTIC RUBY

THE white moon dawned; the sunset died;
And stars were trembling when we spied
    The rose-red temple of our dreams:
Its lamp-lit gardens glimmered cool
With many an onyx-paven pool,
    Amid soft sounds of flowing streams;
Where star-shine shimmered through the white
Tall fountain-shafts of crystal light
    In ever changing rainbow-gleams.

Priests in flowing yellow robes
Glided under rosy globes
   Through the green pomegranate boughs
Moonbeams poured their coloured rain;
Roofs of sea-green porcelain
   Jutted o'er the rose-red house;
Bells were hung beneath its eaves;
Every wind that stirred the leaves
   Tinkled as tired water does.

The temple had a low broad base
Of black bright marble; all its face
   Was marble bright in rosy bloom;
And where two sea-green pillars rose
Deep in the flower-soft eave-shadows
   We saw, thro' richly sparkling gloom,
Wrought in marvellous years of old
With bulls and peacocks bossed in gold,
   The doors of powdered lacquer loom.

Quietly then the tall thin man,
Holding his turquoise-tinted fan,
   Alighted from the palanquin;
We followed: never painter dreamed
Of how that dark rich temple gleamed
   With gules of jewelled gloom within;
And as we wondered near the door
A priest came o'er the polished floor
   In sandals of soft serpent-skin;
His mitre shimmered bright and blue
With pigeon's breast-plumes. When he knew
   Our quest he stroked his broad white chin,
And looked at us with slanting eyes
And smiled; then through his deep disguise
We knew him! It was Creeping Sin!

But cunningly he bowed his head
Down on his gilded breast and said
   Come: and he led us through the dusk
Of passages whose painted walls
Gleamed with dark old festivals;

Till where the gloom grew sweet with musk
And incense, through a door of amber
We came into a high-arched chamber.

There on a throne of jasper sat
A monstrous idol, black and fat;
    Thick rose-oil dropped upon its head:
Drop by drop, heavy and sweet,
Trickled down to its ebon feet
    Whereon the blood of goats was shed,
And smeared around its perfumed knees
In savage midnight mysteries.

It wore about its bulging waist
A belt of dark green bronze enchased
    With big, soft, cloudy pearls; its wrists
Were clasped about with moony gems
Gathered from dead kings' diadems;
    Its throat was ringed with amethysts,
And in its awful hand it held
A softly smouldering emerald.

Silkily murmured Creeping Sin,
"This is the stone you wished to win!"
    "White Snake," replied the tall thin man,
"Show us the Ruby Stone, or I
Will slay thee with my hands."   The sly
    Long eyelids of the priest began
To slant aside; and then once more
He led us through the fragrant door.

And now along the passage walls
Were painted hideous animals,
    With hooded eyes and cloven stings:
In the incense that like shadowy hair
Streamed over them they seemed to stir
    Their craggy claws and crooked wings.
At last we saw strange moon-wreaths curl
Around a deep, soft porch of pearl.

O, what enchanter wove in dreams
That chapel wild with shadowy gleams
    And prismy colours of the moon?
Shrined like a rainbow in a mist
Of flowers, the fretted amethyst
    Arches rose to a mystic tune;
And never mortal art inlaid
Those cloudy floors of sea-soft jade.

There, in the midst, an idol rose
White as the silent starlit snows
    On lonely Himalayan heights:
Over its head the spikenard spilled
Down to its feet, with myrrh distilled
    In distant, odorous Indian nights:
It held before its ivory face
A flaming yellow chrysoprase.

O, silkily murmured Creeping Sin,
"This is the stone you wished to win."
    But in his ear the tall thin man
Whispered with slow, strange lips—we knew
Not what, but Creeping Sin went blue
    With fear; again his eyes began
To slant aside; then through the porch
He passed, and lit a tall, brown torch.

Down a corridor dark as death,
With beating hearts and bated breath
    We hurried; far away we heard
A dreadful hissing, fierce as fire
When rain begins to quench a pyre;
    And where the smoky torch-light flared
Strange vermin beat their bat-like wings,
And the wet walls dropped with slimy things.

And darker, darker, wound the way,
Beyond all gleams of night and day,
    And still that hideous hissing grew
Louder and louder on our ears,
And tortured us with eyeless fears;

Then suddenly the gloom turned blue,
And, in the wall, a rough rock cave
Gaped, like a phosphorescent grave.

And from the purple mist within
There came a wild tumultuous din
   Of snakes that reared their heads and hissed
As if a witch's cauldron boiled;
All round the door great serpents coiled,
   With eyes of glowing amethyst,
Whose fierce blue flames began to slide
Like shooting stars from side to side.

Ah! with a sickly gasping grin
And quivering eyelids, Creeping Sin
   Stole to the cave; but, suddenly,
As through its glimmering mouth he passed,
The serpents flashed and gripped him fast:
   He wriggled and gave one awful cry,
Then all at once the cave was cleared;
The snakes with their victim had disappeared.

And fearlessly the tall thin man
Opened his turquoise-tinted fan
   And entered; and the mists grew bright,
And we saw that the cave was a diamond hall
Lit with lamps for a festival.
   A myriad globes of coloured light
Went gliding deep in its massy sides,
Like the shimmering moons in the glassy tides
   Where a sea-king's palace enchants the night.

Gliding and flowing, a glory and wonder,
Through each other, and over, and under,
   The lucent orbs of green and gold,
Bright with sorrow or soft with sleep,
In music through the glimmering deep,
   Over their secret axles rolled,
And circled by the murmuring spheres
We saw in a frame of frozen tears
   A mirror that made the blood run cold.

For, when we came to it, we found
It imaged everything around
   Except the face that gazed in it;
And where the mirrored face should be
A heart-shaped Ruby fierily
   Smouldered; and round the frame was writ,
Mystery: Time and Tide shall pass,
I am the Wisdom Looking-Glass.

This is the Ruby none can touch:
Many have loved it overmuch;
   Its fathomless fires flutter and sigh,
Being as images of the flame
That shall make earth and heaven the same
   When the fire of the end reddens the sky,
And the world consumes like a burning pall,
Till where there is nothing, there is all.

So we looked up at the tall thin man
And we saw that his face grew sad and wan:
   Tears were glistening in his eyes:
At last, with a breaking sob, he bent
His head upon his breast and went
   Swiftly away!   With dreadful cries
We rushed to the softly glimmering door
And stared at the hideous corridor.
   But his robe was gone as a dream that flies:
Back to the glass in terror we came,
And stared at the writing round the frame.

We could not understand one word:
And suddenly we thought we heard
   The hissing of the snakes again:
How could we front them all alone?
O, madly we clutched at the mirrored stone
   And wished we were back on the flowery plain:
And swifter than thought and swift as fear
The whole world flashed, and behold we were there.

Yes; there was the port of Old Japan,
With its twisted patterns, white and wan,
Shining like a mottled fan
   Spread by the blue sea, faint and far;
And far away we heard once more
A sound of singing on the shore,
Where boys in blue kimonos bore
   Roses in a golden jar:
And we heard, where the cherry orchards blow,
The serpent-charmers fluting low,
And the song of the maidens of Miyako.

And at our feet unbroken lay
The glass that had whirled us thither away:
   And in the grass, among the flowers
We sat and wished all sorts of things:
O, we were wealthier than kings!
   We ruled the world for several hours!
And then, it seemed, we knew not why,
All the daisies began to die.

We wished them alive again; but soon
The trees all fled up towards the moon
   Like peacocks through the sunlit air:
And the butterflies flapped into silver fish;
And each wish spoiled another wish;
   Till we threw the glass down in despair;
For, getting whatever you want to get,
Is like drinking tea from a fishing net.

At last we thought we'd wish once more
That all should be as it was before;
   And then we'd shatter the glass, if we could;
But just as the world grew right again,
We heard a wanderer out on the plain
   Singing what none of us understood;
Yet we thought that the world grew thrice more sweet
And the meadows were blossoming under his feet.

And we felt a grand and beautiful fear,
For we knew that a marvellous thought drew near;
  So we kept the glass for a little while:
And the skies grew deeper and twice as bright,
And the seas grew soft as a flower of light,
  And the meadows rippled from stile to stile;
And memories danced in a musical throng
Thro' the blossom that scented the wonderful song.

SONG

We sailed across the silver seas
  And saw the sea-blue bowers,
We saw the purple cherry trees,
  And all the foreign flowers,
We travelled in a palanquin
  Beyond the caravan,
And yet our hearts had never seen
  The Flower of Old Japan.

The Flower above all other flowers,
  The Flower that never dies;
Before whose throne the scented hours
  Offer their sacrifice;
The Flower that here on earth below
  Reveals the heavenly plan;
But only little children know
  The Flower of Old Japan.

There, in the dim blue flowery plain
We wished with the magic glass again
  To go to the Flower of the song's desire:
And o'er us the whole of the soft blue sky
Flashed like fire as the world went by,
  And far beneath us the sea like fire
Flashed in one swift blue brilliant stream,
And the journey was done, like a change in a dream.

PART IV

THE END OF THE QUEST

LIKE the dawn upon a dream
  Slowly through the scented gloom
Crept once more the ruddy gleam
  O'er the friendly nursery room.
There, before our waking eyes,
  Large and ghostly, white and dim,
Dreamed the Flower that never dies,
  Opening wide its rosy rim.

Spreading like a ghostly fan,
  Petals white as porcelain,
There the Flower of Old Japan
  Told us we were home again;
For a soft and curious light
  Suddenly was o'er it shed,
And we saw it was a white
  English daisy, ringed with red.

Slowly, as a wavering mist
  Waned the wonder out of sight,
To a sigh of amethyst,
  To a wraith of scented light.
Flower and magic glass had gone;
  Near the clutching fire we sat
Dreaming, dreaming, all alone,
  Each upon a furry mat.

While the firelight, red and clear,
  Fluttered in the black wet pane,
It was very good to hear
  Howling winds and trotting rain.
For we found at last we knew
  More than all our fancy planned,
All the fairy tales were true,
  And home the heart of fairyland.

EPILOGUE

Carol, every violet has
Heaven for a looking-glass!

Every little valley lies
Under many-clouded skies;
Every little cottage stands
Girt about with boundless lands.
Every little glimmering pond
Claims the mighty shores beyond—
Shores no seamen ever hailed,
Seas no ship has ever sailed.

All the shores when day is done
Fade into the setting sun,
So the story tries to teach
More than can be told in speech.

Beauty is a fading flower,
Truth is but a wizard's tower,
Where a solemn death-bell tolls,
And a forest round it rolls.

We have come by curious ways
To the Light that holds the days;
We have sought in haunts of fear
For that all-enfolding sphere:
And lo! it was not far, but near.

We have found, O foolish-fond,
The shore that has no shore beyond.

Deep in every heart it lies
With its untranscended skies;
For what heaven should bend above
Hearts that own the heaven of love?

Carol, Carol, we have come
Back to heaven, back to home.

APES AND IVORY

Apes and ivory, skulls and roses, in junks of old Hong-Kong,
Gliding over a sea of dreams to a haunted shore of song,
Masts of gold and sails of satin, shimmering out of the East,
O, Love has little need of you now to make his heart a feast.

Or is it an elephant, white as milk and bearing a severed head
That tatters his broad soft wrinkled flank in tawdry patches
    of red,
With a negro giant to walk beside and a temple dome above,
Where ruby and emerald shatter the sun,—is it these that
    should please my love?

Or is it a palace of pomegranates, where ivory-limbed young
    slaves
Lure a luxury out of the noon in the swooning fountain's
    waves;
Or couch like cats and sun themselves on the warm white
    marble brink?
O, Love has little to ask of these, this day in May, I think.

Is it Lebanon cedars or purple fruits of the honeyed southron
    air,
Spikenard, saffron, roses of Sharon, cinnamon, calamus, myrrh,
A bed of spices, a fountain of waters, or the wild white wings
    of a dove,
Now, when the winter is over and gone, is it these that should
    please my love?

The leaves outburst on the hazel-bough and the hawthorn's
    heaped wi' flower,
And God has bidden the crisp clouds build my love a lordlier
    tower,
Taller than Lebanon, whiter than snow, in the fresh blue skies
    above;
And the wild rose wakes in the winding lanes of the radiant
    land I love.

Apes and ivory, skulls and roses, in junks of old Hong-Kong,
Gliding over a sea of dreams to a haunted shore of song,
Masts of gold and sails of satin, shimmering out of the East,
O, Love has little need of you now to make his heart a feast.

A SONG OF SHERWOOD

Sherwood in the twilight, is Robin Hood awake?
Grey and ghostly shadows are gliding through the brake,
Shadows of the dappled deer, dreaming of the morn,
Dreaming of a shadowy man that winds a shadowy horn.

Robin Hood is here again: all his merry thieves
Hear a ghostly bugle-note shivering through the leaves,
Calling as he used to call, faint and far away,
In Sherwood, in Sherwood, about the break of day.

Merry, merry England has kissed the lips of June:
All the wings of fairyland were here beneath the moon,
Like a flight of rose-leaves fluttering in a mist
Of opal and ruby and pearl and amethyst.

Merry, merry England is waking as of old,
With eyes of blither hazel and hair of brighter gold:
For Robin Hood is here again beneath the bursting spray
In Sherwood, in Sherwood, about the break of day.

Love is in the greenwood building him a house
Of wild rose and hawthorn and honeysuckle boughs:
Love is in the greenwood, dawn is in the skies,
And Marian is waiting with a glory in her eyes.

Hark! The dazzled laverock climbs the golden steep!
Marian is waiting: is Robin Hood asleep?
Round the fairy grass-rings frolic elf and fay,
In Sherwood, in Sherwood, about the break of day.

Oberon, Oberon, rake away the gold,
Rake away the red leaves, roll away the mould,
Rake away the gold leaves, roll away the red,
And wake Will Scarlett from his leafy forest bed.

4

Friar Tuck and Little John are riding down together
With quarter-staff and drinking-can and grey goose-feather.
The dead are coming back again, the years are rolled away
In Sherwood, in Sherwood, about the break of day.

Softly over Sherwood the south wind blows.
All the heart of England hid in every rose
Hears across the greenwood the sunny whisper leap,
Sherwood in the red dawn, is Robin Hood asleep?

Hark, the voice of England wakes him as of old
And, shattering the silence with a cry of brighter gold
Bugles in the greenwood echo from the steep,
Sherwood in the red dawn, is Robin Hood asleep?

Where the deer are gliding down the shadowy glen
All across the glades of fern he calls his merry men—
Doublets of the Lincoln green glancing through the May
In Sherwood, in Sherwood, about the break of day—

Calls them and they answer: from aisles of oak and ash
Rings the *Follow! Follow!* and the boughs begin to crash,
The ferns begin to flutter and the flowers begin to fly,
And through the crimson dawning the robber band goes by.

Robin! Robin! Robin!   All his merry thieves
Answer as the bugle-note shivers through the leaves,
Calling as he used to call, faint and far away,
In Sherwood, in Sherwood, about the break of day.

THE WORLD'S MAY–QUEEN

I

WHITHER away is the Spring to-day?
    To England, to England!
In France they heard the South wind say,
"She's off on a quest for a Queen o' the May,
So she's over the hills far away,
        To England!"

And why did she fly with her golden feet
  To England, to England?
In Italy, too, they heard the sweet
Roses whisper and flutter and beat—
"She's an old and a true, true love to greet
  In England!"

A moon ago there came a cry
  From England, from England,
Faintly, fondly it faltered nigh
The throne of the Spring in the Southern sky,
And it whispered "Come," and the world went by,
And with one long loving blissful sigh
  The Spring was away to England!

II

When Spring comes back to England
 And crowns her brows with May,
Round the merry moonlit world
 She goes the greenwood way:
She throws a rose to Italy,
 A fleur-de-lys to France;
But round her regal morris-ring
 The seas of England dance.

When Spring comes back to England
 And dons her robe of green,
There's many a nation garlanded
 But England is the Queen;
She's Queen, she's Queen of all the world
 Beneath the laughing sky,
For the nations go a-Maying
 When they hear the New Year cry—

"Come over the water to England,
 My old love, my new love,
Come over the water to England,
 In showers of flowery rain;

Come over the water to England,
    April, my true love;
And tell the heart of England
    The Spring is here again!"

III

So it's here, she is here with her eyes of blue
        In England, in England!
She has brought us the rainbows with her, too,
And a glory of shimmering glimmering dew
And a heaven of quivering scent and hue
And a lily for me and a rose for you
        In England.

There's many a wanderer far away
        From England, from England,
Will toss upon his couch and say—
Though Spain is proud and France is gay,
And there's many a foot on the primrose way,
The world has never a Queen o' the May
        But England.

IV

When Drake went out to seek for gold
    Across the uncharted sea,
And saw the Western skies unfold
    Their veils of mystery;
To lure him through the fevered hours
    As nigh to death he lay,
There floated o'er the foreign flowers
    A breath of English May:

And back to Devon shores again
    His dreaming spirit flew
Over the splendid Spanish Main
    To haunts his childhood knew,
Whispering "God forgive the blind
    Desire that bade me roam,
I've sailed around the world to find
    The sweetest way to home."

V

And it's whither away is the Spring to-day?
          To England, to England!
In France you'll hear the South wind say,
"She off on a quest for a Queen o' the May,
So she's over the hills and far away,
          To England!"

She's flown with the swallows across the sea
          To England, to England!
For there's many a land of the brave and free
But never a home o' the hawthorn-tree,
And never a Queen o' the May for me
          But England!

And round the fairy revels whirl
          In England, in England!
And the buds outbreak and the leaves unfurl,
And where the crisp white cloudlets curl
The Dawn comes up like a primrose girl
With a crowd of flowers in a basket of pearl
          For England!

PIRATES

Come to me, you with the laughing face, in the night as I lie
Dreaming of days that are dead and of joys gone by;
Come to me, comrade, come through the slow-dropping rain,
Come from your grave in the darkness and let us be pirates
          again.

Let us be boys together to-night, and pretend as of old
We are pirates at rest in a cave among huge heaps of gold,
Red Spanish doubloons and great pieces of eight, and muskets
          and swords,
And a smoky red camp-fire to glint, you know how, on our ill-
          gotten hoards.

The old cave in the fir-wood that slopes down the hills to the
    sea
Still is haunted, perhaps, by young pirates as wicked as we:
Though the fir with the magpie's big mud-plastered nest used
    to hide it so well,
And the boys in the gang had to swear that they never would
    tell.

Ah, that tree; I have sat in its boughs and looked seaward for
    hours.
I remember the creak of its branches, the scent of the flowers
That climbed round the mouth of the cave.   It is odd I recall
Those little things best, that I scarcely took heed of at all.

I remember how brightly the brass on the butt of my spy-glass
    gleamed
As I climbed through the purple heather and thyme to our
    eyrie and dreamed;
I remember the smooth glossy sun-burn that darkened our
    faces and hands
As we gazed at the merchantmen sailing away to those wonder-
    ful lands.

I remember the long, slow sigh of the sea as we raced in the
    sun,
To dry ourselves after our swimming; and how we would run
With a cry and a crash through the foam as it creamed on the
    shore,
Then back to bask in the warm dry gold of the sand once more.

Come to me, you with the laughing face, in the gloom as I lie
Dreaming of days that are dead and of joys gone by;
Let us be boys together to-night and pretend as of old
We are pirates at rest in a cave among great heaps of gold.

Come; you shall be chief.   We'll not quarrel, the time flies so
    fast.
There are ships to be grappled, there's blood to be shed, ere
    our playtime be past.
No; perhaps we *will* quarrel, just once, or it scarcely will seem
So like the old days that have flown from us both like a dream.

Still; you shall be chief in the end; and then we'll go home
To the hearth and the tea and the books that we loved: ah,
　　　　but come,
Come to me, come through the night and the slow-dropping
　　　　rain;
Come, old friend, come thro' the darkness and let us be play-
　　　　mates again.

A SONG OF ENGLAND

THERE is a song of England that none shall ever sing;
　　　　So sweet it is and fleet it is
That none whose words are not as fleet as birds upon
　　　　the wing,
　　　　And regal as her mountains,
　　　　And radiant as the fountains
Of rainbow-coloured sea-spray that every wave can fling
Against the cliffs of England, the sturdy cliffs of England,
　　　　Could more than seem to dream of it,
　　　　Or catch one flying gleam of it,
Above the seas of England that never cease to sing.

There is a song of England that only lovers know;
　　　　So rare it is and fair it is,
O, like a fairy rose it is upon a drift of snow,
　　　　So cold and sweet and sunny,
　　　　So full of hidden honey,
So like a flight of butterflies where rose and lily blow
Along the lanes of England, the leafy lanes of England;
　　　　When flowers are at their vespers
　　　　And full of little whispers,
The boys and girls of England shall sing it as they go.

There is a song of England that only love may sing,
　　　　So sure it is and pure it is;
And seaward with the sea-mew it spreads a whiter wing,
　　　　And with the sky-lark hovers
　　　　Above the tryst of lovers,
Above the kiss and whisper that led the lovely Spring

Through all the glades of England, the ferny glades of **England,**
        Until the way enwound her
        With sprays of May, and crowned her
With stars of frosty blossom in a merry morris-ring.

There is a song of England that haunts her hours of rest:
        The calm of it and balm of it
Are breathed from every hedgerow that blushes to the West·
        From the cottage doors that nightly
        Cast their welcome out so brightly
On the lanes where laughing children are lifted and caressed
By the tenderest hands in England, hard and blistered hands of
        England:
        And from the restful sighing
        Of the sleepers that are lying
With the arms of God around them on the night's contented
        breast.

There is a song of England that wanders on the wind;
        So sad it is and glad it is
That men who hear it madden and their eyes are wet and blind,
        For the lowlands and the highlands
        Of the unforgotten islands,
For the Islands of the Blesséd and the rest they cannot find
As they grope in dreams to England and the love they left in
        England;
        Little feet that danced to meet them
        And the lips that used to greet them,
And the watcher at the window in the home they left behind.

There is a song of England that thrills the beating blood
        With burning cries and yearning
Tides of hidden aspiration hardly known or understood;
        Aspirations of the creature
        Tow'rds the unity of Nature;
Sudden chivalries revealing whence the longing is renewed
In the men that live for England, live and love and die **for**
        England:
        By the light of their desire
        They shall blindly blunder higher,
To a wider, grander Kingdom and a deeper, nobler Good.

There is a song of England that only heaven can hear;
          So gloriously victorious,
It soars above the choral stars that sing the Golden Year;
          Till even the cloudy shadows
          That wander o'er her meadows
In silent purple harmonies declare His glory there,
Along the hills of England, the billowy hills of England;
          While heaven rolls and ranges
          Through all the myriad changes
That mirror God in music to the mortal eye and ear.

There is a song of England that none shall ever sing;
          So sweet it is and fleet it is
That none whose words are not as fleet as birds upon the wing,
          And regal as her mountains,
          And radiant as her fountains
Of rainbow-coloured sea-spray that every wave can fling
Against the cliffs of England, the sturdy cliffs of England,
          Could more than seem to dream of it,
          Or catch one flying gleam of it,
Above the seas of England that never cease to sing.

THE OLD SCEPTIC

I AM weary of disbelieving: why should I wound my love
    To pleasure a sophist's pride in a graven image of truth?
I will go back to my home, with the clouds and the stars above,
    And the heaven I used to know, and the God of my buried
        youth.

I will go back to the home where of old in my boyish pride
    I pierced my father's heart with a murmur of unbelief.
He only looked in my face as I spoke, but his mute eyes
        cried
    Night after night in my dreams; and he died in **grief, in**
        grief.

Books? I have read the books, the books that we write ourselves,
  Extolling our love of an abstract truth and our pride of
debate:
I will go back to the love of the cotter who sings as he delves
  To that childish infinite love and the God above fact and
date.

To that ignorant infinite God who colours the meaningless
flowers,
  To that lawless infinite Poet who crowns the law with the
crime;
To the Weaver who covers the world with a garment of wonderful hours,
  And holds in His hand like threads the tales and the truth
of time.

Is the faith of the cotter so simple and narrow as this? Ah,
well,
  It is hardly so narrow as yours who daub and plaster with
dyes
The shining mirrors of heaven, the shadowy mirrors of hell,
  And blot out the dark deep vision, if it seem to be framed
with lies.

No faith I hurl against you, no fact to freeze your sneers.
  Only the doubt you taught me to weld in the fires of youth
Leaps to my hand like the flaming sword of nineteen hundred
years,
  The sword of the high God's answer, *O Pilate, what is truth?*

Your laughter has killed more hearts than ever were pierced
with swords,
  Ever you daub new mirrors and turn the old to the wall;
And more than blood is lost in the weary battle of words;
  For creeds are many; but God is One, and contains them all.

Ah, why should we strive or cry? Surely the end is close!
  Hold by your little truths: deem your triumph complete!
But nothing is true or false in the infinite heart of the rose;
  And the earth is a little dust that clings to our travelling feet

I will go back to my home and look at the wayside flowers,
  And hear from the wayside cabins the kind old hymns again,
Where Christ holds out His arms in the quiet evening hours,
  And the light of the chapel porches broods on the peaceful
    lane.

And there I shall hear men praying the deep old foolish prayers,
  And there I shall see, once more, the fond old faith confessed,
And the strange old light on their faces who hear as a blind
    man hears,—
  Come unto Me, ye weary. and I will give you rest.

I will go back and believe in the deep old foolish tales,
  And pray the simple prayers that I learned at my mother's
    knee,
Where the Sabbath tolls its peace thro' the breathless moun-
    tain-vales,
  And the sunset's evening hymn hallows the listening sea.

THE DEATH OF CHOPIN

Sing to me!   Ah, remember how
    Poor Heine here in Paris leant
Watching me play at the fall of day
    And following where the music went,
Till that old cloud upon his brow
    Was almost smoothed away.

"Do roses in the moonlight flame
    Like this and this?" he said and smiled;
Then bent his head as o'er his dead
    Brother might breathe some little child
The accustomed old half-jesting name,
    With all its mockery fled,

Like summer lightnings, far away,
    In heaven.   O, what Bohemian nights
We passed down there for that brief year
    When art revealed her last delights;
And then, that night, that night in May
    When Hugo came to hear!

"Do roses in the moonlight glow
 Like this and this?"   I could not see
His eyes, and yet—they were quite wet,
 Blinded, I think!   What should I be
If in that hour I did not know
 My own diviner debt?

For God has made this world of ours
 Out of His own exceeding pain,
As here in art man's bleeding heart
 Slow drop by drop completes the strain;
And dreams of death make sweet the flowers
 Where lovers meet to part.

Recall, recall my little room
 Where all the masters came that night,
Came just to hear me, Meyerbeer,
 Lamartine, Balzac; and no light
But my two candles in the gloom;
 Though she, she too was there,

George Sand.   This music once unlocked
 My heart, she took the gold she prized:
Her novel gleams no richer: dreams
 Like mine are best unanalysed:
And she forgets her poor bemocked
 Prince Karol, now, it seems.

I was Prince Karol; yes, and Liszt
 Count Salvator Albani: she
My Floriani—all so far
 Away!—My dreams are like the sea
That round Majorca sighed and kissed
 Each softly mirrored star.

O, what a golden round of hours
 Our island villa knew: we two
Alone with sky and sea, the sigh
 Of waves, the warm unfathomed blue;
With what a chain of nights like flowers
 We bound Love, she and I.

What music, what harmonious
   Glad triumphs of the world's desire
Where passion yearns to God and burns
   Earth's dross out with its own pure fire,
Or tolls like some deep angelus
   Through Death's divine nocturnes.

"Do roses in the moonlight glow
   Like this and this?"   What did she think
Of him whose hands at Love's command
   Made Life as honey o'er the brink
Of Death drip slow, darkling and slow?
   Ah, did she understand?

She studied every sob she heard,
   She watched each dying hope she found;
And yet she understood not one
   Poor sorrow there that like a wound
Gaped, bleeding, pleading—for one word—
   No?   And the dream was done.

For her—I am "wrapped in incense gloom,
   In drifting clouds and golden light;"
Once I was shod with fire and trod
   Beethoven's path through storm and night:
It is too late now to resume
   My monologue with God.

Well, my lost love, you were so kind
   In those old days: ah, yes; you came
When I was ill!   In dreams you still
   Will come?   (Do roses always flame
By moonlight, thus?)   I, too, grow blind
   With wondering if she will.

Yet, Floriani, what am I
   To you, though love was life to me?
My life consumed like some perfumed
   Pale altar-flame beside the sea:
You stood and smiled and watched it die!
   You, you whom it illumed,

Could you not feed it with your love?
   Am I not starving here and now?
Sing, sing! I'd miss no smile or kiss—
   No roses in Majorca glow
Like this and this—so death may prove
   Best—ah, how sweet life is!

SONG

(AFTER THE FRENCH OF ROSTAND)

O, MANY a lover sighs
Beneath the summer skies
For black or hazel eyes
     All day.
No light of hope can mar
My whiter brighter star;
I love a Princess far
     Away.

Now you that haste to meet
Your love's returning feet
Must plead for every sweet
     Caress;
But, day and night and day,
Without a prayer to pray,
I love my far away
     Princess.

BUTTERFLIES

SUN-CHILD, as you watched the rain
    Beat the pane,
Saw the garden of your dreams
   Where the clove carnation grows
    And the rose
Veiled with shimmering shades and gleams,

Mirrored colours, mystic gleams,
    Fairy dreams,
Drifting in your radiant eyes
  Half in earnest asked, that day,
    Half in play,
Where were all the butterflies?

Where were all the butterflies
    When the skies
Clouded and their bowers of clover
  Bowed beneath the golden shower?
    Every flower
Shook and the rose was brimming over.

Ah, the dog-rose trembling over
    Thyme and clover,
How it glitters in the sun,
  Now the hare-bells lift again
    Bright with rain
After all the showers are done!

See, when all the showers are done,
    How the sun
Softly smiling o'er the scene
  Bids the white wings come and go
    To and fro
Through the maze of gold and green.

Magic webs of gold and green
    Rainbow sheen
Mesh the maze of flower and fern,
  Cuckoo-grass and meadow-sweet,
    And the wheat
Where the crimson poppies burn.

Ay; and where the poppies burn,
    They return
All across the dreamy downs,
  Little wings that flutter and beat
    O'er the sweet
Bluffs the purple clover crowns.

Where the fairy clover crowns
Dreamy downs,
And amidst the golden grass
Buttercups and daisies blow
To and fro
When the shadowy billows pass;

Time has watched them pause and pass
Where Love was;
Ah, what fairy butterflies,
Little wild incarnate blisses,
Coloured kisses,
Floating under azure skies!

Under those eternal skies
See, they rise:
Mottled wings of moony sheen,
Wings in whitest star-shine dipped,
Orange tipped,
Eyed with black and veined with green.

They were fairies plumed with green
Rainbow-sheen
Ere Time bade their host begone
From that palace built of roses
Which still dozes
In the greenwood all alone.

In the greenwood all alone
And unknown:
Now they roam these mortal dells
Wondering where that happy glade is,
Painted Ladies,
Admirals, and Tortoise-shells.

O, Fritillaries, Admirals,
Tortoise-shells;
You, like fragments of the skies
Fringed with Autumn's richest hues,
Dainty blues
Patterned with mosaic dyes;

Oh, and you whose peacock dyes
       Gleam with eyes;
You, whose wings of burnished copper
  Burn upon the sunburnt brae
      Where all day
Whirrs the hot and grey grasshopper;

While the grey grasshopper whirrs
      In the furze,
You that with your sulphur wings
  Melt into the gold perfume
      Of the broom
Where the linnet sits and sings;

 You that, as a poet sings,
      On your wings
Image forth the dreams of earth,
  Quickening them in form and hue
      To the new
Glory of a brighter birth;

You that bring to a brighter birth
      Dust and earth,
Rapt to glory on your wings,
  All transfigured in the white
      Living light
Shed from out the soul of things;

Heralds of the soul of things,
      You whose wings
Carry heaven through every glade;
  Thus transfigured from the petals
      Death unsettles,
Little souls of leaf and blade;

You that mimic bud and blade,
      Light and shade;
Tinted souls of leaf and stone,
  Flower and sunny bank of sand,
      Fairyland
Calls her children to their own;

Calls them back into their own
Great unknown;
Where the harmonies they cull
On their wings are made complete
As they beat
Through the Gate called Beautiful.

SONG OF THE WOODEN-LEGGED FIDDLER

(PORTSMOUTH 1805)

I LIVED in a cottage adown in the West
When I was a boy, a boy;
But I knew no peace and I took no rest
Though the roses nigh smothered my snug little nest;
For the smell of the sea
Was much rarer to me,
And the life of a sailor was all my joy.

CHORUS.—*The life of a sailor was all my joy!*

My mother she wept, and she begged me to stay
Anchored for life to her apron-string,
And soon she would want me to help with the hay;
So I bided her time, then I flitted away
On a night of delight in the following spring,
With a pair of stout shoon
And a seafaring tune
And a bundle and stick in the light of the moon,
Down the long road
To Portsmouth I strode,
To fight like a sailor for country and king.

CHORUS.—*To fight like a sailor for country and king.*

And now that my feet are turned homeward again
My heart is still crying Ahoy! Ahoy!
And my thoughts are still out on the Spanish main
A-chasing the frigates of France and Spain,
For at heart an old sailor is always a boy;

And his nose will still itch
For the powder and pitch
Till the days when he can't tell t'other from which,
  Nor a grin o' the guns from a glint o' the sea,
  Nor a skipper like Nelson from lubbers like me.

    CHORUS.—*Nor a skipper like Nelson from lubbers like me.*

Ay! Now that I'm old I'm as bold as the best,
  And the life of a sailor is all my joy;
      Though I've swapped my leg
      For a wooden peg
And my head is as bald as a new-laid egg,
      The smell of the sea
      Is like victuals to me,
And I think in the grave I'll be crying Ahoy!
  For, though my old carcass is ready to rest,
  At heart an old sailor is always a boy.

    CHORUS.—*At heart an old sailor is always a boy.*

THE FISHER-GIRL

WHERE the old grey churchyard slopes to the sea,
  On the sunny side of a mossed headstone;
Watching the wild white butterflies pass
Through the fairy forests of grass,
Two little children with brown legs bare
    Were merrily, merrily
Weaving a wonderful daisy-chain,
And chanting the rhyme that was graven there
    Over and over and over again;
While the warm wind came and played with their **hair**
    And laughed and was gone
Out, far out to the foam-flowered lea
Like an ocean-wandering memory.

    Eighteen hundred and forty-three,
    Dan Trevennick was lost at sea;
    And, buried here at her husband's side
    Lies the body of Joan, his bride,
    Who, a little while after she lost him, died.

This was the rhyme that was graven there,
　　And the children chanted it quietly;
As the warm wind came and played with their hair,
And rustled the golden grasses against the stone,
　　And laughed and was gone
To waken the wild white flowers of the sea,
And sing a song of the days that were,
A song of memory, gay and blind
As the sun on the graves that it left behind;
For this, ah this, was the song of the wind.

I

She sat on the tarred old jetty, with a sailor's careless ease,
And the clear waves danced around her feet and kissed her
　　　　tawny knees;
Her head was bare, and her thick black hair was coiled behind
　　　　a throat
Chiselled as hard and bright and bold as the bow of a sailing
　　　　boat.

II

Her eyes were blue, and her jersey was blue as the lapping,
　　　　slapping seas,
And the rose in her cheek was painted red by the brisk Atlantic
　　　　breeze;
And she sat and waited her father's craft, while Dan Treven-
　　　　nick's eyes
Were sheepishly watching her sunlit smiles and her soft con-
　　　　tented sighs.

III

For he thought he would give up his good black pipe and his
　　　　evening glasses of beer,
And blunder to chapel on Sundays again for a holy Christian
　　　　year,
To hold that foot in his hard rough hand and kiss the least
　　　　of its toes:
Then he swore at himself for a great damned fool; which he
　　　　probably was, God knows.

IV

Often in summer twilights, too, he would sit on a coil of rope,
As the stars came out in their twinkling crowds to play with
wonder and hope,
While he watched the side of her clear-cut face as she sat on the
jetty and fished,
And even to help her coil her line was more than he hoped
or wished.

V

But once or twice o'er the dark green tide he saw with a
solemn delight,
Hooked and splashing after her line, a flash and a streak of
white;
As hand over hand she hauled it up, a great black conger eel,
For Dan Trevennick to kill as it squirmed with its head beneath
his heel.

VI

And at last, with a crash and a sunset cry from the low soft
evening star,
A shadowy schooner suddenly loomed o'er the dark green oily
bar;
With fairy-like spars and misty masts in the golden dusk of
gloaming,
Where the last white seamew's wide-spread wings were wistfully westward roaming;

VII

Then the song of the foreign seamen rose in the magical
evening air,
Faint and far away, as it seemed, but they knew it was, ah, so
near;
Far away as her heart from Dan's as he sheepishly drew to
her side,
And near as her heart when he kissed the lips of his newly
promised bride.

VIII

And when they were riding away in the train on the night of
their honeymoon,
What a whisper tingled against her cheek as it blushed like a
rose in June;
For she said, "I am tired and ready for bed," and Dan said,
"So am I;"
And she murmured, "Are you tired, too, poor Dan?" and he
answered her, "No, dear, why?"

IX

It was never a problem-play, at least, and the end of it all is
this;
They were drowned in the bliss of their ignorance and buried
the rest in a kiss;
And they loved one another their whole life long, as lovers
will often do;
For it never was only the fairy-tales that rang so royally true.

X

*The rose in her cheek was painted red by the brisk Atlantic
breeze;*
*Her eyes were blue, and her jersey was blue as the lapping, slapping
seas;*
*Her head was bare, and her thick black hair was coiled behind a
throat*
*Chiselled as hard and bright and bold as the bow of a sailing
boat.*

XI

Eighteen hundred and forty-three,
Dan Trevennick was lost at sea;
And, buried here at her husband's side
Lies the body of Joan, his bride,
Who, a little while after she lost him, died.

A SONG OF TWO BURDENS

THE round brown sails were reefed and struggling home
    Over the glitter and gloom of the angry deep:
Dark in the cottage she sang, "Soon, soon, he will come,
    Dreamikin, Drowsy-head, sleep, my little one, sleep."

Over the glitter and gloom of the angry deep
    Was it only a dream or a shadow that vanished away?
"Lullaby, little one, sleep, my little one, sleep."
    She sang in a dream as the shadows covered the day.

Was it only a sail or a shadow that vanished away?
    The boats come home: there is one that will never return;
But she sang in a dream as the shadows buried the day;
    And she set the supper and begged the fire to burn.

The boats come home; but one will never return;
    And a strangled cry went up from the struggling sea.
She sank on her knees and begged the fire to burn,
    "Burn, oh burn, for my love is coming to me!"

A strangled cry went up from the struggling sea,
    A cry where the ghastly surf to the moon-dawn rolled;
"Burn, oh burn; for my love is coming to me,
    His hands will be scarred with the ropes and starved with
        the cold."

A strangled cry where the foam in the moonlight rolled,
    A bitter cry from the heart of the ghastly sea;
"His hands will be frozen, the night is dark and cold,
    Burn, oh burn, for my love is coming to me."

One cry to God from the soul of the shuddering sea,
    One moment of stifling lips and struggling hands;
"Burn, oh burn; for my love is coming to me;
    And oh, I think the little one understands."

One moment of stifling lips and struggling hands,
    Then only the glitter and gloom of the angry deep;
"And oh, I think the little one understands;
    Dreamikin, Drowsy-head, sleep, my little one, sleep."

EARTH-BOUND

GHOSTS?   Love would fain believe,
    Earth being so fair, the dead might wish to return!
    Is it so strange if, even in heaven, they yearn
For the May-time and the dreams it used to give?

Through dark abysms of Space,
    From strange new spheres where Death has called them
        now
    May they not, with a crown on every brow,
Still cry to the loved earth's lost familiar face?

We two, love, we should come
    Seeking a little refuge from the light
    Of the blinding terrible star-sown Infinite,
Seeking some sheltering roof, some four-walled home,

From that too high, too wide
    Communion with the universe and God,
    How glad to creep back to some lane we trod
Hemmed in with a hawthorn hedge on either side.

Fresh from death's boundless birth,
    How fond the circled vision of the sea
    Would seem to souls tired of Infinity,
How kind the soft blue boundaries of earth,

How rich the nodding spray
    Of pale green leaves that made the sapphire deep
    A background to the dreams of that brief sleep
We called our life when heaven was far away.

How strange would be the sight
    Of the little towns and twisted streets again,
    Where all the hurrying works and ways of men
Would seem a children's game for our delight.

What boundless heaven could give
    This joy in the strait austere restraints of earth,
    Whereof the dead have felt the immortal dearth
Who look upon God's face and cannot live?

Our ghosts would clutch at flowers
    As drowning men at straws, for fear the sea
    Should sweep them back to God's Eternity,
Still clinging to the day that once was ours.

No more with fevered brain
    Plunging across the gulfs of Space and Time
    Would we revisit this our earthly clime
We two, if we could ever come again;

Not as we came of old,
    But reverencing the flesh we now despise
    And gazing out with consecrated eyes,
Each of us glad of the other's hand to hold.

So we should wander nigh
    Our mortal home, and see its little roof
    Keeping the deep eternal night aloof
And yielding us a refuge from the sky.

We should steal in, once more,
    Under the cloudy lilac at the gate,
    Up the walled garden, then with hearts elate
Forget the stars and close our cottage door.

Oh then, as children use
    To make themselves a little hiding-place,
    We would rejoice in narrowness of space,
And God should give us nothing more to lose.

How good it all would seem
    To souls that from the æonian ebb and flow
    Came down to hear once more the to and fro
Swing o' the clock dictate its hourly theme.

How dear the strange recall
  From vast antiphonies of joy and pain
  Beyond the grave, to these old books again,
That cosy lamp, those pictures on the wall.

Home! Home! The old desire!
  We would shut out the innumerable skies,
  Draw close the curtains, then with patient eyes
  Bend o'er the hearth; laugh at our memories,
Or watch them crumbling in the crimson fire.

ART, THE HERALD

"The voice of one crying in the wilderness"

I

BEYOND; beyond; and yet again beyond!
What went ye out to seek, oh foolish-fond?
  Is not the heart of all things here and now?
Is not the circle infinite, and the centre
Everywhere, if ye would but hear and enter?
  Come; the porch bends and the great pillars bow.

II

Come; come and see the secret of the sun;
The sorrow that holds the warring worlds in one;
  The pain that holds Eternity in an hour;
One God in every seed self-sacrificed,
One star-eyed, star-crowned universal Christ,
  Re-crucified in every wayside flower.

THE OPTIMIST

TEACH me to live and to forgive
  The death that all must die
Who pass in slumber through this heaven
  Of earth and sea and sky;

Who live by grace of Time and Space
    At which their peace is priced;
And cast their lots upon the robe
    That wraps the cosmic Christ;

Who cannot see the world-wide Tree
    Where Love lies bleeding still;
This universal cross of God
    Our star-crowned Igdrasil.

Teach me to live; I do not ask
    For length of earthly days,
Or that my heaven-appointed task
    Should fall in pleasant ways;

If in this hour of warmth and light
    The last great knell were knolled;
If Death should close mine eyes to-night
    And all the tale be told;

While I have lips to speak or sing
    And power to draw this breath,
Shall I not praise my Lord and King
    Above all else, for death?

When on a golden eve he drove
    His keenest sorrow deep
Deep in my heart, and called it love;
    I did not wince or weep.

A wild Hosanna shook the world
    And wakened all the sky,
As through a white and burning light
    Her passionate face went by.

When on a golden dawn he called
    My best beloved away,
I did not shrink or stand appalled
    Before the hopeless day.

The joy of that triumphant dearth
    And anguish cannot die;
The joy that casts aside this earth
    For immortality.

I would not change one word of doom
    Upon the dreadful scroll,
That gave her body to the tomb
    And freed her fettered soul.

For now each idle breeze can bring
    The kiss I never seek;
The nightingale has heard her sing,
    The rose caressed her cheek.

And every pang of every grief
    That ruled my soul an hour,
Has given new splendours to the leaf,
    New glories to the flower;

And melting earth into the heaven
    Whose inmost heart is pain,
Has drawn the veils apart and given
    Her soul to mine again.

A POST-IMPRESSION

I

HE sat with his foolish mouth agape at the golden glare of
        the sea,
    And his wizened and wintry flaxen locks fluttered around his
        ears,
    And his foolish infinite eyes were full of the sky's own glitter
        and glee,
    As he dandled an old Dutch Doll on his knee and sang the
        song of the spheres.

II

*Blue and red and yellow and green they are melting away in
the white;*
*Hey! but the wise old world was wrong and my idiot heart was
right;*
*Yes; and the merry-go-round of the stars rolls to my cracked
old tune,*
*Hey! diddle, diddle, the cat and the fiddle, the cow jumped over
the moon.*

III

Then he cradled his doll on his crooning heart and cried as a
sea-bird cries;
And the hot sun reeled like a drunken god through the
violent violet vault:
And the hillside cottage that danced to the deep debauch of
the perfumed skies
Grew palsied and white in the purple heath as a pillar of
Dead Sea salt.

IV

There were three gaunt sun-flowers nigh his chair: they were
yellow as death and tall;
And they threw their sharp blue shadowy stars on the blind
white wizard wall;
And they nodded their heads to the weird old hymn that
daunted the light of the noon,
*Hey! diddle, diddle, the cat and the fiddle, the cow jumped over
the moon.*

V

The little dog laughed and leered with the white of his eye as
he sidled away
To stare at the dwarfish hunchback waves that crawled to
the foot of the hill,
For his master's infinite mind was wide to the wealth of the
night and the day;
The walls were down: it was one with the Deep that only
a God can fill.

VI

Then a tiny maiden of ten sweet summers arrived with a
    song and a smile,
And she swung on the elfin garden-gate and sung to the sea
    for a while,
And a phantom face went weeping by and a ghost began to
    croon
*Hey! diddle, diddle, the cat and the fiddle, the cow jumped over
    the moon.*

VII

And she followed a butterfly up to his chair; and the moon-calf
    caught at her hand
  And stared at her wide blue startled eyes and muttered,
    "My dear, I have been,
In fact, I am there at this moment, I think, in a wonderful
    fairy-land:"
  And he bent and he whispered it low in her ear—"*I know
    why the grass is green.*

VIII

"I know why the daisy is white, my dear, I know why the
    seas are blue;
I know that the world is a dream, my dear, and I know that the
    dream is true;
I know why the rose and the toad-stool grow, as a curse and
    a crimson boon,
*Hey! diddle, diddle, the cat and the fiddle, the cow jumped over
    the moon.*

IX

"If I gaze at a rose, do you know, it grows till it overshadows
    the earth,
  Like a wonderful Tree of Knowledge, my dear, the Tree
    of our evil and good;
But I dare not tell you the terrible vision that gave the toad-
    stool birth,
  The dream of a heart that breaks, my dear, and a Tree
    that is bitter with blood.

X

"Oh, Love may wander wide as the wind that blows from
    sea to sea,
But a wooden dream, for me, my dear, and a painted memory;
For the God that has bidden the toad-stool grow has writ
    in his cosmic rune,
Hey! diddle, diddle, the cat and the fiddle, the cow jumped over
    the moon."

XI

Then he stared at the child and he laughed aloud, and she sud-
    denly screamed and fled,
  As he dreamed of enticing her out thro' the ferns to a quarry
    that gapped the hill,
To hurtle her down and grin as her gold hair scattered around
    her head
  Far, far below, like a sunflower disk, so crimson-spattered
    and still.

XII

"Ah, hush!" he cried; and his dark old eyes were wet with a
    sacred love
As he kissed the wooden face of his doll and winked at the
    skies above,
"I know, I know why the toad-stools grow, and the rest of the
    world will, soon;
Hey! diddle, diddle, the cat and the fiddle, the cow jumped over
    the moon."

XIII

Blue and red and yellow and green they are all mixed up in the
    white;
Hey! but the wise old world was wrong and my idiot heart was
    right;
Yes; and the merry-go-round of the stars rolls to my cracked
    old tune,
Hey! diddle, diddle, the cat and the fiddle, the cow jumped over
    the moon."

THE BARREL-ORGAN

THERE'S a barrel-organ carolling across a golden street
   In the City as the sun sinks low;
And the music's not immortal; but the world has made it
     sweet
   And fulfilled it with the sunset glow;
And it pulses through the pleasures of the City and the pain
   That surround the singing organ like a large eternal light;
And they've given it a glory and a part to play again
   In the Symphony that rules the day and night.

And now it's marching onward through the realms of old
     romance,
   And trolling out a fond familiar tune,
And now it's roaring cannon down to fight the King of France,
   And now it's prattling softly to the moon,
And all around the organ there's a sea without a shore
   Of human joys and wonders and regrets;
To remember and to recompense the music evermore
   For what the cold machinery forgets. . . .

     Yes; as the music changes,
       Like a prismatic glass,
     It takes the light and ranges
       Through all the moods that pass;
     Dissects the common carnival
       Of passions and regrets,
     And gives the world a glimpse of all
       The colours it forgets.

     And there *La Traviata* sighs
       Another sadder song;
     And there *Il Trovatore* cries
       A tale of deeper wrong;
     And bolder knights to battle go
       With sword and shield and lance,
     Than ever here on earth below
       Have whirled into—*a dance!*—

Go down to Kew in lilac-time, in lilac-time, in lilac-time;
 Go down to Kew in lilac-time (it isn't far from London!)
And you shall wander hand in hand with love in summer's
  wonderland;
 Go down to Kew in lilac-time (it isn't far from London!'

The cherry-trees are seas of bloom and soft perfume and
  sweet perfume,
 The cherry-trees are seas of bloom (and oh, so near to
  London!)
And there they say, when dawn is high and all the world's
  a blaze of sky
 The cuckoo, though he's very shy, will sing a song for London.

The Dorian nightingale is rare and yet they say you'll hear
  him there
 At Kew, at Kew in lilac-time (and oh, so near to London!)
The linnet and the throstle, too, and after dark the long halloo
 And golden-eyed *tu-whit, tu-whoo* of owls that ogle London.

For Noah hardly knew a bird of any kind that isn't heard
 At Kew, at Kew in lilac-time (and oh, so near to London!)
And when the rose begins to pout and all the chestnut spires
  are out
 You'll hear the rest without a doubt, all chorussing for
  London:—

Come down to Kew in lilac-time, in lilac-time, in lilac-time;
 Come down to Kew in lilac-time (it isn't far from London!)
And you shall wander hand in hand with love in summer's
  wonderland;
 Come down to Kew in lilac-time (it isn't far from London!)

And then the troubadour begins to thrill the golden street,
 In the City as the sun sinks low;
And in all the gaudy busses there are scores of weary feet
Marking time, sweet time, with a dull mechanic beat,
And a thousand hearts are plunging to a love they'll never
  meet,
Through the meadows of the sunset, through the poppies and
  the wheat,
 In the land where the dead dreams go.

6

Verdi, Verdi, when you wrote *Il Trovatore* did you dream
   Of the City when the sun sinks low,
Of the organ and the monkey and the many-coloured stream
On the Piccadilly pavement, of the myriad eyes that seem
To be litten for a moment with a wild Italian gleam
As *A che la morte* parodies the world's eternal theme
   And pulses with the sunset-glow.

There's a thief, perhaps, that listens with a face of frozen
        stone
   In the City as the sun sinks low;
There's a portly man of business with a balance of his own,
There's a clerk and there's a butcher of a soft reposeful tone.
And they're all of them returning to the heavens they have
        known:
They are crammed and jammed in busses and—they're each
      of them alone
   In the land where the dead dreams go.

There's a very modish woman and her smile is very bland
   In the City as the sun sinks low;
And her hansom jingles onward, but her little jewelled hand
Is clenched a little tighter and she cannot understand
What she wants or why she wanders to that undiscovered land,
For the parties there are not at all the sort of thing she planned,
   In the land where the dead dreams go.

There's a rowing man that listens and his heart is crying
        out
   In the City as the sun sinks low;
For the barge, the eight, the Isis, and the coach's whoop
      and shout,
For the minute-gun, the counting and the long dishevelled
      rout,
For the howl along the tow-path and a fate that's still in
      doubt,
For a roughened oar to handle and a race to think about
   In the land where the dead dreams go.

There's a labourer that listens to the voices of the dead
    In the City as the sun sinks low;
And his hand begins to tremble and his face to smoulder red
As he sees a loafer watching him and—there he turns his head
And stares into the sunset where his April love is fled,
For he hears her softly singing and his lonely soul is led
    Through the land where the dead dreams go.

There's an old and haggard demi-rep, it's ringing in her ears,
    In the City as the sun sinks low;
With the wild and empty sorrow of the love that blights and
      sears,
Oh, and if she hurries onward, then be sure, be sure she hears,
Hears and bears the bitter burden of the unforgotten years,
And her laugh's a little harsher and her eyes are brimmed with
      tears
    For the land where the dead dreams go.

There's a barrel-organ carolling across a golden street
    In the City as the sun sinks low;
Though the music's only Verdi there's a world to make it
      sweet
Just as yonder yellow sunset where the earth and heaven
      meet
Mellows all the sooty City! Hark, a hundred thousand feet
Are marching on to glory through the poppies and the wheat
    In the land where the dead dreams go.

        So it's Jeremiah, Jeremiah,
          What have you to say
        When you meet the garland girls
          Tripping on their way?.

        All around my gala hat
          I wear a wreath of roses
        (A long and lonely year it is
          I've waited for the May!)
        If any one should ask you,
          The reason why I wear it is—
        My own love, my true love
          Is coming home to-day.

And it's buy a bunch of violets for the lady
  (*It's lilac-time in London; it's lilac-time in London!*)
Buy a bunch of violets for the lady
  While the sky burns blue above:

On the other side the street you'll find it shady
  (*It's lilac-time in London; it's lilac-time in London!*)
But buy a bunch of violets for the lady,
  And tell her she's your own true love.

There's a barrel-organ carolling across a golden street
  In the City as the sun sinks glittering and slow;
And the music's not immortal; but the world has made it
      sweet
And enriched it with the harmonies that make a song complete
In the deeper heavens of music where the night and morning
      meet,
  As it dies into the sunset-glow;
And it pulses through the pleasures of the City and the pain
  That surround the singing organ like a large eternal light,
And they've given it a glory and a part to play again
  In the Symphony that rules the day and night.

And there, as the music changes,
  The song runs round again.
Once more it turns and ranges
  Through all its joy and pain,
Dissects the common carnival
  Of passions and regrets;
And the wheeling world remembers all
  The wheeling song forgets.

Once more *La Traviata* sighs
  Another sadder song:
Once more *Il Trovatore* cries
  A tale of deeper wrong;
Once more the knights to battle go
  With sword and shield and lance
Till once, once more, the shattered foe
  Has whirled into—*a dance!*

Come down to Kew in lilac-time, in lilac-time, in lilac-time;
  Come down to Kew in lilac-time (it isn't far from London!)
And you shall wander hand in hand with love in summer's
          wonderland;
  Come down to Kew in lilac-time (it isn't far from London!)

THE LITANY OF WAR

Sandalphon, whose white wings to heaven upbear
          The weight of human prayer,
Stood silent in the still eternal Light
          Of God, one dreadful night.
His wings were clogged with blood and foul with mire,
          His body seared with fire.
"Hast thou no word for Me?" the Master said.
          The angel sank his head:

"Word from the nations of the East and West,"
          He moaned, "that blood is best.
The patriot prayers of either half of earth,
          Hear Thou, and judge their worth.
Out of the obscene seas of slaughter, hear,
          First, the first nation's prayer:
'O God, deliver Thy people.   Let Thy sword
          Destroy our enemies, Lord!'

Pure as the first, as passionate in trust
          That their own cause is just;
Puppets as fond in those dark hands of greed;
          As fervent in their creed;
As blindly moved, as utterly betrayed,
          As urgent for Thine aid;
Out of the obscene seas of slaughter, hear
          The second nation's prayer:
'O God, deliver Thy people.   Let Thy sword
          Destroy our enemies, Lord.'

Over their slaughtered children, one great cry
          From either enemy!
From either host, thigh-deep in filth and shame,
          One prayer, one and the same;

Out of the obscene seas of slaughter, hear,
            From East and West, one prayer:
'*O God, deliver Thy people.   Let Thy sword
            Destroy our enemies, Lord.*'"

Then, on the Cross of His creative pain,
            God bowed His head again.
Then, East and West, over all seas and lands,
            Out-stretched His piercèd hands.
"And yet," Sandalphon whispered, "men deny
            The Eternal Calvary."

THE ORIGIN OF LIFE

[Written in answer to certain scientific pronouncements]

I

In the beginning?—Slowly grope we back
            Along the narrowing track,
Back to the deserts of the world's pale prime,
            The mire, the clay, the slime;
And then . . . what then?   Surely to something less;
            Back, back, to Nothingness!

II

You dare not halt upon that dwindling way!
            There is no gulf to stay
Your footsteps to the last.   Go back you must!
            Far, far below the dust,
Descend, descend!   Grade by dissolving grade,
            We follow, unafraid!
Dissolve, dissolve this moving world of men
            Into thin air—and then?

III

O pioneers, O warriors of the Light,
            In that abysmal night,
Will you have courage, then, to rise and tell
            Earth of this miracle?
Will you have courage, then, to bow the head,
            And say, when all is said—

"Out of this Nothingness arose our thought!
    This blank abysmal Nought
Woke, and brought forth that lighted City street,
    Those towers, that armoured fleet?" . . .

IV

When you have seen those vacant primal skies
    Beyond the centuries.
Watched the pale mists across their darkness flow,
    As in a lantern-show,
Weaving, by merest "chance," out of thin air,
    Pageants of praise and prayer;
Watched the great hills like clouds arise and set,
    And one—named Olivet;
When you have seen, as a shadow passing away,
    One child clasp hands and pray;
When you have seen emerge from that dark mire
    One martyr, ringed with fire;
Or, from that Nothingness, by special grace,
    One woman's love-lit face, ...

V

Will you have courage, then, to front that law
    (From which your sophists draw
Their only right to flout one human creed)
    That nothing can proceed—
Not even thought, not even love—from less
    Than its own nothingness?
The law is yours!   But dare you waive your pride,
    And kneel where you denied?
The law is yours!   Dare you re-kindle, then,
    One faith for faithless men,
And say you found, on that dark road you trod,
    In the beginning—GOD?

THE LAST BATTLE

KINGS of the earth, Kings of the earth, the trumpet rings
    for warning,
  And like the golden swords that ray from out the setting
    sun
The shout goes out of the trumpet mouth across the hills of
    morning,
  Wake; for the last great battle dawns and all the wars are
    done.

Now all the plains of Europe smoke with marching hooves of
    thunder,
  And through each ragged mountain-gorge the guns begin to
    gleam;
And round a hundred cities where the women watch and
    wonder,
  The tramp of passing armies aches and faints into a dream.

The King of Ind is drawing nigh: a hundred leagues are
    clouded
  Along his loud earth-shaking march from east to western
    sea:
The King o' the Setting Sun is here and all the seas are
    shrouded
  With sails that carry half the world to front Eternity.

Soon shall the darkness roll around the grappling of the nations,
  A darkness lit with deadly gleams of blood and steel and fire;
Soon shall the last great pæan of earth's war-worn generations
  Roar through the thunder-clouded air round War's red
    funeral pyre.

But here defeat and victory are both allied with heaven,
  The enfolding sky makes every foe the centre of her dome,
Each fights for God and his own right, and unto each is given
  The right to find the heart of heaven where'er he finds
    his home.

O, who shall win, and who shall lose, and who shall take the
    glory
  Here at the meeting of the roads, where every cause is right?
O, who shall live, and who shall die, and who shall tell the
    story?
  Each strikes for faith and fatherland in that immortal fight.

High on the grey old hills of Time the last immortal rally,
  Under the storm of the last great tattered flag, shall laugh
    to see
The blood of Armageddon roll from every smoking valley,
  Shall laugh aloud, then rush on death for God and chivalry.

Kings of the earth, Kings of the earth, O, which of you then
    shall inherit
  The Kingdom, the Power and the Glory? for the world's
    old light grows dim
And the cry of you all goes up all night to the dark enfolding
    Spirit,
  Each of you fights for God and home; but God, ah, what
    of Him?

THE PARADOX

"I Am that I Am"

I

ALL that is broken shall be mended;
  All that is lost shall be found;
  I will bind up every wound
When that which is begun shall be ended.
Not peace I brought among you but a sword
  To divide the night from the day,
When I sent My worlds forth in their battle-array
  To die and to live,
  To give and to receive,
    Saith the Lord.

II

Of old time they said none is good save our God;
But ye that have seen how the ages have shrunk from my rod,
And how red is the wine-press wherein at my bidding they
            trod,
Have answered and said that with Eden I fashioned the snake,
That I mould you of clay for a moment, then mar you and
            break,
And there is none evil but I, the supreme Evil, God.
      Lo, I say unto both, I am neither;
      But greater than either;
For meeting and mingling in Me they become neither evil nor
            good;
Their cycle is rounded, they know neither hunger nor food,
They need neither sickle nor seed-time, nor root nor fruit,
      They are ultimate, infinite, absolute.
Therefore I say unto all that have sinned,
      East and West and South and North
      The wings of my measureless love go forth
To cover you all: they are free as the wings of the wind.

III

Consider the troubled waters of the sea
      Which never rest;
As the wandering waves are ye;
      Yet assuaged and appeased and forgiven,
      As the seas are gathered together under the infinite glory
            of heaven,
      I gather you all to my breast.
But the sins and the creeds and the sorrows that trouble the
            sea
      Relapse and subside,
Chiming like chords in a world-wide symphony
      As they cease to chide;
For they break and they are broken of sound and hue,
And they meet and they murmur and they mingle anew,
Interweaving, intervolving, like waves: they have no stay:
They are all made as one with the deep, when they sink and
            are vanished away;

Yea, all is toned at a turn of the tide
To a calm and golden harmony;
But I—shall I wonder or greatly care,
    For their depth or their height?
Shall it be more than a song in my sight
How many wandering waves there were,
Or how many colours and changes of light?
    It is your eyes that see
And take heed of these things: they were fashioned for
    you, not for Me.

IV

With the stars and the clouds I have clothed Myself here
    for your eyes
To behold That which Is.   I have set forth the strength of the
    skies
As one draweth a picture before you to make your hearts wise;
That the infinite souls I have fashioned may know as I know,
    Visibly revealed
    In the flowers of the field,
Yea, declared by the stars in their courses, the tides in their
    flow,
And the clash of the world's wide battle as it sways to and fro,
    Flashing forth as a flame
    The unnameable Name,
    The ineffable Word,
    I am the Lord.

V

I am the End to which the whole world strives:
    Therefore are ye girdled with a wild desire and shod
With sorrow; for among you all no soul
Shall ever cease or sleep or reach its goal
Of union and communion with the Whole,
    Or rest content with less than being God.
Still, as unending asymptotes, your lives
    In all their myriad wandering ways
Approach Me with the progress of the golden days;

Approach Me; for my love contrives
That ye should have the glory of this
    For ever; yea, that life should blend
    With life and only vanish away
    From day to wider wealthier day,
Like still increasing spheres of light that melt and merge in
      wider spheres
Even as the infinite years of the past melt in the infinite future
      years.
    Each new delight of sense,
    Each hope, each love, each fear,
    Widens, relumes and recreates each sphere,
From a new ring and nimbus of pre-eminence.
I am the Sphere without circumference:
I only and for ever comprehend
All others that within me meet and blend.
    Death is but the blinding kiss
    Of two finite infinities;
    Two finite infinite orbs
  The splendour of the greater of which absorbs
The less, though both like Love have no beginning and no end

VI

Therefore is Love's own breath
Like Knowledge, a continual death;
And all his laughter and kisses and tears,
    And woven wiles of peace and strife,
That ever widen thus your temporal spheres,
Are making of the memory of your former years
    A very death in life.

VII

I am that I am;
Ye are evil and good;
With colour and glory and story and song ye are fed as with
    food:
      The cold and the heat,
      The bitter and the sweet,
The calm and the tempest fulfil my Word;
Yet will ye complain of my two-edged sword

That has fashioned the finite and mortal and given you the
        sweetness of strife,
              The blackness and whiteness,
              The darkness and brightness,
Which sever your souls from the formless and void and hold
        you fast-fettered to life?

VIII

    Behold now, is Life not good?
    Yea, is it not also much more than the food,
More than the raiment, more than the breath?
    Yet Strife is its name!
Say, which will ye cast out first from the furnace, the fuel or the
        flame?
Would ye all be as I am; and know neither evil nor good;
        neither life; neither death;
Or mix with the void and the formless till all were as one and
        the same?

IX

I am that I am; the Container of all things: kneel, lift up your
        hands
To the high Consummation of good and of evil which none
        understands;
The divine Paradox, the ineffable Word, in whose light the
        poor souls that ye trod
Underfoot as too vile for their fellows are at terrible union with
        God!
    Am I not over both evil and good,
    The righteous man and the shedder of blood?
        Shall I save or slay?
    I am neither the night nor the day,
        Saith the Lord.
Judge not, oh ye that are round my footstool, judge not, ere
        the hour be born
    That shall laugh you also to scorn.

X

Ah, yet I say unto all that have sinned,
  East and West and South and North
  The wings of my measureless love go forth
To cover you all: they are free as the wings of the wind.

XI

But one thing is needful; and ye shall be true
  To yourselves and the goal and the God that ye seek;
Yea, the day and the night shall requite it to you
  If ye love one another, if your love be not weak.

XII

Since I sent out my worlds in their battle-array
      To die and to live,
      To give and to receive,
Not peace, not peace, I have brought among you but a sword,
    To divide the night from the day,
        Saith the Lord;
Yet all that is broken shall be mended,
      And all that is lost shall be found,
      I will bind up every wound,
When that which is begun shall be ended.

THE PROGRESS OF LOVE

(A LYRICAL SYMPHONY)

I

In other worlds I loved you, long ago:
  Love that hath no beginning hath no end.
The woodbine whispers, low and sweet and low,
In other worlds I loved you, long ago;
The firwoods murmur and the sea-waves know
  The message that the setting sun shall send.
In other worlds I loved you, long ago:
  Love that hath no beginning hath no end.

II

And God sighed in the sunset; and the sea
   Chanted the soft recessional of Time
Against the golden shores of mystery;

And ever as that long low change and chime
   With one slow sob of molten music yearned
Westward, it seemed as if the Love sublime

Almost uttered itself, where the waves burned
   In little flower-soft flames of rose and green
That woke to seaward, while the tides returned

Rising and falling, ruffled and serene,
   With all the mirrored tints of heaven above
Shimmering through their mystic myriad sheen.

As a dove's burnished breast throbbing with love
   Swells and subsides to call her soft-eyed mate
Home through the rosy gloom of glen or grove,

So when the greenwood noon was growing late
   The sea called softly through the waste of years,
Called to the star that still can consecrate

The holy golden haze of human tears
   Which tinges every sunset with our grief
Until the perfect Paraclete appears.

Ah, the long sigh that yields the world relief
   Rose and relapsed across Eternity,
Making a joy of sorrows that are brief,

As, o'er the bright enchantment of the sea,
   Facing the towers of that old City of Pain
Which stands upon the shores of mystery

And frowns across the immeasurable main,
   Venus among her cloudy sunset flowers
Woke; and earth melted into heaven again.

For even the City's immemorial towers
  Were tinted into secret tone and time,
Like old forgotten tombs that age embowers

With muffling roses and with mossy rime
  Until they seem no monument of ours,
But one more note in earth's accordant chime.

O Love, Love, Love, all dreams, desires and powers,
  Were but as chords of that ineffable psalm;
And all the long blue lapse of summer hours,

And all the breathing sunset's golden balm
  By that æonian sorrow were resolved
As dew into the music's infinite calm,

Through which the suns and moons and stars revolve
  According to the song's divine decree,
Till Time was but a tide of intervolved

And interweaving worlds of melody;
  In other worlds I loved you, long ago,—
The angelic citoles fainted o'er the sea;

And seraph citerns answered, sweet and low,
  From where the sunset and the moonrise blend,—
In other worlds I loved you, long ago;

Love that hath no beginning hath no end;
  O Love, Love, Love, the bitter City of Pain
Bidding the golden echoes westward wend,

Chimed in accordant undertone again:
  Though every grey old tower rose like a tomb
To mock the glory of the shoreless main

They could but strike such discords as illume
  The music with strange gleams of utter light
And hallow all the valley's rosy gloom.

And there, though greyly sinking out of sight
  Before the wonders of the sky and sea,
Back through the valley, back into the night,

While mystery melted into mystery,
  The City still rebuffed the far sweet West
That dimmed her sorrows with infinity;

Yet sometimes yearning o'er the sea's bright breast
  To that remote Avilion would she gaze
Where all lost loves and weary warriors rest.

Then she remembered, through that golden haze,
  (Oh faint as flowers the rose-white waves resound)
Her Arthur whom she loved in the dead days,

And how he sailed to heal him of his wound,
  And how he lives and reigns eternally
Where now that unknown love is throned and crowned

Who laid his bleeding head against her knee
  And loosed the bitter breast-plate and unbound
His casque and brought him strangely o'er the sea,

And how she reigns beside him on that shore
  For ever (Yrma, queen, bend down to me)
And they twain have no sorrow any more.

III

They have forgotten all that vanished away
When life's dark night died into death's bright day
They have forgotten all except the gleam
Of light when once he kissed her in a dream
Once on the lips and once upon the brow
In the white orb of God's transcendent Now;
And even then he knew that, long before,
Their eyes had met upon some distant shore;
Yea; that most lonely and immortal face
Which dwells beyond the dreams of time and space
Bowed down to him from out the happy place

And whispered to him, low and sweet and low
In other worlds I loved you, long ago;
And then he knew his love could never die
Because his queen was throned beyond the sky
And called him to his own immortal sphere
Forgetting Launcelot and Guinevere.

So Yrma reigns with Arthur, and they know
They loved on earth a million years ago;
    And watched the sea-waves wistfully westward wend;
And heard a voice whispering in their flow,
And calling through the silent sunset-glow,
Love that hath no beginning hath no end.

IV

It was about the dawn of day
    I heard Etain and Anwyl say
The waving ferns are a fairy forest,
    It is time, it is time to wander away;

For the dew is bright on the heather bells,
And the breeze in the clover sways and swells,
    As the waves on the blue sea wake and wander,
Over and under the braes and dells.

She was eight years old that day,
Full of laughter and play;
    Eight years old and Anwyl nine,—
Two young lovers were they.

Two young lovers were they,
    Born in the City of Pain;
There was never a song in the world so gay
    As the song of the child, Etain;

There was never a laugh so sweet
    With the ripple of fairy bells,
And never a fairy foot so fleet
    Dancing down the woodland dells!

She was eight years old that day,
Two young lovers were they.

There was never a sea of mystical gleams
   Glooming under enchanted skies
Deep as the dark miraculous dreams
   In Anwyl's haunted eyes.

There was never a glory of light
   Around the carolling lark
As Etain's eyes were brave and bright
   To daunt the coming dark.

Two young lovers were they
   Born in the City of Pain;
There was never a song in the world so gay
   As the song of the child, Etain;

Blithe as the wind in the trees,
   Blithe as the bird on the bough,
Blithe as the bees in the sweet Heart's-ease
   Where Love lies bleeding now.

V

And God sighed in the sunset; and the sea
   Forgot her sorrow, and all the breathless West
Grew quiet as the blue tranquillity

That clad the broken mountain's brilliant breast,
   Over the City, with deep heather-bloom
Heaving from crag to crag in sweet unrest,

A sea of dim rich colour and warm perfume
   Whose billows rocked the drowsy honey-bee
Among the golden isles of gorse and broom

Like some enchanted ancient argosy
   Drunkenly blundering over seas of dream
Past unimagined isles of mystery,

Over whose yellow sands the soft waves cream,
    And sunbeams float and toss across the bare
Rose-white arms and perilous breasts that gleam

Where sirens wind their glossy golden hair;
    Oh, miles on miles, the honeyed heather-bloom
Heaving its purple through the high bright air

Rolled a silent glory of gleam and gloom
    From mossy crag to crag and crest to crest
Untroubled by the valley's depth of doom.

The hawk dropped down into the pine-forest
    And, far below, the lavrock ruffled her wings
Blossomwise over her winsome secret nest.

Then suddenly, softly, as when a fairy sings
    Out of the heart of a rose in the heart of the fern,
Or in the floating starlight faintly rings

The frail blue hare-bells—turn again, and turn,
    Under and over, the silvery crescents cry
To where the crimson fox-glove belfries burn

And with a deeper softer peal reply,
    There came a ripple of music through the roses
That rustled on the dimmest rim of sky

Where many a frame of fretted leaves encloses
    For lovers wandering in the fern-wet wood
An arch of summer sea that softly dozes

As if all mysteries were understood:
    Yrma, my queen, what love could understand
That faint sweet music, *God saith all is good,*

As those two children, hand in sunburnt hand,
    Over the blithe blue hills and far away
Wandered into their own green fairyland?

VI

For the song is lost that shook the dew
  Where the wild musk-roses glisten,
When the sunset dreamed that a dream was true
  And the birds were hushed to listen.

The song is lost that shook the night
  With wings of richer fire,
Where the years had touched their eyes with light
  And their souls with a new desire;

And the new delight of the strange old story
  Burned in the flower-soft skies,
And nine more years with a darker glory
  Had deepened the light of her eyes;

But lost, oh more than lost the song
  That shook the rose to tears,
As hand in hand they danced along
  Through childhood's everlasting years.

"Oh, Love has wings," the linnet sings;
  But the dead return no more, no more;
And the sea is breaking its old grey heart
  Against the golden shore.

She was eight years old that day,
Two young lovers were they.

If every song as they danced along
  Paused on the springing spray;
Is there never a bird in the wide greenwood
  Will hush its heart to-day?

There's never a leaf with dew impearled
  To make their pathway sweet,
And never a blossom in all the world
  That knows the kiss of their feet.

No light to-night declares the word
  That thrilled the blossomed bough,
And stilled the happy singing bird
  That none can silence now.

The weary nightingale may sob
  With her bleeding breast against a thorn,
And the wild white rose with every throb
  Grow red as the laugh of morn;

With wings outspread she sinks her head
  But Love returns no more, no more;
And the sea is breaking its old grey heart
  Against the golden shore.

Born in the City of Pain;
  Ah, who knows, who knows
When Death shall turn to delight again
  Or a wound to a red, red rose?

Eight years old that day,
Full of laughter and play;
  Eight years old and Anwyl nine,—
Two young lovers were they.

VII

And down the scented heather-drowsy hills
  The bare-foot children wandered, hand in hand,
And paddled through the laughing silver rills
  In quest of fairyland;
And in each little sunburnt hand a spray,
  A purple fox-glove bell-branch lightly swung,
And Anwyl told Etain how, far away,
  One day he wandered through the dreamland dells
And watched the moonlit fairies as they sung
  And tolled the fox-glove bells;
And oh, how sweetly, sweetly to and fro
The fragrance of the music reeled and rung
  Under the loaded boughs of starry May.

And God sighed in the sunset, and the sea
Grew quieter than the hills: the mystery
Of ocean, earth and sky was like a word
    Uttered, but all unheard,
Uttered by every wave and cloud and leaf
With all the immortal glory of mortal grief;
And every wave that broke its heart of gold
    In music on the rainbow-dazzled shore
Seemed telling, strangely telling, evermore
    A story that must still remain untold.

Oh, *Once upon a time*, and o'er and o'er
    As aye the *Happy ever after* came
The enchanted waves lavished their faery lore

And tossed a foam-bow and a rosy flame
    Around the whispers of the creaming foam,
Till the old rapture with the new sweet name

Through all the old romance began to roam,
    And Anwyl, gazing out across the sea,
Dreamed that he heard the distance whisper "Come."

"Etain," he murmured softly and wistfully,
    With the soul's wakening wonder in his eyes,
"Is it not strange to think that there can be

"No end for ever and ever to those skies,
    No shore beyond, or if there be a shore
Still without end the world beyond it lies;

"Think; think, Etain;" and all his faery lore
    Mixed with the faith that brought all gods to birth
And sees new heavens transcend for evermore

The poor impossibilities of earth;
    But Etain only laughed: the world to her
Was one sweet smile of very present mirth;

Its flowers were only flowers, common or rare;
    Her soul was like a little garden closed
By rose-clad walls, a place of southern air

Islanded from the Mystery that reposed
  Its vast and brooding wings on that abyss
Through which like little clouds that dreamed and dozed

The thoughts of Anwyl wandered toward some bliss
  Unknown, unfathomed, far, how far away,
Where God has gathered all the eternities
  Into strange heavens, beyond the night and day.

VIII

And over the rolling golden bay,
In the funeral pomp of the dying day,
  The bell of Time was wistfully tolling
A million million years away;

And over the heather-drowsy hill
Where the burdened bees were buzzing still,
  The two little sun-bright barefoot children
Wandered down at the flowers' own will;

For still as the bell in the sunset tolled,
The meadow-sweet and the mary-gold
  And the purple orchis kissed their ankles
And lured them over the listening wold.

And the feathery billows of blue-gold grass
Bowed and murmured and bade them pass,
  Where a sigh of the sea-wind softly told them
There is no Time—Time never was.

And what if a sorrow were tolled to rest
Where the rich light mellowed away in the West,
  As a glory of fruit in an autumn orchard
Heaped and asleep o'er the sea's ripe breast?

Why should they heed it, what should they know
Of the years that come or the years that go,
  With the warm blue sky around and above them
And the wild thyme whispering to and fro?

For they heard in the dreamy dawn of day
A fairy harper faintly play,
  Follow me, follow me, little children,
Over the hills and far away;

Where the dew is bright on the heather-bells,
And the breeze in the clover sways and swells,
  As the waves on the blue sea wake and wander,
Over and under the braes and dells.

And the hare-bells tinkled and rang Ding dong
Bell in the dell as they danced along,
  And their feet were stained on the hills with honey,
And crushing the clover till evensong.

And, oh the ripples that rolled in rhyme
Under the wild blue banks of thyme,
  To the answering rhyme of the rolling ocean's
Golden glory of change and chime!

For they came to a stream and her fairy lover
Caught at her hand and swung her over,
  And the broad wet buttercups laughed and gilded
Their golden knees in the deep sweet clover.

There was never a lavrock up in the skies
Blithe as the laugh of their lips and eyes,
  As they glanced and glittered across the meadows
To waken the sleepy butterflies.

There was never a wave on the sea so gay
As the light that danced on their homeward way
  Where the waving ferns were a fairy forest
And a thousand years as yesterday.

> *She was eight years old that day,*
> *Full of laughter and play;*
>   *Eight years old and Anwyl nine,—*
> *Two young lovers were they.*

And when the clouds like folded sheep
Were drowsing over the drowsy deep,
    And like a rose in a golden cradle
Anwyl breathed on the breast of sleep,

Or ever the petals and leaves were furled
At the vesper-song of the sunset-world,
    The sleepy young rose of nine sweet summers
Dreamed in his rose-bed cosily curled.

And what if the light of his nine bright years
Glistened with laughter or glimmered with tears,
    Or gleamed like a mystic globe around him
White as the light of the sphere of spheres?

And what if a glory of angels there,
Starring an orb of ineffable air,
    Came floating down from the Gates of jasper
That melt into flowers at a maiden's prayer?

And what if he dreamed of a fairy face
Wondering out of some happy place,
    Quietly as a star at sunset
Shines in the rosy dreams of space?

For only as far as the west wind blows
The sweets of a swinging full-blown rose,
    Eight years old and queen of the lilies
Little Etain slept—ah, how close!

At a flower-cry over the moonlit lane
In a cottage of roses dreamed Etain,
    And their purple shadows kissed at her lattice
And dappled her sigh-soft counterpane;

And or ever Etain with her golden head
Had nestled to sleep in her lily-white bed,
    She breathed a dream to her fairy lover,
Please, God, bless Anwyl and me, she said.

And a song arose in the rose-white West,
And a whisper of wings o'er the sea's bright breast,
   And a cry where the moon's old miracle wakened
A glory of pearl o'er the pine-forest.

Why should they heed it?   What should they know
Of the years to come or the years to go?
   With the starry skies around and above them
And the roses whispering to and fro.

Ah, was it a song of the mystic morn
When into their beating hearts the thorn
   Should pierce through the red wet crumpled roses
And all the sorrow of love be born?

Ah, was it a cry of the wild wayside
Whereby one day they must surely ride,
   Out of the purple garden of passion
To Calvary, to be crucified?

Only the sound of the distant sea
Broke on the shores of Mystery,
   And tolled as a bell might toll for sorrow
Till Time be tombed in Eternity;

And in their dreams they only heard
Far away, one secret bird
   Sing, till the passionate purple twilight
Throbbed with the wonder of one sweet word:

One sweet word and the wonder awoke,
And the leaves and the flowers and the starlight spoke
   In silent rapture the strange old secret
That none e'er knew till the death-dawn broke;

One sweet whisper, and hand in hand
They wandered in dreams through fairyland,
   Rapt in the star-bright mystical music
Which only a child can understand.

But never a child in the world can tell
The wonderful tale he knows so well,
   Though ever as old Time dies in the sunset
It tolls and tolls like a distant bell.

Love, love, love; and they hardly knew
The sense of the glory that round them grew;
   But the world was a wide enchanted garden;
And the song, the song, the song rang true.

And they danced with the fairies in emerald rings
Arched by the light of their rainbow wings,
   And they heard the wild green Harper striking
A starlight over the golden strings.

Love, oh love; and they roamed once more
Through a forest of flowers on a fairy shore,
   And the sky was a wild bright laugh of wonder
And the West was a dream of the years of yore.

In other worlds I loved you, long ago:
   Love that hath no beginning hath no end:
The heather whispers low and sweet and low,
In other worlds I loved you, long ago;
The meadows murmur and the firwoods know
   The message that the kindling East shall send;
In other worlds I loved you, long ago:
   Love that hath no beginning hath no end.

IX

Out of the deep, my dream, out of the deep,
Yrma, thy voice came to me in my sleep,
And through a rainbow woven of human tears
I saw two lovers wandering down the years;
Two children, first, that roamed a sunset land,
And then two lovers wandering hand in hand,
Forgetful of their childhood's Paradise,
For nine more years had darkened in their eyes,
And heaven itself could hardly find again
Anwyl, the star-child, or the flower, Etain.

For on a day in May, as through the wood
With earth's new passion beating in his blood
He went alone, an empty-hearted youth,
Seeking he knew not what white flower of truth
Or beauty, on all sides he seemed to see
Swift subtle hints of some new harmony,
Yet all unheard, ideal, and incomplete,
A silent song compact of hopes and fears,
A music such as lights the wandering feet
Of Yrma when on earth she reappears.
And he forgot that sad grey City of Pain,
For all earth's old romance returned again,
And as he went, his dreaming soul grew glad
To think that he might meet with Galahad
Or Parsifal in some green glade of fern,
Or see between the boughs a helmet burn
And hear a joyous laugh kindle the sky
As through the wood Sir Launcelot rode by
With face upturned to take the sun like wine.
Ah, was it love that made the whole world shine
Like some great angel's face, blinded with bliss,
While Anwyl dreamed of bold Sir Amadis
And Guinevere's white arms and Iseult's kiss,
And that glad island in a golden sea
Where Arthur lives and reigns eternally?
Surely the heavens were one wide rose-white flame
As down the path to meet him Yrma came;
Ah, was it Yrma, with those radiant eyes,
That came to greet and lead him through the skies,
The skies that gloomed and gleamed so far above
The little wandering prayers of human love? . . .
He had forgotten all except the gleam
Of light when once he kissed her in a dream, . . .
For surely then he knew that long before
Their eyes had met upon some distant shore. . . .
Ah, was it Yrma whose red lips he met
Between the branches, where the leaves were wet?
Etain or Yrma, for it seemed her face
Bent down upon him from some happy place
And whispered to him, low and sweet and low,
In other worlds I loved you, long ago!

And he, too, knew his love could never die,
Because his queen was throned beyond the sky.

Yet in sweet mortal eyes he met her now
And kissed Etain beneath the hawthorn bough,
And dared to dream his infinite dream was true
On earth and reign with Etain, dream he knew
Why leaves were green and skies were fresh and blue;
Yea, dream he knew, as children dream they know
They knew all this a million years ago,
  And watched the sea-waves wistfully westward wend
And heard a voice whispering in their flow
And calling through the silent sunset-glow
  Love that hath no beginning hath no end.

Ah, could they see in the Valley of Gloom
That clove the cliffs behind the City;
Ah, could they hear in the forest of Doom
The peril that neared without pause or pity?
Behind the veils of ivy and vine,
Wild musk-roses and white woodbine,
In glens that were wan as with moonlit tears
And rosy with ghosts of eglantine
And pale as with lilies of long-past years,
Ah, could they see, could they hear, could they know
Behind that beautiful outward show,
Behind the pomp and glory of life
That seething old anarchic strife?
For there in many a dim blue glade
Where the rank red poppies burned,
And if perchance some dreamer strayed
He nevermore returned,
Cold incarnate memories
Of earth's retributory throes,
Deadly desires and agonies
Dark as the worm that never dies,
In the outer night arose,
And waited under those wonderful skies
With Hydra heads and mocking eyes
That winked upon the waning West
From out the gloom of the oak-forest,

Till all the wild profound of wood
That o'er the haunted valley slept
Glowed with eyes like pools of blood
As, lusting after a hideous food,
Through the haggard vistas crept
Without a cry, without a hiss,
The serpent broods of the abyss.
Ancestral folds in darkness furled
Since the beginnings of the world.
Ring upon awful ring uprose
That obscure heritage of foes,
The exceeding bitter heritage
Which still a jealous God bestows
From inappellable age to age,
The ghostly worms that softly move
Through every grey old corse of love
And creep across the coffined years
To batten on our blood and tears;
And there were hooded shapes of death
Gaunt and grey, cruel and blind,
Stealing softly as a breath
Through the woods that lcured behind
The City; hooded shapes of fear
Slowly, slowly stealing near;
While all the gloom that round them rolled
With intertwisting coils grew cold.
And there with leer and gap-toothed grin
Many a gaunt ancestral Sin
With clutching fingers, white and thin,
Strove to put the boughs aside;
And still before them all would glide
Down the wavering moon-white track
One lissom figure, clad in black;
Who wept at mirth and mocked at pain
And murmured a song of the wind and the rain;
His laugh was wild with a secret grief;
His eyes were deep like woodland pools;
And, once and again, as his face drew near
In a rosy gloaming of eglantere,
All the ghosts that gathered there

Bowed together, naming his name:
Lead us, ah thou *Shadow of a Leaf*,
Child and master of all our shame,
Fool of Doubt and King of Fools.

Now the linnet had ended his even-song,
And the lark dropt down from his last wild ditty
And ruffled his wings and his speckled breast
Blossom-wise over his June-sweet nest;
While winging wistfully into the West
As a fallen petal is wafted along
The last white sea-mew sought for rest;
And, over the gleaming heave and swell
Of the swinging seas,
Drowsily breathed the dreaming breeze.
Then, suddenly, out of the Valley of Gloom
That clove the cliffs behind the City,
Out of the silent forest of Doom
That clothed the valley with clouds of fear
Swelled the boom of a distant bell
Once, and the towers of the City of Pain
Echoed it, without hope or pity.
The tale of that tolling who can tell?
That dark old music who shall declare?
Who shall interpret the song of the bell?

Is it nothing to you, all ye that hear,
Sorrowed the bell, *Is it nothing to you?*
Is it nothing to you? the shore-wind cried,
Is it nothing to you? the cliffs replied.
But the low light laughed and the skies were blue,
And this was only the song of the bell.

X

ANWYL

A darkened casement in a darker room
    Was all his home, whence weary and bowed and wh
He watched across the slowly gathering gloom
    The slowly westering light.

Bitterness in his heavy-clouded eyes,
   Bitterness as of heaven's intestine wars
Brooded; he looked upon the unfathomed skies
   And whispered—to the stars—

Some day, he said, she will forget all this
   That she calls life, and looking far above
See throned among the great eternities
   This dream of mine, this love;

Love that has given my soul these wings of fire
   To beat in glory above the sapphire sea,
Until the wings of the infinite desire
   Close in infinity;

Love that has taken the glory of hawthorn boughs,
   And all the dreaming beauty of hazel skies,
As ministers to the radiance of her brows
   And haunted April eyes;

Love that is hidden so deep beneath the dust
   Of little daily duties and delights,
Till that reproachful face of hers grows just
   And God at last requites

A soul whose dream was deeper than the skies,
   A heart whose hope was wider than the sea,
Yet could not enter through his true love's eyes
   Their grey infinity.

And so I know I wound her all day long
   Because my heart must seem so far away;
And even my love completes the silent wrong
   For all that it can say

Seems vast and meaningless to mortal sense;
   Its vague desire can never reach its goal
Till knowledge vanishes in omniscience
   And God surrounds her soul,

8

Breaking its barriers down and flooding in
  Through all her wounds in one almighty tide,
Mingling her soul with that great Love wherein
  My soul waits, glorified.

XI

ETAIN

My love is dying, dying in my heart;
  There is no song in heaven for such as I
Who watch the days and years of youth depart,
  The bloom decay and die;

The rose that withers in the hollow cheek,
  The leaden rings that mark us old and wise;
And Time that writes what Pity dares not speak
  Around the fading eyes.

He dreams he loves; but only loves his dream;
  And in his dream he never can forget
Abana seems a so much mightier stream
  And Pharpar wider yet;

The little deeds of love that light the shrine
  Of common daily duties with such gleams
Of heaven, to me are scarcely less divine
  Than those poor wandering dreams

Of deeds that never happen!   I give him this,
  This heart he cannot find in heaven above;
This heart, this heart of all the eternities,
  This life of mine, this love;

Love that is lord of all the world at once
  And never bade the encircled spirit roam
To the circle's bound, beyond the moons and suns,
  But makes each heart its home.

And every home the heart of Space and Time,
    And each and all a heaven if love could reign;
One infinite untranscended heaven sublime
    With God's own joy and pain.

Why, that was what God meant, to set us here
    In Eden, when he saw that all was good;
And we have made the sun black with despair,
    And turned the moon to blood.

So has Love taught me that too learnèd tongue,
    And in his poorer wisdom made me wise;
I grew so proud of the red drops we wrung
    From all philosophies.

My heart is narrow, foolish, what you will;
    But this I know God meant who set us here,
And gave each soul the Infinities to fulfil
    From its own widening sphere.

To annex new regions to the soul's domain,
    To expand the circle of the golden hours,
Till it enfolds again and yet again
    New heavens, new fields, new flowers,

Oh, this is well; but still the central heart
    Is here at home, not wandering like the wind
That gathers nothing, but must still depart
    Leaving a waste behind.

Where is the song I sang that April morn,
    When all the poet in his eyes awoke
My sleeping heart to heaven; and love was born?
    For while the glad day broke

We met; and as the softly kindling skies
    Thrilled through the scented vistas of the wood
I felt the sudden love-light in his eyes
    Kindle my beating blood.

Happy day, happy day,
Chasing the clouds of the night away
   And bidding the dreams of the dawn depart
Over the freshening April blue,
   Till the blossoms awake to welcome the May,
And the world is made anew;
   And the blackbird sings on the dancing spray
With eyes of glistening dew;
   "Happy, happy, happy day;"
For he knows that his love is true;
   He knows that his love is true, my heart,
He knows that his love is true!

I cannot sing it: these tears blind me: love,
   O love, come back before it is too late,
Why, even Christ came down to us from above:
   I think His love was great;

Yet he stood knocking, knocking at the door
   Until his piteous hands were worn with scars;
He did not hide that crown of love he wore
   Among the lonely stars.

This round of hours, the daily flowers I cull
   Are more to me than all the rolling spheres,
A wounded bird at hand more pitiful
   Than some great seraph's tears.

How should I join the great wise choir above
   With my starved spirit's pale inhuman dearth,
Who never heard the cry of heavenly love
   Rise from the sweet-souled earth?

Yet it is I he needs, and I for whom
   His greed exceeds, his dreams fly wide of the mark!
Is it all self?   I wander in the gloom;
   The ways of God grow dark;

I watch the rose that withers in the cheek,
  The leaden rings that mark us old and wise;
And Time that writes what Pity dares not speak
  Around the fading eyes.

XII

And ever as Anwyl went the unknown end
  Faded before him, back and back and back
He saw new empty heavens for ever bend
  Over his endless track;

And memory, burning with new hopeless fire,
  Showed him how every passing infinite hour
Made some new Crucifix for the World's Desire
  Is some new wayside flower:

He saw what joy and beauty owed to death;
  How all the world was one great sacrifice
Of Him, in whom all creatures that draw breath
  Share God's eternal skies;

How Love is lord of all the world at once;
  And never bids the encircled spirit roam
To the circle's bound, beyond the moons and suns,
  But makes each heart its home,

And every home the heart of Space and Time,
  And each and all a heaven if love could reign
One infnite untranscended heaven sublime
  With God's own joy and pain.

XIII

Out of the deep, my dream, out of the deep,
A little child came to him in his sleep
And led him back to what was Paradise
Before the years had darkened in his eyes,
And showed him what he ne'er could lose again—
The light that once enshrined the child Etain.

Ah, was it Yrma with those radiant eyes
That came to greet and lead him through the skies;
Ay; all the world was one wide rose-white flame,
As down the path to meet him Yrma came
And caught the child up in her arms and cried,
This is my child that moved in Etain's side,
Thy child and Etain's: I the unknown ideal
And she the rich, the incarnate, breathing real
Are one; for me thou never canst attain
But by the love I yield thee for Etain;
Even as through Christ thy soul allays its dearth,
Love's heaven is only compassed upon earth;
And by that love, in thine own Etain's eyes
Thou shalt find all God's untranscended skies.

As of old, as of old, with Etain that day,
Over the hills, and far away,
    He roamed thro' the fairy forests of fern:
Two young lovers were they.

And God sighed in the sunset, and the sea
Grew quieter than the hills: the mystery
Of ocean, earth and sky was like a word
    Uttered, but all unheard,
Uttered by every wave and cloud and leaf
With all the immortal glory of mortal grief;
And every wave that broke its heart of gold
    In music on the rainbow-dazzled shore
Seemed telling, strangely telling, evermore
    A story that must still remain untold.

Oh, *Once upon a time*, and o'er and o'er
    As aye the *Happy ever after* came
The enchanted waves lavished their faery lore

And tossed a foam-bow and a rosy flame
    Around the whispers of the creaming foam,
Till the old rapture with the new sweet name
    Through all the old romance began to roam.

XIV

And those two lovers only heard
   —Oh, love is a dream that knows no waking—
Far away, one secret bird,
Where all the roses breathed one word,
And every crispel on the beach—
   Oh, love is a sea that is ever breaking!—
Lisped it in a sweeter speech;
As hand in hand, by the sunset sea
That breaks on the shores of mystery,
They stood in the gates of the City of Pain
To watch the wild waves flutter and beat
In roses of white soft light at their feet,
Roses of delicate music and light,
Music and moonlight under their feet.
Crumbling and flashing and softly crashing
In rainbow colours that dazzle and wane
And wither and waken and, wild with delight,
Dance and dance to a mystic tune
And scatter their leaves in a flower-soft rain
Over the shimmering golden shore
Between the West and the waking moon,
Between the sunset and the night;
And then they sigh for the years of yore
And gather their glory together again,
Petal by petal and gleam by gleam,
Till, all in one rushing rose-bright stream
They dazzle back to the deep once more,
For the dream of the sea is an endless dream,
And love is a sea that hath no shore,
And the roses dance as they danced before.

XV

In other worlds I loved you, long ago:
   Love that hath no beginning hath no end:
Low to her heart he breathed it, sweet and low;
In other worlds I loved you, long ago;
This is a word that all the sea-waves know
   And whisper as through the shoreless West they wend,
In other worlds I loved you, long ago:
   Love that hath no beginning hath no end.

XVI

"Yet love can die!" she murmured once again;
   For this was in that City by the Sea,
That old grey City of Pain,
   Built on the shifting shores of Mystery
And mocked by all the immeasurable main.
   "Love lives to die!"
Under the deep eternal sky
   His deeper voice caught up that deep refrain;

"A year ago, and under yonder sun
Earth had no Heaven to hold our hearts in one!
   For me there was no love, afar or nigh:
And, O, if love were thus in time begun,
   Love, even our love, in time must surely die."
Then memory murmured, "No";
And he remembered, a million years ago,
   He saw the sea-waves wistfully westward wend;
And heard her voice whispering in their flow
And calling through the silent sunset-glow.
   Love that hath no beginning hath no end.

"Love dies to live!"   How wild, how deep the joy
That knows no death can e'er destroy
   What cannot bear destruction!   By these eyes
   I know that, ere the fashioning of the skies,
Or ever the sun and moon and stars were made
I loved you.   Sweet, I am no more afraid.

"Love lives to die!"
Under the deep eternal sky
   Her wild sweet voice caught up that deep refrain:
There, in that silent City by the Sea,
Listening the wild-wave music of Infinity,
   There, in that old grey City of mortal pain,
Their voices mingled in mystic unison
   With that immortal harmony
Which holds the warring worlds in one.

Their Voice, one Voice, yet manifold,
Possessed the seas, the fields, the sky,
With utterance of the dream that cannot die;
Possessed the West's wild rose and dappled gold,
And that old secret of the setting sun
Which, to the glory of Eternity,
Time, tolling like a distant bell,
Evermore faints to tell,
And, ever telling, never yet has told.
 One, and yet manifold
Arose their Voice, oh strangely one again
With murmurs of the immeasurable main;
 As, far beyond earth's cloudy bars,
Their Soul surpassed the sunset and the stars,
 And all the heights and depths of temporal pain,
Till seas of seraph music round them rolled.

 And in that mystic plane
 They felt their mortal years
 Break away as a dream of pain
 Breaks in a stream of tears.

 Love, of whom life had birth,
 See now, is death not sweet?
 Love, is this heaven or earth?
 Both are beneath thy feet.

 Nay, both within thy heart!
 O Love, the glory nears;
 The Gates of Pearl are flung apart,
 The Rose of Heaven appears.

 Across the deeps of change,
 Like pangs of visible song,
 What angel-spirits, remote and strange,
 Thrill through the starry throng?

 And oh, what wind that blows
 Over the mystic Tree,
 What whisper of the sacred Rose,
 What murmur of the sapphire Sea,

What dreams that faint and fail
From harps of burning gold,
But tell in heaven the sweet old tale
An earthly sunset told?

Hark! like a holy bell
Over that spirit Sea,
Time, in the world it loves so well,
Tolls for Eternity.

Earth calls us once again,
And, through the mystic Gleam,
The grey old City of mortal pain
Dawns on the heavenly dream.

Sweet as the voice of birds
At dawn, the years return,
With little songs and sacred words
Of human hearts that yearn.

The sweet same waves resound
Along our earthly shore;
But now this earth we lost and found
Is heaven for evermore.

Hark! how the cosmic choir,
In sea and flower and sun,
Recalls that triumph of desire
Which made all music one:

One universal soul,
Completing joy with pain,
And harmonising with the Whole
The temporal refrain,

Until from hill and plain,
From bud and blossom and tree,
From shadow and shining after rain,
From cloud and clovered bee,

From earth and sea and sky,
From laughter and from tears,
One molten golden harmony
Fulfils the yearning years.

Love, of whom death had birth,
See now, is life not sweet?
Love, is this heaven or earth?
Both are beneath thy feet.

In other worlds I loved you, long ago;
  Love that hath no beginning hath no end;
The sea-waves whisper, low and sweet and low,
In other worlds I loved you, long ago;
The May-boughs murmur and the roses know
  The message that the dawning moon shall send;
In other worlds I loved you, long ago;
  Love that hath no beginning hath no end.

THE FOREST OF WILD THYME

DEDICATED TO
HELEN, ROSIE, AND BEATRIX

PERSONS OF THE TALE

OURSELVES   THE HIDEOUS HERMIT
FATHER   THE KING OF FAIRY-LAND
MOTHER   PEASE-BLOSSOM
LITTLE BOY BLUE   MUSTARD-SEED
     Dragons, Fairies, Mammoths, Angels, etc.

APOLOGIA

ONE more hour to wander free
With Puck on his unbridled bee
  Thro' heather-forests, leagues of bloom,
Our childhood's maze of scent and sun!
  Forbear awhile your notes of doom,
Dear Critics, give me still this one
  Swift hour to hunt the fairy gleam
  That flutters thro' the unfettered dream.

It mocks me as it flies, I know:
All too soon the gleam will go;
    Yet I love it and shall love
My dream that brooks no narrower bars
    Than bind the darkening heavens above,
My Jack o'Lanthorn of the stars:
    Then, I'll follow it no more,
    I'll light the lamp: I'll close the door.

PRELUDE

Hush! if you remember how we sailed to old Japan,
    Peterkin was with us then, our little brother Peterkin!
Now we've lost him, so they say: I think the tall thin man
Must have come and touched him with his curious twinkling
        fan
    And taken him away again, our merry little Peterkin;
He'll be frightened all alone; we'll find him if we can;
    Come and look for Peterkin, poor little Peterkin.

No one would believe us if we told them what we know,
    Or they wouldn't grieve for Peterkin, merry little Peterkin!
If they'd only watched us roaming through the streets of
        Miyako,
And travelling in a palanquin where parents never go,
    And seen the golden gardens where we wandered once with
        Peterkin,
And smelt the purple orchards where the cherry-blossoms blow,
    They wouldn't mourn for Peterkin, merry little Peterkin.

Put away your muskets, lay aside the drum,
    Hang it by the wooden sword we made for little Peterkin!
He was once our trumpeter, now his bugle's dumb,
Pile your arms beneath it, for the owlet light is come,
    We'll wander through the roses where we marched of old
        with Peterkin,
We'll search the summer sunset where the Hybla beehives
        hum,
    And—if we meet a fairy there—we'll ask for news of Peterkin

He was once our cabin-boy and cooked the sweets for tea;
   And O, we've sailed around the world with laughing little
       Peterkin;
From nursery floor to pantry door we've roamed the mighty
       sea,
And come to port below the stairs in distant Caribee,
   But wheresoe'er we sailed we took our little lubber Peterkin,
Because his wide grey eyes believed much more than ours
       could see,
   And so we liked our Peterkin, our trusty little Peterkin.

Peterkin, Peterkin, I think if you came back
   The captain of our host to-day should be the bugler Peterkin,
And he should lead our smugglers up that steep and narrow
       track,
A band of noble brigands, bearing each a mighty pack
   Crammed with lace and jewels to the secret cave of Peterkin,
And he should wear the biggest boots and make his pistol
       crack,—
   The Spanish cloak, the velvet mask, we'd give them all to
       Peterkin.

Come, my brother pirates, I am tired of play;
   Come and look for Peterkin, little brother Peterkin,
Our merry little comrade that the fairies took away,
For people think we've lost him, and when we come to say
   Our good-night prayers to mother, if we pray for little
       Peterkin
Her eyes are very sorrowful, she turns her head away.
   Come and look for Peterkin, merry little Peterkin.

God bless little Peterkin, wherever he may be!
   Come and look for Peterkin, lonely little Peterkin:
I wonder if they've taken him again across the sea
From the town of Wonder-Wander and the Amfalula tree
   To the land of many marvels where we roamed of old with
       Peterkin,
The land of blue pagodas and the flowery fields of tea!
   Come and look for Peterkin, poor little Peterkin.

PART I

THE SPLENDID SECRET

Now father stood engaged in talk
With mother on that narrow walk
Between the laurels (where we play
At Red-skins lurking for their prey)
And the grey old wall of roses
Where the Persian kitten dozes
And the sunlight sleeps upon
Crannies of the crumbling stone
—So hot it is you scarce can bear
Your naked hand upon it there,
Though there luxuriating in heat
With a slow and gorgeous beat
White-winged currant-moths display
Their spots of black and gold all day.—

Well, since we greatly wished to know
Whether we too might some day go
Where little Peterkin had gone
Without one word and all alone,
We crept up through the laurels there
Hoping that we might overhear
The splendid secret, darkly great,
Of Peterkin's mysterious fate;
And on what high adventure bound
He left our pleasant garden-ground,
Whether for old Japan once more
He voyaged from the dim blue shore,
Or whether he set out to run
By candle-light to Babylon.

We just missed something father said
About a young prince that was dead,
A little warrior that had fought
And failed: how hopes were brought to nought

He said, and mortals made to bow
  Before the Juggernaut of Death,
And all the world was darker now,
  For Time's grey lips and icy breath
Had blown out all the enchanted lights
That burned in Love's Arabian nights;
And now he could not understand
Mother's mystic fairy-land,
"Land of the dead, poor fairy-tale,"
He murmured, and her face grew pale,
And then with great soft shining eyes
She leant to him—she looked so wise—
And, with her cheek against his cheek,
We heard her, ah so softly, speak.

"Husband, there was a happy day,
Long ago, in love's young May,
When with a wild-flower in your hand
  You echoed that dead poet's cry—
'*Little flower, but if I could understand!*'
  And you saw it had roots in the depths of the sky
And there in that smallest bud lay furled
The secret and meaning of all the world."

He shook his head and then he tried
To kiss her, but she only cried
And turned her face away and said,
"You come between me and my dead!
His soul is near me, night and day,
But you would drive it far away;
And you shall never kiss me now
Until you lift that brave old brow
Of faith I know so well; or else
Refute the tale the skylark tells,
Tarnish the glory of that May,
Explain the Smallest Flower away."
And still he said, "Poor fairy-tales,
How terribly their starlight pales
Before the solemn sun of truth
That rises o'er the grave of youth!"

"Is heaven a fairy-tale?" she said,—
And once again he shook his head;
And yet we ne'er could understand
Why heaven should *not* be fairy-land,
A part of heaven at least, and why
The thought of it made mother cry,
And why they went away so sad,
  And father still quite unforgiven,
For what could children be but glad
  To find a fairy-land in heaven?

And as we talked it o'er we found
Our brains were really spinning round;
But Dick, our, eldest, late returned
From school, by all the lore he'd learned
Declared that we should seek the lost
Smallest Flower at any cost.
For, since within its leaves lay furled
The secret of the whole wide world,
He thought that we might learn therein
The whereabouts of Peterkin;
And, if we found the Flower, we knew
Father would be forgiven, too;
And mother's kiss atone for all
The quarrel by the rose-hung wall;
We knew, not how we knew not why,
  But Dick it was who bade us try,
Dick made it all seem plain and clear,
And Dick it is who helps us here
To tell this tale of fairy-land
In words we scarce can understand.
For ere another golden hour
  Had passed, our anxious parents found
  We'd left the scented garden-ground
To seek—the Smallest Flower.

PART II

THE FIRST DISCOVERY

O, grown-ups cannot understand
  And grown-ups never will,
How short's the way to fairy-land
  Across the purple hill:
They smile: their smile is very bland,
  Their eyes are wise and chill;
And yet—at just a child's command—
  The world's an Eden still.

Under the cloudy lilac-tree,
  Out at the garden-gate,
We stole, a little band of three,
  To tempt our fairy fate.
There was no human eye to see,
  No voice to bid us wait;
The gardener had gone home to tea,
  The hour was very late.

I wonder if you've ever dreamed,
  In summer's noonday sleep,
Of what the thyme and heather seemed
  To ladybirds that creep
Like little crimson shimmering gems
Between the tiny twisted stems
  Of fairy forests deep;
And what it looks like as they pass
Through jungles of the golden grass.

If you could suddenly become
  As small a thing as they,
A midget-child, a new Tom Thumb,
  A little gauze-winged fay,
Oh then, as through the mighty shades
Of wild thyme woods and violet glades
  You groped your forest-way,
How fraught each fragrant bough would be
With dark o'erhanging mystery.

9

How high the forest aisles would loom,
   What wondrous wings would beat
Through gloamings loaded with perfume
   In many a rich retreat,
While trees like purple censers bowed
And swung beneath a swooning cloud
   Mysteriously sweet,
Where flowers that haunt no mortal clime
Burden the Forest of Wild Thyme.

We'd watched the bats and beetles flit
   Through sunset-coloured air
The night that we discovered it
   And all the heavens were bare:
We'd seen the colours melt and pass
Like silent ghosts across the grass
   To sleep—our hearts knew where;
And so we rose, and hand in hand
We sought the gates of fairy-land.

For Peterkin, oh Peterkin,
   The cry was in our ears,
A fairy clamour, clear and thin
   From lands beyond the years;
A wistful note, a dying fall
As of the fairy bugle-call
   Some dreamful changeling hears,
And pines within his mortal home
Once more through fairy-land to roam.

We left behind the pleasant row
   Of cottage window-panes,
The village inn's red-curtained glow,
   The lovers in the lanes;
And stout of heart and strong of will
We climbed the purple perfumed hill,
   And hummed the sweet refrains
Of fairy tunes the tall thin man
Taught us of old in Old Japan.

So by the tall wide-barred church-gate
　　Through which we all could pass
We came to where that curious plate,
　　That foolish plate of brass,
Said Peterkin was fast asleep
Beneath a cold and ugly heap
　　Of earth and stones and grass.
It was a splendid place for play,
That churchyard, on a summer's day;

A splendid place for hide-and-seek
　　Between the grey old stones;
Where even grown-ups used to speak
　　In awestruck whispering tones;
And here and there the grass ran wild
In jungles for the creeping child,
　　And there were elfin zones
Of twisted flowers and words in rhyme
And great sweet cushions of wild thyme.

So in a wild thyme snuggery there
　　We stayed awhile to rest;
A bell was calling folk to prayer:
　　One star was in the West:
The cottage lights grew far away,
The whole sky seemed to waver and sway
　　Above our fragrant nest;
And from a distant dreamland moon
Once more we heard that fairy tune:

Why, mother once had sung it us
　　When, ere we went to bed,
She told the tale of Pyramus,
　　How Thisbe found him dead
And mourned his eyes as green as leeks,
His cherry nose, his cowslip cheeks.

That tune would oft around us float
　　Since on a golden noon
We saw the play that Shakespeare wrote
　　Of Lion, Wall, and Moon;

Ah, hark—the ancient fairy theme—
Following darkness like a dream!

The very song Will Shakespeare sang,
The music that through Sherwood rang
And Arden and that forest glade
Where Hermie and Lysander strayed,
And Puck cried out with impish glee,
Lord, what fools these mortals be!
Though the masquerade was mute
Of Quince and Snout and Snug and Flute,
And Bottom with his donkey's head
Decked with roses, white and red,
Though the fairies had forsaken
Sherwood now and faintly shaken
The forest-scents from off their feet,
Yet from some divine retreat
Came the music, sweet and clear,
To hang upon the raptured ear
With the free unfettered sway
Of blossoms in the moon of May.
Hark! the luscious fluttering
Of flower-soft words that kiss and cling,
And part again with sweet farewells,
And rhyme and chime like fairy-bells.

"I know a bank where the wild thyme blows
Where oxlips and the nodding violet grows,
Quite over-canopied with luscious woodbine,
With sweet musk-roses and with eglantine."

Out of the undiscovered land
    So sweetly rang the song,
We dreamed we wandered, hand in hand,
    The fragrant aisles along,
Where long ago had gone to dwell
In some enchanted distant dell
    The outlawed fairy throng
When out of Sherwood's wildest glen
They sank, forsaking mortal men.

And as we dreamed, the shadowy ground
   Seemed gradually to swell;
And a strange forest rose around,
   But how—we could not tell—
Purple against a rose-red sky
The big boughs brooded silently:
   Far off we heard a bell;
And, suddenly, a great red light
Smouldered before our startled sight.

Then came a cry, a fiercer flash,
   And down between the trees
We saw great crimson figures crash,
   Wild-eyed monstrosities;
Great dragon-shapes that breathed a flame
From roaring nostrils as they came:
   We sank upon our knees;
And looming o'er us, ten yards high,
Like battleships they thundered by.

And then, as down that mighty dell
   We followed, faint with fear,
We understood the tolling bell
   That called the monsters there;
For right in front we saw a house
Woven of wild mysterious boughs
   Bursting out everywhere
In crimson flames, and with a shout
The monsters rushed to put it out.

And, in a flash, the truth was ours;
   And there we knew—we knew—
The meaning of those trees like flowers,
   Those boughs of rose and blue,
And from the world we'd left above
A voice came crooning like a dove
   To prove the dream was true:
And this—we knew it by the rhyme
Must be—the Forest of Wild Thyme.

For out of the mystical rose-red dome
  Of heaven the voice came murmuring down:
Oh, Ladybird, Ladybird, fly away home;
  Your house is on fire and your children are gone.

  We knew, we knew it by the rhyme,
    Though *we* seemed, after all,
  No tinier, yet the sweet wild thyme
    Towered like a forest tall   .
  All round us; oh, we knew not how,
  And yet—we knew those monsters now:
    Our dream's divine recall
  Had dwarfed us, as with magic words;
  The dragons were but ladybirds!

  And all around us as we gazed,
  Half glad, half frightened, all amazed,
  The scented clouds of purple smoke
  In lurid gleams of crimson broke;
  And o'er our heads the huge black trees
  Obscured the sky's red mysteries;
  While here and there gigantic wings
  Beat o'er us, and great scaly things
  Fold over monstrous leathern fold
  Out of the smouldering copses rolled;
  And eyes like blood-red pits of flame
  From many a forest-cavern came
  To glare across the blazing glade,
  Till, with the sudden thought dismayed,
  We wondered if we e'er should find
  The mortal home we left behind:
  Fear clutched us in a grisly grasp,
  We gave one wild and white-lipped gasp,
  Then turned and ran, with streaming hair,
  Away, away, and anywhere!

And hurry-skurry, heart and heel and hand, we tore along,
  And still our flying feet kept time and pattered on for
    Peterkin,
For Peterkin, oh Peterkin, it made a kind of song

To prove the road was right although it seemed so dark and
    wrong,
    As through the desperate woods we plunged and ploughed
      for little Peterkin,
Where many a hidden jungle-beast made noises like a gong
    That rolled and roared and rumbled as we rushed along to
      Peterkin.

Peterkin, Peterkin, if you could only hear
    And answer us, one little word from little lonely Peterkin
To take and comfort father, he is sitting in his chair
    In the library: he's listening for your footstep on the stair
And your patter down the passage, he can only think of
      Peterkin:
Come back, come back to father, for to-day he'd let us tear
    His newest book to make a paper-boat for little Peterkin.

PART III

THE HIDEOUS HERMIT

Ah, what wonders round us rose
    When we dared to pause and look,
Curious things that seemed all toes,
    Goblins from a picture-book;
Ants like witches, four feet high,
    Waving all their skinny arms,
Glared at us and wandered by,
    Muttering their ancestral charms.

Stately forms in green and gold
    Armour strutted through the glades,
Just as Hamlet's ghost, we're told,
    Mooned among the midnight shades:

Once a sort of devil came
Scattering broken trees about,

Winged with leather, eyed with flame,—
  He was but a moth, no doubt.

Here and there, above us clomb
  Feathery clumps of palm on high:
Those were ferns, of course, but some
  Really seemed to touch the sky;
Yes; and down one fragrant glade,
  Listening as we onward stole,
Half delighted, half afraid,
  Dong, we heard the hare-bells toll!

Something told us what that gleam
  Down the glen was brooding o'er;
Something told us in a dream
  What the bells were tolling for!
Something told us there was fear,
  Horror, peril, on our way!
Was it far or was it near?
  Near, we heard the night-wind say.

Toll, the music reeled and pealed
  Through the vast and sombre trees,
Where a rosy light revealed
  Dimmer, sweeter mysteries;
And, like petals of the rose,
  Fairy fans in beauty beat,
Light in light—ah, what were those
  Rhymes we heard the night repeat?

Toll, a dream within a dream,
  Up an aisle of rose and blue,
Up the music's perfumed stream
  Came the words, and then we knew,

Knew that in that distant glen
  Once again the case was tried,

Hark!—*Who killed Cock Robin, then?*
  And a tiny voice replied,
        "I
        killed
        Cock
        Robin!"

"I!" And who are *You*, sir, pray?"
  Growled a voice that froze our marrow:
"Who!" we heard the murderer say,
  "Lord, sir, I'm the famous Sparrow,
And this 'ere's my bow and arrow!
        "I
        killed
        Cock
        Robin!"

Then, with one great indrawn breath,
  Such a sighin' and a sobbin'
Rose all round us for the death
  Of poor, poor Cock Robin,
Oh, we couldn't bear to wait
Even to hear the murderer's fate,
Which we'd often wished to know
 Sitting in the fireside glow
And with hot revengeful looks
Searched for in the nursery-books;
For the Robin and the Wren
Are such friends to mortal men,
  Such dear friends to mortal men!

Toll; and through the woods once more
  Stole we, drenched with fragrant dew;
Toll; the hare-bell's burden bore
  Deeper meanings than we knew:
Still it told us there was fear,
  Horror, peril on our way!
Was it far or was it near?
  Near, we heard the night-wind say!

Near; and once or twice we saw
    Something like a monstrous eye,
Something like a hideous claw
    Steal between us and the sky:
Still we hummed a dauntless tune
    Trying to think such things might be
Glimpses of the fairy moon
    Hiding in some hairy tree.

Yet around us as we went
    Through the glades of rose and blue
Sweetness with the horror blent
    Wonder-wild in scent and hue:
Here Aladdin's cavern yawned,
    Jewelled thick with gorgeous dyes;
There a head of clover dawned
    Like a cloud in eastern skies.

Hills of topaz, lakes of dew,
    Fairy cliffs of crystal sheen
Passed we; and the forest's blue
    Sea of branches tossed between:
Once we saw a gryphon make
    One soft iris as it passed
Like the curving meteor's wake
    O'er the forest, far and fast.

Winged with purple, breathing flame,
    Crimson-eyed we saw him go,
Where—ah! could it be the same
    Cockchafer we used to know?—
Valley-lilies overhead,
    High aloof in clustered spray,
Far through heaven their splendour spread,
    Glimmering like the Milky Way.

Mammoths father calls "extinct,"
    Creatures that the cave-men feared,
Through that forest walked and blinked,
    Through that jungle crawled and leered;

Beasts no Nimrod ever knew,
   Woolly bears back and red;
Crocodiles, we wondered who
   Ever dared to see *them* fed,

Were they lizards?   If they were,
   They could swallow *us* with ease;
But they slumbered quietly there
   In among the mighty trees;
Red and silver, blue and green,
   Played the moonlight on their scales;
Golden eyes they had, and lean
   Crookèd legs with cruel nails.

Yet again, oh, faint and far,
   Came the shadow of a cry,
Like the calling of a star
   To its brother in the sky;
Like an echo in a cave
   Where young mermen sound their shells,
Like the wind across a grave
   Bright with scent of lily-bells.

Like a fairy hunter's horn
   Sounding in some purple glen
Sweet revelly to the morn
   And the fairy quest again:
Then, all round it surged a song
   We could never understand
Though it lingered with us long,
   And it seemed so sad and grand.

SONG

Little Boy Blue, come blow up your horn,
Summon the day of deliverance in:

We are weary of bearing the burden of scorn
  As we yearn for the home that we never shall win;
For here there is weeping and sorrow and sin.
  And the poor and the weak are a spoil for the strong!
Ah, when shall the song of the ransomed begin?
  The world is grown weary with waiting so long.

Little Boy Blue, you are gallant and brave,
  There was never a doubt in those clear bright eyes.
Come, challenge the grim dark Gates of the Grave
  As the skylark sings to those infinite skies!
This world is a dream, say the old and the wise,
  And its rainbows arise o'er the false and the true;
But the mists of the morning are made of our sighs,—
  Ah, shatter them, scatter them, Little Boy Blue!

Little Boy Blue, if the child-heart knows,
  Sound but a note as a little one may;
And the thorns of the desert shall bloom with the rose,
  And the Healer shall wipe all tears away;
Little Boy Blue, we are all astray,
  The sheep's in the meadow, the cow's in the corn,
Ah, set the world right, as a little one may;
  Little Boy Blue, come blow up your horn!

Yes; and there between the trees
    Circled with a misty gleam
Like the light a mourner sees
    Round an angel in a dream;
Was it he? oh, brave and slim,
    Straight and clad in æry blue,
Lifting to his lips the dim
    Golden horn?   We never knew!

Never; for a witch's hair
    Flooded all the moonlit sky,
And he vanished, then and there,
    In the twinkling of an eye:

Just as either boyish cheek
    Puffed to set the world aright,
Ere the golden horn could speak
    Round him flowed the purple night.

*   *   *   *   *   *   *

At last we came to a round black road
That tunnelled through the woods and showed,
Or so we thought, a good clear way
Back to the upper lands of day;
Great silken cables overhead
In many a mighty mesh were spread
Netting the rounded arch, no doubt
To keep the weight of leafage out.
And, as the tunnel narrowed down,
So thick and close the cords had grown
No leaf could through their meshes stray,
And the faint moonlight died away;
Only a strange grey glimmer shone
To guide our weary footsteps on,
Until, tired out, we stood before
The end, a great grey silken door.

Then from out a weird old wicket, overgrown with shaggy
        hair
Like a weird and wicked eyebrow round a weird and wicked
        eye,
                Two great eyeballs and a beard
                For one ghastly moment peered
At our faces with a sudden stealthy stare:
                Then the door was open wide,
                And a hideous hermit cried
With a shy and soothing smile from out his lair,
Won't you walk into my parlour?   I can make you cosy there!

And we couldn't quite remember where we'd heard that
          phrase before,
As the great grey-bearded ogre stood beside his open door;
But an echo seemed to answer from a land beyond the sky—
Won't you walk into my parlour? said the spider to the fly.

Then we looked a little closer at the ogre as he stood
With his great red eyeballs glowing like two torches in a wood,
And his mighty speckled belly and his dreadful clutching claws
And his nose—a horny parrot's beak, his whiskers and his
          jaws;
Yet he seemed so sympathetic, and we saw two tears descend
As he murmured, "I'm so ugly, but I've lost my dearest
          friend!
I tell you most lymphatic'ly, I've yearnings in my soul,"—
And right along his parrot's beak we saw the tear-drops roll
He's an arrant sentimentalist, we heard a distant sigh,
Won't you weep upon my bosom? said the spider to the fly

"If you'd dreamed my dreams of beauty, if you'd seen my
          works of art,
If you'd felt the cruel hunger that is gnawing at my heart
And the grief that never leaves me and the love I can't forget
(For I loved with all the letters in the Chinese alphabet!
Oh, you'd all come in to comfort me: you ought to help the
          weak;
And I'm full of melting moments; and—I—know—the—thing
          —you—seek!"
And the haunting echo answered, *Well, I'm sure you ought to
          try;*
There's a duty to one's neighbour, said the spider to the fly

          So we walked into his parlour
               Though a gleam was in his eye;
          And it *was* the prettiest parlour
               That ever we did spy!

But we saw by the uncertain
    Misty light, shot through with gleams
Of many a silken curtain
    Broidered o'er with dreadful dreams,
That he locked the door behind us!   So we stood with bated
    breath
        In a silence deep as death.

There were scarlet gleams and crimson
    In the curious foggy grey,
Like the blood-red light that swims on
    Old canals at fall of day,
Where the smoke of some great city loops and droops in
    gorgeous veils
        Round the heavy purple barges' tawny sails.

Were those creatures gagged and muffled,
    See—there—by that severed head?
Was it but a breeze that ruffled
    Those dark curtains, splashed with red,
Ruffled the dark figures on them, made them moan like things
    in pain?
        How we wished that we were safe at home again.

     *   *   *   *   *

"Oh, we want to hear of Peterkin; good sir, you say you know;
Won't you tell us, won't you put us in the way we want to go?"
So we pleaded, for he seemed so very full of sighs and tears
That we couldn't doubt his kindness, and we smothered all
        our fears;
But he said, "You must be crazy if you come to me for help;
Why should I desire to send you to your horrid little whelp?"

And again the foolish echo made a far-away reply,
Oh, don't come to me for comfort,
Pray don't look to me for comfort,
Heavens! you mustn't be so selfish, said the spider to the fly.

"Still, when the King of Scotland, so to speak, was in a hole,
He was aided by my brother; it's a story to console
The convict of the treadmill and the infant with a sum,
For it teaches you to try again until your kingdom's come!
The monarch dawdled in that hole for centuries of time
Until my own twin-brother rose and showed him how to
     climb:
He showed him how to swing and sway upon a tiny thread
Across a mighty precipice, and light upon his head
Without a single fracture and without a single pain
If he only did it frequently and tried and tried again:"
And once again the whisper like a moral wandered by,
Perseverance is a virtue, said the spider to the fly.

Then he moaned, "My heart is hungry; but I fear I cannot
     eat,
(Of course I speak entirely now of spiritual meat!)
For I only fed an hour ago, but if we calmly sat
While I told you all my troubles in a confidential chat
It would give me *such* an appetite to hear you sympathise,
And I should sleep the better—see, the tears are in my eyes!
Dead yearnings are such dreadful things, let's keep 'em all
     alive,—
Let's sit and talk awhile, my dears; we'll dine, I think, at
     five."
And he brought his chair beside us in his most engaging
     style,
And began to tell his story with a melancholy smile.—

"You remember Miss Muffet
Who sat on a tuffet
     Partaking of curds and whey;

Well, *I* am the spider
Who sat down beside her
  And frightened Miss Muffet away!

"There was nothing against her!
An elderly spinster
  Were such a grammatical mate
For a spider and spinner,
I swore I would win her,
  I knew I had met with my fate!

"That love was the purest
And strongest and surest
  I'd felt since my first thread was spun;
I know I'm a bogey,
But *she's* an old fogey,
  So why in the world did she run?

"When Bruce was in trouble,
A spider, my double,
  Encouraged him greatly, they say!
Now, *why* should the spider
Who sat down beside her
  Have frightened Miss Muffet away?"

He seemed to have much more to tell,
But we could scarce be listening well,
Although we tried with all our might
To look attentive and polite;
For still afar we heard the thin
Clear fairy-call to Peterkin;
Clear as a skylark's mounting song
It drew our wandering thoughts along.
Afar, it seemed, yet, ah, so nigh,
Deep in our dreams it scaled the sky,
In captive dreams that brooked no bars
It touched the love that moves the stars,

And with sweet music's golden tether
It bound our hearts and heaven together.

SONG

Wake, arise, the lake, the skies
*   Fade into the faery day;*
Come and sing before our king,
*   Heed not Time, the dotard grey;*
Time has given his crown to heaven—
*   Ah, how long?   Awake, away!*

Then, as the Hermit rambled on
In one long listless monotone,
We heard a wild and mournful groan
Come rumbling down the tunnelled way;
A voice, an awful mournful bray,
Singing some old funereal lay;
Then solemn footsteps, muffled, dull,
Approached as if they trod on wool,
And as they nearer, nearer drew,
We saw our Host was listening too!

His bulging eyes began to glow
    Like great red match-heads rubbed at night,
And then he stole with a grim "O-ho!"
    To that grey old wicket where, out of sight,
Blandly rubbing his hands and humming,
He could see, at one glance, whatever was coming.

He had never been so jubilant or frolicsome before,
As he scurried on his cruel hairy crutches to the door;
            And flung it open wide
            And most hospitably cried,
"Won't you walk into my parlour?   I've some little friends
            to tea,—
They'll be highly entertaining to a man of sympathy,
            Such as you yourself must be!"

Then the man, for so he seemed,
  (Doubtless one who'd lost his way
And was dwarfed as we had been!)
  In his ancient suit of black,
Black upon the verge of green,
  Entered like a ghost that dreamed
Sadly of some bygone day;
  And he never ceased to sing
In that awful mournful bray.

The door closed behind his back;
  He walked round us in a ring,
And we hoped that he might free us,
  But his tears appeared to blind him,
For he didn't seem to see us,
  And the Hermit crept behind him
Like a cat about to spring.

And the song he sang was this;
  And his nose looked very grand
As he sang it, with a bliss
  Which we could not understand;
For his voice was very sad,
While his nose was proud and glad.

Rain, April, rain, thy sunny, sunny tears!
Through the black boughs the robe of Spring appears,
Yet, for the ghosts of all the bygone years,
        Rain, April, rain.

Rain, April, rain; the rose will soon be glad;
Spring will rejoice, a Spring I, too, have had;
A little while, till I no more be sad,
        Rain, April, rain.

And then the spider sprang
  Before we could breathe or speak,
And one great scream out-rang
  As the terrible horny beak

Crunched into the Sad Man's head,
  And the terrible hairy claws
Clutched him around his middle;
  And he opened his lantern-jaws,
And he gave one twist, one twiddle,
  One kick, and his sorrow was dead.

And there, as he sucked his bleeding prey,
  The spider leered at us—"You will do,
My sweet little dears, for another day;
  But this is the sort I like; huh! huh!"

And there we stood, in frozen fear,
        Whiter than death,
        With bated breath;
And lo! as we thought of Peterkin,
Father and home and Peterkin,
Once more that music clear and thin,
Clear as a skylark's mounting song,
But nearer now, more sweet, more strong,
Drew all our wandering thoughts along,
Until it seemed, a mystic sea
Of hidden delight and harmony
Began to ripple and rise all round
The prison where our hearts lay bound;
And from sweet heaven's most rosy rim
There swelled a distant marching hymn
Which made the hideous Hermit pause
And listen with lank down-dropt jaws,
Till, with great bulging eyes of fear,
He sought the wicket again to peer
Along the tunnel, as like sweet rain
We heard the still approaching strain,
And, under it, the rhythmic beat
Of multitudinous marching feet.
Nearer, nearer, they rippled and rang,
And this was the marching song they sang:—

SONG

A fairy band are we
In fairy-land:
Singing march we, hand in hand;
Singing, singing all day long:
(Some folk never heard a fairy-song!)

Singing, singing,
When the merry thrush is swinging
On a springing spray;
Or when the witch that lives in gloomy caves
And creeps by night among the graves
Calls a cloud across the day;
Cease we never our fairy song,
March we ever, along, along,
Down the dale, or up the hill,
Singing, singing still.

And suddenly the Hermit turned and ran with all his might
  Through the back-door of his parlour as we thought of little
      Peterkin;
And the great grey roof was shattered by a shower of rosy
      light,
And the spider-house went floating, torn and tattered through
      the night
  In a flight of prismy streamers, as a shout went up for
      Peterkin;
And lo, the glistening fairy-host stood there arrayed for fight,
  In arms of rose and green and gold, to lead us on to
      Peterkin.

And all around us, rippling like a pearl and opal sea,
  The host of fairy faces winked a kindly hint of Peterkin;
And all around the rosy glade a laugh of fairy glee
Watched spider-streamers floating up from fragrant tree to
      tree
  Till the moonlight caught the gossamers and, oh we wished
      for Peterkin!

Each rope became a rainbow; but it made us ache to see
    Such a fairy forest-pomp without explaining it to Peterkin.

        Then all the glittering crowd
        With a courtly gesture bowed
        Like a rosy jewelled cloud
           Round a flame,
        As the King of Fairy-land,
        Very dignified and grand,
        Stepped forward to demand
           Whence we came.

        He'd a cloak of gold and green
        Such as caterpillars spin,
        For the fairy ways, I ween,
           Are very frugal;
        He'd a bow that he had borne
        Since the crimson Eden morn,
        And a honeysuckle horn
           For his bugle.

So we told our tale of faëry to the King of Fairy-land,
    And asked if he could let us know the latest news of Peterkin;
And he turned him with a courtly smile and waved his jewelled
        wand
And cried, *Pease-blossom, Mustard-seed! You know the old
        command;*
    *Well; these are little children; you must lead them on to
        Peterkin.*
Then he knelt, the King of Faëry knelt; his eyes were great
        and grand
    As he took our hands and kissed them, saying, *Father loves
        your Peterkin!*

        So out they sprang, on either side,
        A light fantastic fairy guide,
        To lead us to the land unknown
        Where little Peterkin was gone;

And, as we went with timid pace,
We saw that every fairy face
In all that moonlit host was wet
With tears: we never shall forget
The mystic hush that seemed to fade
Away like sound, as down the glade
We passed beyond their zone of light.
Then through the forest's purple night
We trotted, at a pleasant speed,
With gay Pease-blossom and Mustard-seed.

PART IV

PEASE–BLOSSOM AND MUSTARD–SEED

SHYLY we surveyed our guides
As through the gloomy woods we went
In the light that the straggling moonbeams lent:
We envied them their easy strides!
Pease-blossom in his crimson cap
And delicate suit of rose-leaf green,
His crimson sash and his jewelled dagger,
Strutted along with an elegant swagger
Which showed that he didn't care one rap
For anything less than a Fairy Queen:
His eyes were deep like the eyes of a poet,
Although his crisp and curly hair
Certainly didn't seem to show it!
While Mustard-seed was a devil-may-care
Epigrammatic and pungent fellow
Clad in a splendid suit of yellow,
With emerald stars on his glittering breast
And eyes that shone with a diamond light:
They made you feel sure it would always be best
To tell him the truth: he was not perhaps *quite*
So polite as Pease-blossom, but then who could be
Quite such a debonair fairy as he?

We never could tell you one-half that we heard
And saw on that journey.   For instance, a bird
Ten times as big as an elephant stood
By the side of a nest like a great thick wood:
The clouds in glimmering wreaths were spread
Behind its vast and shadowy head
Which rolled at us trembling below.   (Its eyes
Were like great black moons in those pearl-pale skies.)
And we feared he might take us, perhaps, for a worm.

But he ruffled his breast with the sound of a storm,
And snuggled his head with a careless disdain
Under his huge hunched wing again;
And Mustard-seed said, as we stole thro' the dark,
There was nothing to fear: it was only a Lark!

And so he cheered the way along
    With many a neat little epigram,
    While dear Pease-blossom before him swam
On a billow of lovely moonlit song,
Telling us why they had left their home
In Sherwood, and had hither come
To dwell in this magical scented clime,
This dim old Forest of sweet Wild Thyme.

"Men toil," he said, "from morn till night
With bleeding hands and blinded sight
For gold, more gold!   They have betrayed
The trust that in their souls was laid;
Their fairy birthright they have sold
For little disks of mortal gold;
And now they cannot even see
The gold upon the greenwood tree,
The wealth of coloured lights that pass
In soft gradations through the grass,
The riches of the love untold
That wakes the day from grey to gold;
And howsoe'er the moonlight weaves
Magic webs among the leaves

Englishmen care little now
For elves beneath the hawthorn bough:
Nor if Robin should return
Dare they of an outlaw learn;
For them the Smallest Flower is furled,
Mute is the music of the world;
And unbelief has driven away
Beauty from the blossomed spray."

Then Mustard-seed with diamond eyes
Taught us to be laughter-wise,
And he showed us how that Time
Is much less powerful than a rhyme;
And that Space is but a dream;
"For look," he said, with eyes agleam,
"Now you are become so small
You think the Thyme a forest tall;
But underneath your feet you see
A world of wilder mystery
Where, if you were smaller yet,
You would just as soon forget
This forest, which you'd leave above
As you have left the home you love!
For, since the Thyme you used to know
Seems a forest here below,
What if you should sink again
And find there stretched a mighty plain
Between each grass-blade and the next?
You'd think till you were quite perplexed!
Especially if all the flowers
That lit the sweet Thyme-forest bowers
Were in that wild transcendent change
Turned to Temples, great and strange,
With many a pillared portal high
And domes that swelled against the sky!
How foolish, then, you will agree,
Are those who think that all must see
The world alike, or those who scorn
Another who, perchance, was born
Where—in a different dream from theirs—
What they call sins to him are prayers!

We cannot judge; we cannot know;
All things mingle; all things flow;
There's only one thing constant here—
Love—that untranscended sphere:
Love, that while all ages run
Holds the wheeling worlds in one;
Love that, as your sages tell,
Soars to heaven and sinks to hell."

Even as he spoke, we seemed to grow
Smaller, the Thyme trees seemed to go
Farther away from us: new dreams
Flashed out on us with mystic gleams
Of mighty Temple-domes: deep awe
Held us all breathless as we saw
A carven portal glimmering out
Between new flowers that put to rout
Our other fancies: in sweet fear
We tiptoed past, and seemed to hear
A sound of singing from within
That told our souls of Peterkin:
Our thoughts of *him* were still the same
Howe'er the shadows went and came,
So, on we wandered, hand in hand,
And all the world was fairy-land.

    *   *   *   *   *

And as we went we seemed to hear
    Surging up from distant dells
A solemn music, soft and clear
    As if a field of lily-bells
Were tolling all together, sweet
    But sad and low and keeping time
To multitudinous marching feet
With a slow funereal beat
    And a deep harmonious chime
That told us by its dark refrain
The reason fairies suffered pain.

SONG

Bear her along
Keep ye your song
Tender and sweet and low:
Fairies must die!
Ask ye not why
Ye that have hurt her so.

*Passing away—flower from the spray! Colour and light from
the leaf!*
*Soon, soon will the year shed its bloom on her bier, and the dust of
its dreams on our grief.*

Men upon earth
Bring us to birth
Gently at even and morn!
When as brother and brother
They greet one another
And smile—then a fairy is born!

But at each cruel word
Upon earth that is heard,
Each deed of unkindness or hate,
Some fairy must pass
From the games in the grass
And steal thro' the terrible Gate.

*Passing away—flower from the spray! Colour and light from
the leaf!*
*Soon, soon will the year shed its bloom on her bier, and the dust
of its dreams on our grief.*

If ye knew, if ye knew
All the wrong that ye do
By the thought that ye harbour alone,
How the face of some fairy
Grows wistful and weary
And the heart in her cold as a stone!

Ah, she was born
Blithe as the morn
Under an April sky,
Born of the greeting
Of two lovers meeting.
They parted, and so she must die.

*Passing away—flower from the spray!   Colour and light from
the leaf!*
*Soon, soon will the year shed its bloom on her bier, and the dust
of its dreams on our grief.*

Cradled in blisses,
Yea, born of your kisses.
Oh, ye lovers that met by the moon,
She would not have cried
In the darkness and died
If ye had not forgotten so soon.

Cruel mortals, they say,
Live for ever and aye,
And they pray in the dark on their knees.
But the flowers that are fled
And the loves that are dead,
What heaven takes pity on these?

Bear her along—singing your song—tender and sweet and low!
Fairies must die!   Ask ye not why—ye that have hurt her so.

Passing away—
Flower from the spray!
Colour and light from the leaf!
Soon, soon will the year
Shed its bloom on her bier
And the dust of its dreams on our grief.

*   *   *   *   *

Then we came through a glittering crystal grot
By a path like a pale moonbeam,
And a broad blue bridge of Forget-me-not
Over a shimmering stream,

To where, through the deep blue dusk, a gleam
   Rose like the soul of the setting sun;
A sunset breaking through the earth,
   A crimson sea of the poppies of dream,
Deep as the sleep that gave them birth
   In the night where all earthly dreams are done.

And then, like a pearl-pale porch of the moon,
   Faint and sweet as a starlit shrine,
        Over the gloom
        Of the crimson bloom
   We saw the Gates of Ivory shine;
And, lulled and lured by the lullaby tune
   Of the cradling airs that drowsily creep
From blossom to blossom, and lazily croon
Through the heart of the midnight's mystic noon,
   We came to the Gates of the City of Sleep.

Faint and sweet as a lily's repose
   On the broad black breast of a midnight lake,
   The City delighted the cradling night:
Like a straggling palace of cloud it rose;
   The towers were crowned with a crystal light
   Like the starry crown of a white snowflake
As they pierced in a wild white pinnacled crowd,
Through the dusky wreaths of enchanted cloud
   That swirled all round like a witch's hair.

And we heard, as the sound of a great sea sighing,
   The sigh of the sleepless world of care;
And we saw strange shadowy figures flying
Up to the Ivory Gates and beating
   With pale hands, long and famished and thin;
Like blinded birds we saw them dash
   Against the cruelly gleaming wall:
   We heard them wearily moan and call
With sharp starved lips for ever entreating
   The pale doorkeeper to let them in.

And still, as they beat, again and again,
   We saw on the moon-pale lintels a splash
Of crimson blood like a poppy-stain
Or a wild red rose from the gardens of pain
   That sigh all night like a ghostly sea
   From the City of Sleep to Gethsemane.

And lo, as we neared the mighty crowd
An old blind man came, crying aloud
To greet us, as once the blind man cried
In the Bible picture—you know we tried
To paint that print, with its Eastern sun;
But the reds and the yellows *would* mix and run,
And the blue of the sky made a horrible mess
Right over the edge of the Lord's white dress.
And the old blind man, just as though he had eyes,
Came straight to meet us; and all the cries
Of the crowd were hushed; and a strange sweet calm
Stole through the air like a breath of the balm
That was wafted abroad from the Forest of Thyme
(For it rolled all round that curious clime
With its magical clouds of perfumed trees.)
And the blind man cried, "Our help is at hand,
Oh, brothers, remember the old command,
Remember the frankincense and myrrh,
Make way, make way for those little ones there;
Make way, make way, I have seen them afar
Under a great white Eastern star;
For I am the mad blind man who sees!"
Then he whispered, softly—*Of such as these;*
And through the hush of the cloven crowd
We passed to the gates of the City, and there
Our fairy heralds cried aloud—
Open your Gates; don't stand and stare;
These are the Children for whom our King
Made all the star-worlds dance in a ring!

And lo, like a sorrow that melts from the heart
In tears, the slow gates melted apart;
And into the City we passed like a dream;
And then, in one splendid marching stream

The whole of that host came following through.
We were only children, just like you;
Children, ah, but we felt so grand
As we led them—although we could understand
Nothing at all of the wonderful song
That rose all round as we marched along.

SONG

You that have seen how the world and its glory
  Change and grow old like the love of a friend;
You that have come to the end of the story,
  You that were tired ere you came to the end;
You that are weary of laughter and sorrow,
  Pain and pleasure, labour and sin,
Sick of the midnight and dreading the morrow,
  Ah, come in; come in.

You that are bearing the load of the ages;
  You that have loved overmuch and too late;
You that confute all the saws of the sages;
  You that served only because you must wait,
Knowing your work was a wasted endeavour;
  You that have lost and yet triumphed therein,
Add loss to your losses and triumph for ever;
  Ah, come in; come in.

And we knew as we went up that twisted street,
  With its violet shadows and pearl-pale walls,
We were coming to Something strange and sweet,
  For the dim air echoed with elfin calls;
And, far away, in the heart of the City,
  A murmur of laughter and revelry rose,—
A sound that was faint as the smile of Pity,
  And sweet as a swan-song's golden close.

And then, once more, as we marched along,
There surged all round us that wonderful song;
And it swung to the tramp of our marching feet
But ah, it was tenderer now and so sweet

That it made our eyes grow wet and blind,
And the whole wide-world seem mother-kind,
Folding us round with a gentle embrace,
And pressing our souls to her soft sweet face.

SONG

Dreams; dreams; ah, the memory blinding us,
  Blinding our eyes to the way that we go;
Till the new sorrow come, once more reminding us
  Blindly of kind hearts, ours long ago:
Mother-mine, whisper we, yours was the love for me!
  Still, though our paths lie lone and apart,
Yours is the true love, shining above for me,
  Yours are the kind eyes, hurting my heart.

Dreams; dreams; ah, how shall we sing of them,
  Dreams that we loved with our head on her breast:
Dreams; dreams; and the cradle-sweet swing of them;
  Ay, for her voice was the sound we loved best:
Can we remember at all or, forgetting it,
  Can we recall for a moment the gleam
Of our childhood's delight and the wonder begetting it,
  Wonder awakened in dreams of a dream?

And once again, from the heart of the City
  A murmur of tenderer laughter rose,
A sound that was faint as the smile of Pity,
  And sweet as a swan-song's golden close;
And it seemed as if some wonderful Fair
  Were charming the night of the City of Dreams,
For, over the mystical din out there,
  The clouds were litten with flickering gleams,
And a roseate light like the day's first flush
  Quivered and beat on the towers above,
And we heard through the curious crooning hush
  An elfin song that we used to love.
Little Boy Blue, come blow up your horn . . .
  And the soft wind blew it the other way;
So all that we heard was—*Cow's in the corn;*
  But we never heard anything half so gay!

And ever we seemed to be drawing nearer
 That mystical roseate smoke-wreathed glare,
And the curious music grew louder and clearer,
 Till mustard-seed said, "We are lucky, you see,
 We've arrived at a time of festivity!"
And so to the end of the street we came,
 And turned a corner, and—there we were,
In a place that glowed like the dawn of day,
 A crowded clamouring City square
Like the cloudy heart of an opal, aflame
 With the lights of a great Dream-Fair:
Thousands of children were gathered there,
 Thousands of old men, weary and grey,
And the shouts of the showmen filled the air—
 This way! This way! This way!

And *See-Saw; Margery Daw;* we heard a rollicking shout,
As the swing-boats hurtled over our heads to the tune of the
   roundabout;
And *Little Boy Blue, come blow up your horn,* we heard the
   showmen cry,
And *Dickory Dock, I'm as good as a clock,* we heard the swings
   reply.

This way, this way to your Heart's Desire;
 Come, cast your burdens down;
And the pauper shall mount his throne in the skies,
 And the king be rid of his crown:
And souls that were dead shall be fed with fire
 From the fount of their ancient pain,
And your lost love come with the light in her eyes
 Back to your heart again.

Ah, here be sure she shall never prove
 Less kind than her eyes were bright;
This way, this way to your old lost love,
 You shall kiss her lips to-night;
This way for the smile of a dead man's face
 And the grip of a brother's hand,
This way to your childhood's heart of grace
 And your home in Fairy-land.

11

Dickory Dock, I'm as good as a clock, d'you hear my swivels
    chime?
To and fro as I come and go, I keep eternal time.
O, little Bo-peep, if you've lost your sheep and don't know where
    to find 'em,
Leave 'em alone and they'll come home, and carry their tails
    behind 'em.

And *See-Saw; Margery Daw;* there came the chorussing shout,
As the swing-boats answered the roaring tune of the rollicking
    roundabout;
Dickory, dickory, dickory, dock, d'you hear my swivels
    chime?
Swing; swing; you're as good as a king if you keep eternal
    time.

Then we saw that the tunes of the world were one;
And the metre that guided the rhythmic sun
Was at one, like the ebb and the flow of the sea,
With the tunes that we learned at our mother's knee;
The beat of the horse-hoofs that carried us down
To see the fine Lady of Banbury Town;
And so, by the rhymes that we knew, we could tell
Without knowing the others—that all was well.

And then, our brains began to spin;
For it seemed as if that mighty din
Were no less than the cries of the poets and sages
Of all the nations in all the ages;
And, if they could only beat out the whole
Of their music together, the guerdon and goal
Of the world would be reached with one mighty shout,
And the dark dread secret of Time be out;
And nearer, nearer they seemed to climb,
    And madder and merrier rose the song,
And the swings and the see-saws marked the time;
    For this was the maddest and merriest throng
That ever was met on a holy-day
To dance the dust of the world away;
And madder and merrier, round and round
The whirligigs whirled to the whirling sound,

Till it seemed that the mad song burst its bars
And mixed with the song of the whirling stars,
The song that the rhythmic Time-Tides tell
To seraphs in Heaven and devils in Hell;
Ay; Heaven and Hell in accordant chime
With the universal rhythm and rhyme
Were nearing the secret of Space and Time;
The song of that ultimate mystery
 Which only the mad blind men who see,
Led by the laugh of a little child,
Can utter; ay, wilder and yet more wild
It maddened, till now—full song— it was out!
It roared from the starry roundabout—

A child was born in Bethlehem, in Bethlehem, in Bethlehem,
 A child was born in Bethlehem; ah, hear my fairy fable;
For I have seen the King of Kings, no longer thronged with angel
   wings,
 But crooning like a little babe, and cradled in a stable.

The wise men came to greet him with their gifts of myrrh and
   frankincense,—
 Gold and myrrh and frankincense they brought to make him
   mirth;
And would you know the way to win to little brother Peterkin,
 My childhood's heart shall guide you through the glories of the
   earth.

A child was born in Bethlehem, in Bethlehem, in Bethlehem;
 The wise men came to welcome him: a star stood o'er the gable;
And there they saw the King of Kings, no longer thronged with
   angel wings,
 But crooning like a little babe, and cradled in a stable.

And creeping through the music once again the fairy cry
 Came freezing o'er the snowy towers to lead us on to Peterkin:
Once more the fairy bugles blew from lands beyond the sky,
And we all groped out together, dazed and blind, we knew not
   why;

Out through the City's farther gates we went to look for
    Peterkin;
Out, out into the dark Unknown, and heard the clamour die
  Far, far away behind us as we trotted on to Peterkin.

Then once more along the rare
    Forest-paths we groped our way:
Here the glow-worm's league-long glare
    Turned the Wild Thyme night to day:
There we passed a sort of whale
    Sixty feet in length or more,
But we knew it was a snail
    Even when we heard it snore.

Often through the glamorous gloom
    Almost on the top of us
We beheld a beetle loom
    Like a hippopotamus;
Once or twice a spotted toad
    Like a mountain wobbled by
With a rolling moon that glowed
    Through the skin-fringe of its eye.

Once a caterpillar bowed
    Down a leaf of Ygdrasil
Like a sunset-coloured cloud
    Sleeping on a quiet hill:
Once we came upon a moth
    Fast asleep with outspread wings,
Like a mighty tissued cloth
    Woven for the feet of kings.

There above the woods in state
    Many a temple dome that glows
Delicately like a great
    Rainbow-coloured bubble rose:
Though they were but flowers on earth,
    Oh, we dared not enter in;
For in that divine re-birth
    Less than awe were more than sin.

Yet their mystic anthems came
  Sweetly to our listening ears;
And their burden was the same—
  "No more sorrow, no more tears!
Whither Peterkin has gone
  You, assuredly, shall go:
When your wanderings are done,
  All he knows you, too, shall know!"

So we thought we'd onward roam
  Till earth's Smallest Flower appeared,
With a less tremendous dome
  Less divinely to be feared:
Then, perchance, if we should dare
  Timidly to enter in,
Might some kindly doorkeeper
  Give us news of Peterkin.

At last we saw a crimson porch
Far away, like a dull red torch
Burning in the purple gloom;
And a great ocean of perfume
Rolled round us as we drew anear,
And then we strangely seemed to hear
The shadow of a mighty psalm,
  A sound as if a golden sea
Of music swung in utter calm
  Against the shores of Eternity;
And then we saw the mighty dome
  Of some mysterious Temple tower
On high; and knew that we had come,
  At last, to that sweet House of Grace
Which wise men find in every place—
  The Temple of the Smallest Flower.

And there—alas—our fairy friends
Whispered, "Here our kingdom ends:
  You must enter in alone,
But your souls will surely show
  Whither Peterkin is gone
And the road that you must go:

We, poor fairies, have no souls!
  Hark, the warning hare-bell tolls;"
So "Good-bye, good-bye," they said,
"Dear little seekers-for-the-dead."
They vanished; ah, but as they went
We heard their voices softly blent
In some mysterious fairy song
That seemed to make us wise and strong;

For it was like the holy calm
That fills the bosomed rose with balm,
Or blessings that the twilight breathes
Where the honeysuckle wreathes
Between young lovers and the sky
As on banks of flowers they lie;
And with wings of rose and green
Laughing fairies pass unseen,
Singing their sweet lullaby,—
    Lulla-lulla-lullaby!
    Lulla-lulla-lullaby!
      Ah, good-night, with lullaby!

          *   *   *   *

Only a flower?   Those carven walls,
Those cornices and coronals,
The splendid crimson porch, the thin
Strange sounds of singing from within—
Through the scented arch we stept,
  Pushed back the soft petallic door,
And down the velvet aisles we crept;
    Was it a Flower—no more?

For one of the voices that we heard,
A child's voice, clear as the voice of a bird,
Was it not?—nay, it could not be!
And a woman's voice that tenderly
Answered him in fond refrain,
And pierced our hearts with sweet sweet pain,
As if dear Mary-mother hung
Above some little child, and sung.

Between the waves of that golden sea
The cradle-songs of Eternity;
And, while in her deep smile he basked,
Answered whatsoe'er he asked.

What is there hid in the heart of a rose,
          Mother-mine?
Ah, who knows, who knows, who knows?
A man that died on a lonely hill
May tell you, perhaps, but none other will,
          Little child.

What does it take to make a rose,
          Mother-mine?
The God that died to make it knows
It takes the world's eternal wars,
It takes the moon and all the stars,
It takes the might of heaven and hell
And the everlasting Love as well,
          Little child.

But there, in one great shrine apart
Within the Temple's holiest heart,
We came upon a blinding light,
    Suddenly, and a burning throne
Of pinnacled glory, wild and white;
    We could not see Who reigned thereon:
For, all at once, as a wood-bird sings,
The aisles were full of great white wings
Row above mystic burning row;
And through the splendour and the glow
We saw four angels, great and sweet,
With outspread wings and folded feet,
Come gliding down from a heaven within
    The golden heart of Paradise;
    And in their hands, with laughing eyes,
Lay little brother Peterkin.

And all around the Temple of the Smallest of the Flowers
  The glory of the angels made a star for little Peterkin;
For all the Kings of Splendour and all the Heavenly Powers
Were gathered there together in the fairy forest bowers
  With all their globed and radiant wings to make a star for
        Peterkin,
The star that shone upon the East, a star that still is ours,
  Whene'er we hang our stockings up, a star of wings for
      Peterkin.

Then all, in one great flash, was gone—
    A voice cried, "Hush, all's well!"
And we stood dreaming there alone,
    In darkness.   Who can tell
The mystic quiet that we felt,
As if the woods in worship knelt;
    Far off we heard a bell
Tolling strange human folk to prayer
Through fields of sunset-coloured air.

And then a voice, "Why, here they are!"
    And—as it seemed—we woke;
The sweet old skies, great star by star
    Upon our vision broke;
Field over field of heavenly blue
Rose o'er us; then a voice we knew
    Softly and gently spoke—
"See, they are sleeping by the side
Of that dear little one—who died."

PART V

THE HAPPY ENDING

WE told dear father all our tale
    That night before we went to bed,
And at the end his face grew pale,
    And he bent over us and said
(Was it not strange?) he, too, was there,
    A weary, weary watch to keep
    Before the gates of the City of Sleep;
But, ere we came, he did not dare

Even to dream of entering in,
Or even to hope for Peterkin.
He was the poor blind man, he said,
And we—how low he bent his head!
Then he called mother near; and low
He whispered to us—"Prompt me now;
For I forget that song we heard,
But you remember every word."
Then memory came like a breaking morn,
And we breathed it to him—*A child was born!*
And there he drew us to his breast
And softly murmured all the rest.—

he wise men came to greet him with their gifts of myrrh and
*   frankincense,—*
*   Gold and myrrh and frankincense they brought to make him*
*   mirth;*
nd would you know the way to win to little brother Peterkin,
*   My childhood's heart shall guide you through the glories of the*
*   earth.*

Then he looked up and mother knelt
    Beside us, oh, her eyes were bright;
Her arms were like a lovely belt
    All round us as we said Good-night
To father: *he* was crying now,
But they were happy tears, somehow;
For there we saw dear mother lay
Her cheek against his cheek and say—
Hush, let me kiss those tears away.

DEDICATION

What can a wanderer bring
*   To little ones loved like you?*
You have songs of your own to sing
*   That are far more steadfast and true,*
Crumbs of pity for birds
*   That flit o'er your sun-swept lawn,*
Songs that are dearer than all our words
*   With a love that is clear as the dawn.*

What should a dreamer devise,
  In the depths of his wayward will,
To deepen the gleam of your eyes
  Who can dance with the Sun-child still?
Yet you glanced on his lonely way,
  You cheered him in dream and deed,
And his heart is o'erflowing, o'erflowing to-day
  With a love that—you never will need.

What can a pilgrim teach
  To dwellers in fairy-land?
Truth that excels all speech
  You murmur and understand!
All he can sing you he brings;
  But—one thing more if he may,
One thing more that the King of Kings
  Will take from the child on the way.

Yet how can a child of the night
  Brighten the light of the sun?
How can he add a delight
  To the dances that never are done?
Ah, what if he struggles to turn
  Once more to the sweet old skies
With praise and praise, from the fetters that burn
  To the God that brightened your eyes?

Yes; he is weak, he will fail,
  Yet, what if, in sorrows apart,
One thing, one should avail,
  The cry of a grateful heart;
It has wings: they return through the night
  To a sky where the light lives yet,
To the clouds that kneel on his mountain-height
  And the path that his feet forget.

What if he struggles and still
  Fails and struggles again?
What if his broken will
  Whispers the struggle is vain?

Once at least he has risen
  Because he remembered your eyes;
Once they have brought to his earthly prison
  The passion of Paradise.

Kind little eyes that I love,
  Eyes forgetful of mine,
In a dream I am bending above
  Your sleep, and you open and shine;
And I know as my own grow blind
  With a lonely prayer for your sake,
He will hear—even me—little eyes that were kind,
  God bless you, asleep or awake.

FORTY SINGING SEAMEN AND
OTHER POEMS

TO GARNETT

FORTY SINGING SEAMEN

"In our lands be Beeres and Lyons of dyvers colours as ye redd,
rene, black, and white. And in our land be also unicornes and
aese Unicornes slee many Lyons. . . . Also there dare no
aan make a lye in our lande, for if he dyde he sholde incontynent
e sleyn."—*Mediæval Epistle, of Pope Prester John.*

I.

ACROSS the seas of Wonderland to Mogadore we plodded,
  Forty singing seamen in an old black barque,
nd we landed in the twilight where a Polyphemus nodded
  With his battered moon-eye winking red and yellow through
          the dark!
        For his eye was growing mellow,
        Rich and ripe and red and yellow,
As was time, since old Ulysses made him bellow in the dark!
'ho.—Since Ulysses bunged his eye up with a pine-torch in
          the dark!

II

Were they mountains in the gloaming or the giant's u
  shoulders
 Just beneath the rolling eyeball, with its bleared and vin
   glow,
Red and yellow o'er the purple of the pines among the bould
 And the shaggy horror brooding on the sullen slopes belo
   Were they pines among the boulders
   Or the hair upon his shoulders?
 We were only simple seamen, so of course we didn't knov
Cho.—We were simple singing seamen, so of course we could
   know.

III

But we crossed a plain of poppies, and we came upon a fount
 Not of water, but of jewels, like a spray of leaping fire;
And behind it, in an emerald glade, beneath a golden mount
 There stood a crystal palace, for a sailor to admire;
   For a troop of ghosts came round us,
   Which with leaves of bay they crowned us,
 Then with grog they well nigh drowned us, to the depth
   our desire!
Cho.—And 'twas very friendly of them, as a sailor can admi

IV

There was music all about us, we were growing quite forget
 We were only singing seamen from the dirt of London-tov
Though the nectar that we swallowed seemed to vanish h
  regretful
 As if we wasn't good enough to take such vittles down,
   When we saw a sudden figure,
   Tall and black as any nigger,
 Like the devil—only bigger—drawing near us with a fro
Cho.—Like the devil—but much bigger—and he wore a gol
   crown!

V

nd" What's all this?" he growls at us! With dignity we
chaunted,
"Forty singing seamen, sir, as won't be put upon!"
What? Englishmen?" he cries, "Well, if ye don't mind
being haunted,
Faith you're welcome to my palace; I'm the famous Prester
John!
Will ye walk into my palace?
I don't bear 'ee any malice!
One and all ye shall be welcome in the halls of Prester
John!"
ho.—So we walked into the palace and the halls of Prester
John!

VI

ow the door was one great diamond and the hall a hollow
ruby—
Big as Beachy Head, my lads, nay bigger by a half!
nd I sees the mate wi' mouth agape, a-staring like a booby,
And the skipper close behind him, with his tongue out like a
calf!
Now the way to take it rightly
Was to walk along politely
Just as if you didn't notice—so I couldn't help but laugh!
ho.—For they both forgot their manners and the crew was
bound to laugh!

VII

But he took us through his palace and, my lads, as I'm a sinner,
We walked into an opal like a sunset-coloured cloud—
My dining-room," he says, and, quick as light we saw a
dinner
Spread before us by the fingers of a hidden fairy crowd;
And the skipper, swaying gently
After dinner, murmurs faintly,

"I looks to-wards you, Prester John, you've done us ve
proud!"
Cho.—And we drank his health with honours, for he *done*
very proud!

VIII

Then he walks us to his garden where we sees a feather
demon
Very splendid and important on a sort of spicy tree!
"That's the Phœnix," whispers Prester, "which all eddicat
seamen
Knows the only one existent, and *he's* waiting for to flee
When his hundred years expire
Then he'll set hisself a-fire
And another from his ashes rise most beautiful to see!"
Cho.—With wings of rose and emerald most beautiful to s

IX

Then he says, "In younder forest there's a little silver rive
And whosoever drinks of it, his youth shall never die!
The centuries go by, but Prester John endures for ever
With his music in the mountains and his magic on the sk
While *your* hearts are growing colder,
While your world is growing older,
There's a magic in the distance, where the sea-line mee
the sky."
Cho.—It shall call to singing seamen till the fount o' song
dry!

X

So we thought we'd up and seek it, but that forest fair defi
us,—
First a crimson leopard laughs at us most horrible to see,
Then a sea-green lion came and sniffed and licked his cho
and eyed us,
While a red and yellow unicorn was dancing round a tree

We was trying to look thinner,
     Which was hard, because our dinner
Must ha' made us very tempting to a cat o' high degree!
ho.—Must ha' made us very tempting to the whole
          menarjeree!

XI

o we scuttled from that forest and across the poppy meadows
     Where the awful shaggy horror brooded o'er us in the dark!
And we pushes out from shore again a-jumping at our shadows,
     And pulls away most joyful to the old black barque!
          And home again we plodded
          While the Polyphemus nodded
With his battered moon-eye winking red and yellow through
          the dark.
ho.—Oh, the moon above the mountains, red and yellow
          through the dark!

XII

Across the seas of Wonderland to London-town we blundered,
     Forty singing seamen as was puzzled for to know
f the visions that we saw was caused by—here again we
               pondered—
     A tipple in a vision forty thousand years ago.
          Could the grog we *dreamt* we swallowed
          Make us *dream* of all that followed?
We were only simple seamen, so of course we didn't know!
ho.—We were simple singing seamen, so of course we could
          not know!

THE EMPIRE BUILDERS

WHO are the Empire-builders?   They
     Whose desperate arrogance demands
A self-reflecting power to sway
     A hundred little selfless lands?

Lord God of battles, ere we bow
  To these and to their soulless lust,
Let fall Thy thunders on us now
  And strike us equal to the dust.

Before the stars in heaven were made
  Our great Commander led us forth;
And now the embattled lines are laid
  To East, to West, to South, to North;
According as of old He planned
  We take our station in the field,
Nor dare to dream we understand
  The splendour of the swords we wield.

We know not what the Soul intends
  That lives and moves behind our deeds;
We wheel and march to glorious ends
  Beyond the common soldier's needs:
And some are raised to high rewards,
  And some by regiments are hurled
To die upon the opposing swords
  And sleep—forgotten by the world.

And not where navies churn the foam,
  Nor called to fields of fierce emprize,
In many a country cottage-home
  The Empire-builder lives and dies:
Or through the roaring streets he goes
  A lean and weary City slave,
The conqueror of a thousand foes
  Who walks, unheeded, to his grave.

Leaders unknown of hopes forlorn
  Go past us in the daily mart,
With many a shadowy crown of thorn
  And many a kingly broken heart:
Though England's banner overhead
  Ever the secret signal flew,
We only see its Cross is red
  As children see the skies are blue.

For all are Empire-builders here,
    Whose hearts are true to heaven and home
And, year by slow revolving year,
    Fulfil the duties as they come;
So simple seems the task, and yet
    Many for this are crucified;
Ay, and their brother-men forget
    The simple wounds in palm and side.

But he that to his home is true,
    Where'er the tides of power may flow,
Has built a kingdom great and new
    Which Time nor Fate shall overthrow
These are the Empire-builders, these
    Annex where none shall say them nay
Beyond the world's uncharted seas
    Realms that can never pass away.

NELSON'S YEAR

(1905)

I

"Hasten the Kingdom, England!"
    This year, a hundred years ago,
he world attended, breathless, on the gathering pomp of war,
    While England and her deathless dead, with all their mighty
                        hearts aglow,
wept onward like the dawn of doom to triumph at Trafalgar;
        Then the world was hushed to wonder
        As the cannon's dying thunder
roke out again in muffled peals across the heaving sea,
        And home the Victor came at last,
        Home, home, with England's flag half-mast,
hat never dipped to foe before, on Nelson's Victory.

II

God gave this year to England;
And what He gives He takes again;
He gives us life, He gives us death: our victories have wings
He gives us love and in its heart He hides the whole world
heart of pain:
We gain by loss: impartially the eternal balance swings!
Ay; in the fire we cherish
Our thoughts and dreams may perish;
Yet shall it burn for England's sake triumphant as of old!
What sacrifice could gain for her
Our own shall still maintain for her,
And hold the gates of Freedom wide that take no keys of gold

III

God gave this year to England;
Her eyes are far too bright for tears
Of sorrow; by her silent dead she kneels, too proud for pride
Their blood, their love, have bought her right to claim th
new imperial years
In England's name for Freedom, in whose love her childre
died;
In whose love, though hope may dwindle,
Love and brotherhood shall kindle
Between the striving nations as a choral song takes fire,
Till new hope, new faith, new wonder
Cleave the clouds of doubt asunder,
And speed the union of mankind in one divine desire.

IV

Hasten the Kingdom, England;
This year across the listening world
There came a sound of mingled tears where victory and defea
Clasped hands; and Peace— among the dead— stood wist
fully, with white wings furled,
Knowing the strife was idle; for the night and morning meet,

Yet there is no disunion
In heaven's divine communion
As through the gates of twilight the harmonious morning
pours;
Ah, God speed that grander morrow
When the world's divinest sorrow
Shall show how Love stands knocking at the world's unopened
doors.

V

Hasten the Kingdom, England;
Look up across the narrow seas,
Across the great white nations to thy dark imperial throne
Where now three hundred million souls attend on thine
august decrees;
Ah, bow thine head in humbleness, the Kingdom is thine own:
Not for the pride or power
God gave thee this in dower;
But, now the West and East have met and wept their mortal
loss,
Now that their tears have spoken
And the long dumb spell is broken,
Is it nothing that thy banner bears the red eternal cross?

VI

Ay! Lift the flag of England;
And lo, that Eastern cross is there,
Veiled with a hundred meanings as our English eyes are veiled;
Yet to the grander dawn we move oblivious of the sign we
bear,
Oblivious of the heights we climb until the last be scaled;
Then with all the earth before us
And the great cross floating o'er us
We shall break the sword we forged of old, so weak we were
and blind;
While the inviolate heaven discloses
England's Rose of all the roses
Dawning wide and ever wider o'er the kingdom of mankind.

VII

Hasten the Kingdom, England;
　　For then all nations shall be one;
One as the ordered stars are one that sing upon their way,
　　One with the rhythmic glories of the swinging sea and
　　　　the rolling sun,
One with the flow of life and death, the tides of night and day;
　　　　One with all dreams of beauty,
　　　　One with all laws of duty;
One with the weak and helpless while the one sky burns above;
　　　　Till eyes by tears made glorious
　　　　Look up at last victorious,
And lips that starved break open in one song of life and love.

VIII

Hasten the Kingdom, England;
　　And when the Spring returns again
Rekindle in our English hearts the universal Spring,
　　That we may wait in faith upon the former and the latter
　　　　rain,
Till all waste places burgeon and the wildernesses sing;
　　　　Pour the glory of thy pity
　　　　Through the dark and troubled city;
Pour the splendour of thy beauty over wood and meadow
　　　　fair;
　　　　May the God of battles guide thee
　　　　And the Christ-child walk beside thee
With a word of peace for England in the dawn of Nelson's
　　　　Year.

IN TIME OF WAR

I

TO-NIGHT o'er Bagshot heath the purple heather
　　Rolls like dumb thunder to the splendid West;
And mighty ragged clouds are massed together
　　Above the scarred old common's broken breast;

And there are hints of blood between the boulders,
   Red glints of fiercer blossom, bright and bold;
And round the shaggy mounds and sullen shoulders
   The gorse repays the sun with savage gold.

And now, as in the West the light grows holy,
   And all the hollows of the heath grow dim,
Far off, a sulky rumble rolls up slowly
   Where guns at practice growl their evening hymn.

And here and there in bare clean yellow spaces
   The print of horse-hoofs like an answering cry
Strikes strangely on the sense from lonely places
   Where there is nought but empty heath and sky.

The print of warlike hoofs, where now no figure
   Of horse or man along the sky's red rim
Breaks on the low horizon's rough black rigour
   To make the gorgeous waste less wild and grim;

Strangely the hoof-prints strike, a Crusoe's wonder,
   Framed with sharp furze amongst the footless fells,
A menace and a mystery, rapt asunder,
   As if the whole wide world contained nought else,—

Nought but the grand despair of desolation
   Between us and that wild, how far, how near,
Where, clothed with thunder, nation grapples nation,
   And Slaughter grips the clay-cold hand of Fear.

II

And far above the purple heath the sunset stars awaken,
   And ghostly hosts of cloud across the West begin to stream,
And all the low soft winds with muffled cannonades are
     shaken,
   And all the blood-red blossom draws aloof into a dream;

A dream—no more—and round the dream the clouds are
    curled together;
  A dream of two great stormy hosts embattled in the sky;
For there against the low red heavens each sombre ridge of
    heather
  Up-heaves a hedge of bayonets around a battle-cry;

Melts in the distant battlefield or brings the dream so near it
  That, almost, as the rifted clouds around them swim and reel,
A thousand grey-lipped faces flash—ah, hark, the heart can
    hear it—
  The sharp command that lifts as one the levelled lines of
    steel.

And through the purple thunders there are silent shadows
    creeping
  With murderous gleams of light, and then—a mighty leaping
    roar
Where foe and foe are met; and then—a long low sound of
    weeping
  As Death laughs out from sea to sea, another fight is o'er.

Another fight—but ah, how much is over?   Night descending
  Draws o'er the scene her ghastly moon-shot veil with
    piteous hands;
But all around the bivouac-glare the shadowy pickets wending
  See sights, hear sounds that only war's own madness
    understands.

No circle of the accursed dead where dreaming Dante
    wandered,
  No city of death's eternal dole could match this mortal
    world
Where men, before the living soul and quivering flesh are
    sundered,
  Through all the bestial shapes of pain to one wide grave are
    hurled.

But in the midst for those who dare beyond the fringe to enter
　　Be sure one kingly figure lies with pale and blood-soiled
　　　　face,
And round his brows a ragged crown of thorns; and in the
　　　　centre
　　Of those pale folded hands and feet the sigil of his grace.

See, how the pale limbs, marred and scarred in love's lost
　　　　battle, languish;
　　See how the splendid passion still smiles quietly from his
　　　　eyes:
Come, come and see a king indeed, who triumphs in his
　　　　anguish,
　　Who conquers here in utter loss beneath the eternal skies.

For unto lips so deadly calm what answer shall be given?
　　Oh pale, pale king so deadly still beneath the unshaken stars,
Who shall deny thy kingdom here, though heaven and earth
　　　　were riven,
　　With the last roar of onset in the world's intestine wars?

The laugh is Death's; he laughs as erst o'er hours that England
　　　　cherished,
　　"Count up, count up the stricken homes that wail the first-
　　　　born son,
Count by your starved and fatherless the tale of what hath
　　　　perished;
　　Then gather with your foes and ask if you—or I—have won."

III

　　The world rolls on; and love and peace are mated:
　　　　Still on the breast of England, like a star,
　　The blood-red lonely heath blows, consecrated,
　　　　A brooding practice-ground for blood-red war.

　　Yet is there nothing out of tune with Nature
　　　　There, where the skylark showers his earliest song,
　　Where sun and wind have moulded every feature,
　　　　And one world-music bears each note along.

There many a brown-winged kestrel swoops or hovers
   In poised and patient quest of his own prey;
And there are fern-clad glens where happy lovers
   May kiss the murmuring summer noon away.

There, as the primal earth was—all is glorious
   Perfect and wise and wonderful in view
Of that great heaven through which we rise victorious
   O'er all that strife and change and death can do.

No nation yet has risen o'er earth's first nature;
   Though love illumed each individual mind,
Like some half-blind, half-formed primeval creature
   The State still crawled a thousand years behind.

Still on the standards of the great World-Powers
   Lion and bear and eagle sullenly brood,
Whether the slow folds flap o'er halcyon hours
   Or stream tempestuously o'er fields of blood.

By war's red evolution we have risen
   Far, since fierce Erda chose her conquering few,
And out of Death's red gates and Time's grey prison
   They burst, elect from battle, tried and true.

But now Death mocks at youth and love and glory,
   Chivalry slinks behind his loaded mines,
With meaner murderous lips War tells her story,
   And round her cunning brows no laurel shines.

And here to us the eternal charge is given
   To rise and make our low world touch God's high:
To hasten God's own kingdom, Man's own heaven,
   And teach Love's grander army how to die.

No kingdom then, no long-continuing city
   Shall e'er again be stablished by the sword;
No blood-bought throne defy the powers of pity,
   No despot's crown outweigh one helot's word.

Imperial England, breathe thy marching orders:
  The great host waits; the end, the end is close,
When earth shall know thy peace in all her borders,
  And all her deserts blossom with thy Rose.

Princedoms and peoples rise and flash and perish
  As the dew passes from the flowering thorn;
Yet the one Kingdom that our dreams still cherish
  Lives in a light that blinds the world's red morn.

Hasten the Kingdom, England, the days darken;
  We would not have thee slacken watch or ward,
Nor doff thine armour till the whole world hearken,
  Nor till Time bid thee lay aside the sword.

Hasten the Kingdom; hamlet, heath, and city,
  We are all at war, one bleeding bulk of pain;
Little we know; but one thing—by God's pity—
  We know, and know all else on earth is vain.

We know not yet how much we dare, how little;
  We dare not dream of peace; yet, as at need,
England, God help thee, let no jot or tittle
  Of Love's last law go past thee without heed.

Who saves his life shall lose it!   The great ages
  Bear witness—Rome and Babylon and Tyre
Cry from the dust-stopped lips of all their sages,—
  There is no hope if man can climb no higher.

England, by God's grace set apart to ponder
  A little while from battle, ah, take heed,
Keep watch, keep watch, beside thy sleeping thunder;
  Call down Christ's pity while those others bleed;

Waken the God within thee, while the sorrow
  Of battle surges round a distant shore,
While Time is thine, lest on some deadly morrow
  The moving finger write—*but thine no more.*

Little we know—but though the advancing æons
　　Win every painful step by blood and fire,
Though tortured mouths must chant the world's great pæans,
　　And martyred souls proclaim the world's desire;

Though war be nature's engine of rejection,
　　Soon, soon, across her universal verge
The soul of man in sacred insurrection
　　Shall into God's diviner light emerge.

Hasten the Kingdom, England, queen and mother;
　　Little we know of all Time's works and ways;
Yet this, this, this is sure: we need none other
　　Knowledge or wisdom, hope or aim or praise,

But to keep this one stormy banner flying
　　In this one faith that none shall e'er disprove,
Then drive the embattled world before thee, crying,
　　There is one Emperor, whose name is Love.

ODE FOR THE SEVENTIETH BIRTHDAY OF SWINBURNE

I

He needs no crown of ours, whose golden heart
　　Poured out its wealth so freely in pure praise
　　　Of others: him the imperishable bays
Crown, and on Sunium's height he sits apart:
He hears immortal greetings this great morn:
　　Fain would we bring, we also, all we may,
　　　　Some wayside flower of transitory bloom,
　　　　　　Frail tribute, only born
　　To greet the gladness of this April day
　　　Then waste on death's dark wind its faint perfume.

II

Here on this April day the whole sweet Spring
  Speaks thro' his music only, or seems to speak.
  And we that hear, with hearts uplift and weak,
What can we more than claim him for our king?
Here on this April day (and many a time
  Shall April come and find him singing still)
    He is one with the world's great heart beyond the years,
      One with the pulsing rhyme
  Of tides that work some heavenly rhythmic will
    And hold the secret of all human tears.

III

For he, the last of that immortal race
  Whose music, like a robe of living light
  Re-clothed each new-born age and made it bright
As with the glory of Love's transfiguring face,
Reddened earth's roses, kindled the deep blue
  Of England's radiant, ever-singing sea,
    Recalled the white Thalassian from the foam,
      Woke the dim stars anew
  And triumphed in the triumph of Liberty,
    We claim him; but he hath not here his home.

IV

Not here; round him to-day the clouds divide:
  We know what faces thro' that rose-flushed air
  Now bend above him: Shelley's face is there,
And Hugo's, lit with more than kingly pride.
Replenished there with splendour, the blind eyes
  Of Milton bend from heaven to meet his own,
    Sappho is there, crowned with those queenlier flowers
      Whose graft outgrew our skies,
  His gift: Shakespeare leans earthward from his throne
    With hands outstretched.   He needs no crown of ours.

IN CLOAK OF GREY

I

Love's a pilgrim, cloaked in grey,
    And his feet are pierced and bleeding:
Have ye seen him pass this way
    Sorrowfully pleading?
Ye that weep the world away,
Have ye seen King Love to-day?—

II

Yea, we saw him; but he came
    Poppy-crowned and white of limb!
Song had touched his lips with flame,
    And his eyes were drowsed and dim;
And we kissed the hours away
Till night grew rosier than the day.—

III

Hath he left you?—Yea, he left us
    A little while ago,
Of his laughter quite bereft us
    And his limbs of snow;
We know not why he went away
Who ruled our revels yesterday.—

IV

Because ye did not understand
    Love cometh from afar,
A pilgrim out of Holy Land
    Guided by a star:
Last night he came in cloak of grey,
Begging.   Ye knew him not: he went his way.

A RIDE FOR THE QUEEN

Queen of queens, oh lady mine,
  You who say you love me,
Here's a cup of crimson wine
  To the stars above me;
Here's a cup of blood and gall
  For a soldier's quaffing!
What's the prize to crown it all?
  Death?   I'll take it laughing!
I ride for the Queen to-night!

Though I find no knightly fee
  Waiting on my lealty,
High upon the gallows-tree
  Faithful to my fealty,
What had I but love and youth,
  Hope and fame in season?
She has proved that more than truth
  Glorifies her treason!

Would that other do as much?
  Ah, but if in sorrow
Some forgotten look or touch
  Pierce her heart to-morrow
She might love me yet, I think;
  So her lie befriends me,
Though I know there's darker drink
  Down the road she sends me.

Ay, one more great chance is mine
  (Can I faint or falter?)
She shall pour my blood like wine,
  Make my heart her altar,
Burn it to the dust!   For, there,
  What if o'er the embers
She should stoop and—I should hear—
  "*Hush!   Thy love remembers!*"

One more chance for every word
   Whispered to betray me,
While she buckled on my sword
   Smiling to allay me;
One more chance; ah, let me not
   Mar her perfect pleasure;
Love shall pay me, jot by jot,
   Measure for her measure.

Faith shall think I never knew,
   I will be so fervent!
Doubt shall dream I dreamed her true
   As her war-worn servant!
Whoso flouts her spotless name
   (Love, I wear thy token!)
He shall face one sword of flame
   Ere the lie be spoken!

All the world's a-foam with may,
   (Fragrant as her bosom!)
Could I find a sweeter way
   Through the year's young blossom,
Where her warm red mouth on mine
   Woke my soul's desire? . . .
Hey! The cup of crimson wine,
   Blood and gall and fire!

Castle Doom or Gates of Death?
   (Smile again for pity!)
"Boot and horse," my lady saith,
   "Spur against the City,
Bear this message!" God and she
   Still forget the guerdon;
Nay, the rope is on the tree!
   That shall bear the burden!
I ride for the Queen to-night!

SONG

I

Wʜᴇɴ that I loved a maiden
  My heaven was in her eyes,
And when they bent above me
  I knew no deeper skies;
But when her heart forsook me
  My spirit broke its bars,
For grief beyond the sunset
  And love beyond the stars.

II

When that I loved a maiden
  She seemed the world to me:
Now is my soul the universe,
  My dreams the sky and sea:
There is no heaven above me,
  No glory binds or bars
My grief beyond the sunset,
  My love beyond the stars.

III

When that I loved a maiden
  I worshipped where she trod;
But, when she clove my heart, the cleft
  Set free the imprisoned god:
Then was I king of all the world,
  My soul had burst its bars,
For grief beyond the sunset
  And love beyond the stars.

THE HIGHWAYMAN

PART ONE

I

THE wind was a torrent of darkness among the gusty trees,
The moon was a ghostly galleon tossed upon cloudy seas,
The road was a ribbon of moonlight over the purple moor,
And the highwayman came riding—
   Riding—riding—
The highwayman came riding, up to the old inn-door.

II

He'd a French cocked-hat on his forehead, a bunch of lace at
   his chin,
A coat of the claret velvet, and breeches of brown doe-skin;
They fitted with never a wrinkle: his boots were up to the thigh!
And he rode with a jewelled twinkle,
   His pistol butts a-twinkle,
His rapier hilt a-twinkle, under the jewelled sky.

III

Over the cobbles he clattered and clashed in the dark inn-
   yard,
And he tapped with his whip on the shutters, but all was
   locked and barred;
He whistled a tune to the window, and who should be waiting
   there
But the landlord's black-eyed daughter,
   Bess, the landlord's daughter,
Plaiting a dark red love-knot into her long black hair.

IV

And dark in the dark old inn-yard a stable-wicket creaked
Where Tim the ostler listened; his face was white and peaked;
His eyes were hollows of madness, his hair like mouldy hay,
But he loved the landlord's daughter,
   The landlord's red-lipped daughter,
Dumb as a dog he listened, and he heard the robber say—

V

"One kiss, my bonny sweetheart, I'm after a prize to-night,
But I shall be back with the yellow gold before the morning
      light;
Yet, if they press me sharply, and harry me through the
      day,
Then look for me by moonlight,
      Watch for me by moonlight,
I'll come to thee by moonlight, though hell should bar the
      way."

VI

He rose upright in the stirrups; he scarce could reach her
      hand,
But she loosened her hair i' the casement! His face burnt
      like a brand
As the black cascade of perfume came tumbling over his breast;
And he kissed its waves in the moonlight,
      (Oh, sweet black waves in the moonlight!)
Then he tugged at his rein in the moonlight, and galloped away
      to the West.

PART TWO

I

He did not come in the dawning; he did not come at noon;
And out o' the tawny sunset, before the rise o' the moon,
When the road was a gipsy's ribbon, looping the purple moor,
A red-coat troop came marching—
      Marching—marching—
King George's men came marching, up to the old inn-door.

II

They said no word to the landlord, they drank his ale in-
      stead,
But they gagged his daughter and bound her to the foot of her
      narrow bed;

13

Two of them knelt at her casement, with muskets at their side!
There was death at every window;
And hell at one dark window;
For Bess could see, through her casement, the road that _he_
would ride.

III

They had tied her up to attention, with many a sniggering
jest;
They had bound a musket beside her, with the barrel beneath
her breast!
"Now keep good watch!" and they kissed her.
She heard the dead man say—
Look for me by moonlight;
Watch for me by moonlight;
I'll come to thee by moonlight, though hell should bar the way!

IV

She twisted her hands behind her; but all the knots held
good!
She writhed her hands till her fingers were wet with sweat
or blood!
They stretched and strained in the darkness, and the hours
crawled by like years,
Till, now, on the stroke of midnight,
Cold, on the stroke of midnight,
The tip of one finger touched it! The trigger at least was hers!

V

The tip of one finger touched it; she strove no more for the
rest!
Up, she stood up to attention, with the barrel beneath her
breast,
She would not risk their hearing; she would not strive again;
For the road lay bare in the moonlight;
Blank and bare in the moonlight;
And the blood of her veins in the moonlight throbbed to her
love's refrain.

VI

Tlot-tlot; tlot-tlot! Had they heard it? The horse-hoofs
    ringing clear;
Tlot-tlot, tlot-tlot, in the distance? Were they deaf that they
    did not hear?
Down the ribbon of moonlight, over the brow of the hill,
The highwayman came riding,
       Riding, riding!
The red-coats looked to their priming! She stood up, straight
    and still!

VII

Tlot-tlot, in the frosty silence! *Tlot-tlot,* in the echoing night!
Nearer he came and nearer! Her face was like a light!
Her eyes grew wide for a moment; she drew one last deep
    breath,
Then her finger moved in the moonlight,
       Her musket shattered the moonlight,
Shattered her breast in the moonlight and warned him—with
    her death.

VIII

He turned; he spurred to the West; he did not know who stood
Bowed, with her head o'er the musket, drenched with her own
    red blood!
Not till the dawn he heard it, his face grew grey to hear
How Bess, the landlord's daughter,
       The landlord's black-eyed daughter,
Had watched for her love in the moonlight, and died in the
    darkness there.

IX

Back, he spurred like a madman, shrieking a curse to the sky,
With the white road smoking behind him and his rapier
    brandished high!
Blood-red were his spurs i' the golden noon; wine-red was his
    velvet coat,
When they shot him down on the highway,
       Down like a dog on the highway,
And he lay in his blood on the highway, with the bunch of
    lace at his throat.

    *   *   *   *   *   *

X

And still of a winter's night, they say, when the wind is in the
trees,
When the moon is a ghostly galleon tossed upon cloudy seas,
When the road is a ribbon of moonlight over the purple moor,
A highwayman comes riding—
   Riding—riding—
A highwayman comes riding, up to the old inn-door.

XI

Over the cobbles he clatters and clangs in the dark inn-yard;
He taps with his whip on the shutters, but all is locked and
barred;
He whistles a tune to the window, and who should be waiting
there
But the landlord's black-eyed daughter,
  Bess, the landlord's daughter,
Plaiting a dark red love-knot into her long black hair.

THE HAUNTED PALACE

COME to the haunted palace of my dreams,
 My crumbling palace by the eternal sea,
Which, like a childless mother, still must croon
Her ancient sorrows to the cold white moon,
  Or, ebbing tremulously,
With one pale arm, where the long foam-fringe gleams,
 Will gather her rustling garments, for a space
 Of muffled weeping, round her dim white face.

A princess dwelt here once: long, long ago
 This tower rose in the sunset like a prayer;
And, through the witchery of that casement, rolled
In one soft cataract of faëry gold
  Her wonder-woven hair;
Her face leaned out and took the sacred glow
 Of evening, like the star that listened, high
 Above the gold clouds of the western sky.

Was there no prince behind her in the gloom,
   No crimson shadow of his rich array?
Her face leaned down to me: I saw the tears
Bleed through her eyes with the slow pain of years,
      And her mouth yearned to say—
"Friend, is there any message, from the tomb
   Where love lies buried?"   But she only said—
   "Oh, friend, canst thou not save me from my dead?

"Canst thou not minister to a soul in pain?
   Or hast thou then no comfortable word?
Is there no faith in thee wherewith to atone
For his unfaith who left me here alone,
      Heart-sick with hope deferred;
Oh, since my love will never come again,
   Bring'st thou no respite through the desolate years,
Respite from these most unavailing tears?"

Then saw I, and mine own tears made response,
   Her woman's heart come breaking through her eyes;
And, as I stood beneath the tower's grey wall,
She let the soft waves of her deep hair fall
      Like flowers from Paradise
Over my fevered face: then all at once
   Pity was passion; and like a sea of bliss
   Those waves rolled o'er me drowning for her kiss.

      *   *   *   *   *   *

Seven years we dwelt together in that tower,
   Seven years in that old palace by the sea,
And sitting at that casement, side by side,
She told me all her pain: how love had died
      Now for all else but me;
Yet how she had loved that other: like a flower
   Her red lips parted and with low sweet moan
   She pressed their tender suffering on mine own.

And always with vague eyes she gazed afar,
  Out through the casement o'er the changing tide;
And slowly was my heart's hope brought to nought
That some day I should win each wandering thought
     And make her my soul's bride:
Still, still she gazed across the cold sea-bar;
  Ay; with her hand in mine, still, still and pale,
  Waited and watched for the unreturning sail.

And I, too, watched and waited as the years
  Rolled on; and slowly was I brought to feel
How on my lips she met her lover's kiss,
How my heart's pulse begat an alien bliss;
     And cold and hard as steel
For me those eyes were, though their tender tears
  Were salt upon my cheek; and then one night
  I saw a sail come through the pale moonlight.

And like an alien ghost I stole away,
  And like a breathing lover he returned;
And in the woods I dwelt, or sometimes crept
Out in the grey dawn while the lovers slept
     And the great sea-tides yearned
Against the iron shores; and faint and grey
  The tower and the shut casement rose above:
  And on the earth I sobbed out all my love.

At last, one royal rose-hung night in June,
  When the warm air like purple Hippocrene
Brimmed the dim valley and sparkled into stars,
I saw them cross the foam-lit sandy bars
     And dark pools, glimmering green,
To bathe beneath the honey-coloured moon:
  I saw them swim out from that summer shore,
  Kissed by the sea, but they returned no more.

     *   *   *   *   *   *

And into the dark palace, like a dream
   Remembered after long oblivious years,
Through the strange open doors I crept and saw
As some poor pagan might, with reverent awe,
     And deep adoring tears,
The moonlight through that painted window stream
   Over the soft wave of their vacant bed;
   There sank I on my knees and bowed my head,

For as a father by a cradle bows,
   Remembering two dead children of his own,
I knelt; and by the cry of the great deep
Their love seemed like a murmuring in their sleep,
     A little fevered moan,
A little tossing of childish arms that shows
   How dreams go by! "If I were God," I wept,
   "I would have pity on children while they slept."

   *   *   *   *   *   *

The days, the months, the years drift over me;
   This is my habitation till I die:
Nothing is changed; they left that open book
Beside the window.   Did he sit and look
     Up at her face as I
Looked while she read it, and the enchanted sea
   With rich eternities of love unknown
   Fulfilled the low sweet music of her tone?

So did he listen, looking in her face?
   And did she ever pause, remembering so
   The heart that bore the whole weight of her pain
Until her own heart's love returned again?
     In the still evening glow
I sit and listen in this quiet place,
   And only hear—like notes of phantom birds—
   Their perished kisses and little broken words.

Come to the haunted palace of my dreams,
  My crumbling palace by the eternal sea,
Which, like a childless mother, still must croon
Her ancient sorrows to the cold white moon,
       Or, ebbing tremulously,
With one pale arm, where the long foam-fringe gleams,
  Will gather her rustling garments, for a space
  Of muffled weeping, round her dim white face.

THE SCULPTOR

THIS is my statue: cold and white
It stands and takes the morning light!
    The world may flout my hopes and fears,
    Yet was my life's work washed with tears
Of blood when this poor hand last night
    Finished the pain of years.

Speak for me, patient lips of stone,
Blind eyes my lips have rested on
    So often when the o'er-weary brain
    Would grope to human love again,
And found this grave cold mask alone
    And the tears fell like rain.

Ay; is this all?   Is this the brow
I fondled, never wondering how
    It lived—the face of pain and bliss
    That through the marble met my kiss?
Oh, though the whole world praise it now,
    Let no man dream it is!

They blame; they cannot blame aright
Who never knew what infinite
    Deep loss must shame me most of all!
    They praise; like earth their praises fall
Into a tomb.   The hour of light
    Is flown beyond recall.

Yet have I seen, yet have I known,
And oh, not tombed in cold white stone
The dream I lose on earth below;
And I shall come with face aglow
And find and claim it for my own
Before God's throne, I know.

SUMMER

(AN ODE)

Now like a pageant of the Golden Year
    In rich memorial pomp the hours go by,
With rose-embroidered flags unfurled
And tasselled bugles calling through the world
        Wake, for your hope draws near!
Wake, for in each soft porch of azure sky,
    Seen through each arch of pale green leaves, the Gate
    Of Eden swings apart for Summer's royal state.

Ah, when the Spirit of the moving scene
    Has entered in, the splendour will be spent!
The flutes will cease, the gates will close;
Only the scattered crimson of the rose,
        The wild wood's hapless queen,
Dis-kingdomed, will declare the way he went;
    And, in a little while, her court will go,
    Pass like a cloud and leave no trace on earth below.

Tell us no more of Autumn, the slow gold
    Of fruitage ripening in a world's decay,
The falling leaves, the moist rich breath
Of woods that swoon and crumble into death
        Over the gorgeous mould:
    Give us the flash and scent of keen-edged may
    Where wastes that bear no harvest yield their bloom,
    Rude crofts of flowering nettle, bents of yellow broom.

The very reeds and sedges of the fen
   Open their hearts and blossom to the sky;
The wild thyme on the mountain's knees
Unrolls its purple market to the bees;
     Unharvested of men
The Traveller's Joy can only smile and die.
   Joy, joy alone the throbbing whitethroats bring,
   Joy to themselves and heaven! They were but born to sing

And see, between the northern-scented pines,
   The whole sweet summer sharpens to a glow!
See, as the well-spring plashes cool
Over a shadowy green fern-fretted pool
     The mystic sunbeam shines
For one mad moment on a breast of snow
   A warm white shoulder and a glowing arm
   Up-flung, where some swift Undine sinks in shy alarm.

And if she were not all a dream, and lent
   Life for a little to your own desire,
Oh, lover in the hawthorn lane,
Dream not you hold her, or you dream in vain!
     The violet, spray-besprent
When from that plunge the rainbows flashed like fire,
   Will scarce more swiftly lose its happy dew
   Than eyes which Undine haunts will cease to shine on you

What though the throstle pour his heart away,
   A happy spendthrift of uncounted gold,
Swinging upon a blossomed briar
With soft throat lifted in a wild desire
     To make the world his may.
Ever the pageant through the gates is rolled
   Further away; in vain the rich notes throng
   Flooding the mellow noon with wave on wave of song.

The feathery meadows like a lilac sea,
   Knee-deep, with honeyed clover, red and white,
Roll billowing: the crisp clouds pass
Trailing their soft blue shadows o'er the grass;
     The skylark, mad with glee,

Quivers, up, up, to lose himself in light;
  And, through the forest, like a fairy dream
  Through some dark mind, the ferns in branching beauty
      stream.

Enough of joy! A little respite lend,
  Summer, fair god that hast so little heed
Of these that serve thee but to die,
Mere trappings of thy tragic pageantry!
      Show us the end, the end!
We too, with human hearts that break and bleed,
  March to the night that rounds their fleeting hour,
  And feel we, too, perchance but serve some loftier Power.

O that our hearts might pass away with thee,
  Burning and pierced and full of thy sweet pain,
Burst through the gates with thy swift soul,
Hunt thy most white perfection to the goal,
      Nor wait, once more to see
Thy chaliced lilies rotting in the rain,
  Thy ragged yellowing banners idly hung
  In woods that have forgotten all the songs we sung!

Peace! Like a pageant of the Golden Year
  In rich memorial pomp the hours go by,
With rose-embroidered flags unfurled
And tasselled bugles calling through the world
      Wake, for your hope draws near!
Wake, for in each soft porch of azure sky,
  Seen through each arch of pale green leaves, the Gate
  Of Eden swings apart for Summer's royal state.

Not wait! Forgive, forgive that feeble cry
  Of blinded passion all unworthy thee!
For here the spirit of man may claim
A loftier vision and a nobler aim
      Than e'er was born to die:
Man only, of earth, throned on Eternity,
  From his own sure abiding-place can mark
  How earth's great golden dreams go past into the dark.

AT DAWN

O HESPER-PHOSPHOR, far away
    Shining, the first, the last white star,
Hear'st thou the strange, the ghostly cry,
That moan of an ancient agony
From purple forest to golden sky
    Shivering over the breathless bay?
It is not the wind that wakes with the day;
    For see, the gulls that wheel and call,
    Beyond the tumbling white-topped bar,
Catching the sun-dawn on their wings,
    Like snow-flakes or like rose-leaves fall,
Flutter and fall in airy rings;
    And drift, like lilies ruffling into blossom
    Upon some golden lake's unwrinkled bosom.

Are not the forest's deep-lashed fringes wet
With tears?   Is not the voice of all regret
    Breaking out of the dark earth's heart?
She too, she too, has loved and lost; and we—
We that remember our lost Arcady,
Have we not known, we too,
The primal greenwood's arch of blue,
The radiant clouds at sun-rise curled
Around the brows of the golden world;
The marble temples, washed with dew,
To which with rosy limbs aflame
The violet-eyed Thalassian came,
Came, pitiless, only to display
How soon the youthful splendour dies away;
    Came, only to depart
Laughing across the grey-grown bitter sea;
For each man's life is earth's epitome,
And though the years bring more than aught they take,
Yet might his heart and hers well break
Remembering how one prayer must still be vain.
    How one fair hope is dead,
    One passion quenched, one glory fled
With those first loves that never come again.

How many years, how many generations,
    Have heard that sigh in the dawn,
When the dark earth yearns to the unforgotten nations
    And the old loves withdrawn,
Old loves, old lovers, wonderful and unnumbered
    As waves on the wine-dark sea,
'Neath the tall white towers of Troy and the temples that
    slumbered
    In Thessaly?

From the beautiful palaces, from the miraculous portals,
    The swift white feet are flown!
They were taintless of dust, the proud, the peerless Immortals
    As they sped to their loftier throne!
Perchance they are there, earth dreams, on the shores of
    Hesper,
    Her rosy-bosomed Hours,
Listening the wild fresh forest's enchanted whisper,
    Crowned with its new strange flowers;
Listening the great new ocean's triumphant thunder
    On the stainless unknown shore,
While that perilous queen of the world's delight and wonder
    Comes white from the foam once more.

When the mists divide with the dawn o'er those glittering
    waters,
    Do they gaze over unoared seas—
Naiad and nymph and the woodland's rose-crowned
    daughters
    And the Oceanides?
Do they sing together, perchance, in that diamond splendour,
    That world of dawn and dew,
With eyelids twitching to tears and with eyes grown tender
    The sweet old songs they knew,
The songs of Greece?   Ah, with harp-strings mute do they
    falter
    As the earth like a small star pales?
When the heroes launch their ship by the smoking altar
    Does a memory lure their sails?

Far, far away, do their hearts resume the story
     That never on earth was told,
When all those urgent oars on the waste of glory
     Cast up its gold?

> *Are not the forest fringes wet*
> *With tears?   Is not the voice of all regret*
> *Breaking out of the dark earth's heart?*
> *She too, she too, has loved and lost; and though*
> *She turned last night in disdain*
> *   Away from the sunset-embers,*
> *From her soul she can never depart;*
> *She can never depart from her pain.*
> *Vainly she strives to forget;*
> *Beautiful in her woe,   .*
> *   She awakes in the dawn and remembers.*

THE SWIMMER'S RACE

I

BETWEEN the clover and the trembling sea
     They stand upon the golden-shadowed shore
In naked boyish beauty, a strenuous three,
     Hearing the breakers' deep Olympic roar;
Three young athletes poised on a forward limb,
     Mirrored like marble in the smooth wet sand,
          Three statues moulded by Praxiteles:
               The blue horizon rim
          Recedes, recedes upon a lovelier land,
               And England melts into the skies of Greece.

II

The dome of heaven is like one drop of dew,
     Quivering and clear and cloudless but for one
Crisp bouldered Alpine range that blinds the blue
     With snowy gorges glittering to the sun:
Forward the runners lean, with outstretched hand
     Waiting the word—ah, how the light relieves
          The silken rippling muscles as they start
               Spurning the yellow sand,
          Then skimming lightlier till the goal receives
               The winner, head thrown back and lips apart.

III

Now at the sea-marge on the sand they lie
  At rest for a moment, panting as they breathe,
And gazing upward at the unbounded sky
  While the sand nestles round them from beneath;
And in their hands they gather up the gold
  And through their fingers let it lazily stream
    Over them, dusking all their limbs' fair white,
      Blotting their shape and mould,
    Till, mixed into the distant gazer's dream
     Of earth and heaven, they seem to sink from sight.

IV

But one, in seeming petulance, oppressed
  With heat has cast his brown young body free:
With arms behind his head and heaving breast
  He lies and gazes at the cool bright sea;
So young Leander might when in the noon
  He panted for the starry eyes of eve
    And whispered o'er the waste of wandering waves,
      "Hero, bid night come soon!"
    Nor knew the nymphs were waiting to receive
     And kiss his pale limbs in their cold sea-caves.

V

Now to their feet they leap and, with a shout,
  Plunge through the glittering breakers without fear,
Breast the green-arching billows, and still out,
  As if each dreamed the arms of Hero near;
Now like three sunbeams on an emerald crest,
  Now like three foam-flakes melting out of sight,
    They are blent with all the glory of all the sea;
      One with the golden West;
    Merged in a myriad waves of mystic light
     As life is lost in immortality.

THE VENUS OF MILO

I

BACKWARD she leans, as when the rose unblown
  Slides white from its warm sheath some morn in May
Under the sloping waist, aslant, her zone
  Clings as it slips in tender disarray;
One knee, out-thrust a little, keeps it so
  Lingering ere it fall; her lovely face
    Gazes as o'er her own Eternity!
Those armless radiant shoulders, long ago
  Perchance held arms out wide with yearning grace
    For Adon by the blue Sicilian sea.

II

No; thou eternal fount of these poor gleams,
  Bright axle-star of the wheeling temporal skies,
Daughter of blood and foam and deathless dreams,
  Mother of flying Love that never dies,
To thee, the topmost and consummate flower,
  The last harmonic height, our dull desires
    And our tired souls in dreary discord climb;
The flesh forgets its pale and wandering fires;
  We gaze through heaven as from an ivory tower
    Shining upon the last dark shores of Time.

III

White culmination of the dreams of earth,
  Thy splendour beacons to a loftier goal,
Where, slipping earthward from the great new birth,
  The shadowy senses leave the essential soul!
Oh, naked loveliness, not yet revealed,
  A moment hence that falling robe will show
    No prophecy like this, this great new dawn,
The bare bright breasts, each like a soft white shield,
  And the firm body like a slope of snow
    Out of the slipping dream-stuff half withdrawn.

THE NET OF VULCAN

FROM peaks that clove the heavens asunder
  The hunchback god with sooty claws
Loomed o'er the night, a cloud of thunder,
  And hurled the net of mortal laws;
It flew, and all the world grew dimmer;
  Its blackness blotted out the stars,
Then fell across the rosy glimmer
  That told where Venus couched with Mars.

And, when the steeds that draw the morning
  Spurned from their Orient hooves the spray,
All vainly soared the lavrock, warning
  Those tangled lovers of the day:
Still with those twin white waves in blossom,
  Against the warrior's rock-broad breast,
The netted light of the foam-born bosom
  Breathed like a sea at rest.

And light was all that followed after,
  Light the derision of the sky,
Light the divine Olympian laughter
  Of kindlier gods in days gone by:
Low to her lover whispered Venus,
  "The shameless net be praised for this—
When night herself no more could screen us
  It snared us one more hour of bliss."

NIOBE

How like the sky she bends above her child,
  One with the great horizon of her pain!
No sob from our low seas where woe runs wild,
  No weeping cloud, no momentary rain,
Can mar the heaven-high visage of her grief,
  That frozen anguish, proud, majestic, dumb.
    She stoops in pity above the labouring earth,
      Knowing how fond, how brief
    Is all its hope, past, present, and to come,
      She stoops in pity, and yearns to assuage its dearth.

14

Through that fair face the whole dark universe
   Speaks, as a thorn-tree speaks thro' one white flower;
And all those wrenched Promethean souls that curse
   The gods, but cannot die before their hour,
Find utterance in her beauty.   That fair head
     Bows over all earth's graves.   It was her cry
       Men heard in Rama when the twisted ways
         With children's blood ran red!
     Her silence utters all the sea would sigh;
       And, in her face, the whole earth's anguish prays.

It is the pity, the pity of human love
   That strains her face, upturned to meet the doom,
And her deep bosom, like a snow-white dove
   Frozen upon its nest, ne'er to resume
Its happy breathing o'er the golden brace
     Whose fostering was her death.   Death, death alone
       Can break the anguished horror of that spell!
         The sorrow on her face
     Is sealed: the living flesh is turned to stone;
       She knows all, all, that Life and Time can tell.

Ah, yet, her woman's love, so vast, so tender;
   Her woman's body, hurt by every dart;
Braving the thunder, still, still hide the slender
   Soft frightened child beneath her mighty heart.
She is all one mute immortal cry, one brief
     Infinite pang of such victorious pain
       That she transcends the heavens and bows them down!
         The majesty of grief
     Is hers, and her dominion must remain
       Eternal.   God nor man usurps that crown.

ORPHEUS AND EURYDICE

I

Height over height, the purple pine-woods clung to the
    rich Arcadian mountains,
    Holy-sweet as a sea of incense, under the low dark crimson
      skies:
Glad were the glens where Eurydice bathed, in the beauty
    of dawn, at the haunted fountains
    Deep in the blue hyacinthine hollows, whence all the
      rivers of Arcady rise.

Long ago, ah, white as the Huntress, cold and sweet as
    the petals that crowned her,
    Fair and fleet as the fawn that shakes the dew from the
      fern at break of day,
Wreathed with the clouds of her dusky hair that swept in
    a sun-bright glory around her,
    Down to the valley her light feet stole, ah, soft as the
      budding of flowers in May.

Down to the valley she came, for far and far below in the
    dreaming meadows
    Pleaded ever the Voice of voices, calling his love by her
      golden name;
So she arose from her home in the hills, and down through the
    blossoms that danced with their shadows,
    Out of the blue of the dreaming distance, down to the
      heart of her lover she came.

.   .   .   .

Red were the lips that hovered above her lips in the flowery
    haze of the June-day:
    Red as a rose through the perfumed mist of passion that
      reeled before her eyes;
Strong the smooth young sunburnt arms that folded her
    heart to his heart in the noon-day,
    Strong and supple with throbbing sunshine under the
      blinding southern skies.

Ah, the kisses, the little murmurs, mad with pain for their
    phantom fleetness,
  Mad with pain for the passing of love that lives, they
    dreamed—as we dream—for an hour!
Ah, the sudden tempest of passion, mad with pain for its
    over-sweetness,
  As petal by petal and pang by pang their love broke out into
    perfect flower.

Ah, the wonder as once he wakened, out of a dream of remem-
    bered blisses,
  Couched in the meadows of dreaming blossom to feel,
    like the touch of a flower on his eyes,
Cool and fresh with the fragment dews of dawn the touch
    of her light swift kisses,
  Shed from the shadowy rose of her face between his face and
    the warm blue skies.

II

Lost in his new desire
He dreamed away the hours;
    His lyre
Lay buried in the flowers:

To whom the King of Heaven,
Apollo, lord of light,
    Had given
Beauty and love and might:

Might, if he would, to slay
All evil dreams and pierce
    The grey
Veil of the Universe;

With Love that holds in one
Sacred and ancient bond
    The sun
And all the vast beyond,

And Beauty to enthrall
The soul of man to heaven:
      Yea, all
These gifts to him were given.

Yet in his dream's desire
He drowsed away the hours:
      His lyre
Lay buried in the flowers.

Then in his wrath arose
Apollo, lord of light,
      That shows
The wrong deed from the right;

And by what radiant laws
O'erruling human needs,
      The cause
To consequence proceeds;

How balanced is the sway
He gives each mortal doom:
      How day
Demands the atoning gloom:

How all good things await
The soul that pays the price
      To Fate
By equal sacrifice;

And how on him that sleeps
For less than labour's sake
      There creeps
Uncharmed, the Pythian snake.

III

Lulled by the wash of the feathery grasses, a sea with many a
    sun-swept billow,
    Heart to heart in the heart of the summer, lover by lover
        asleep they lay,
Hearing only the whirring cicala that chirruped awhile at
    their poppied pillow
    Faint and sweet as the murmur of men that laboured in
        villages far away.

Was not the menace indeed more silent?   Ah, what care for
    labour and sorrow?
    Gods in the meadows of moly and amaranth surely might
        envy their deep sweet bed
Here where the butterflies troubled the lilies of peace, and took
    no thought for the morrow,
    And golden-girdled bees made feast as over the lotus the
        soft sun spread.

Nearer, nearer the menace glided, out of the gorgeous gloom
    around them,
    Out of the poppy-haunted shadows deep in the heart of the
        purple brake;
Till through the hush and the heat as they lay, and their own
    sweet listless dreams enwound them,—
    Mailed and mottled with hues of the grape-bloom suddenly,
        quietly, glided the snake.

Subtle as jealousy, supple as falsehood, diamond-headed and
    cruel as pleasure,
    Coil by coil he lengthened and glided, straight to the fragrant
        curve of her throat:
There in the print of the last of the kisses that still glowed red
    from the sweet long pressure,
    Fierce as famine and swift as lightning over the glittering
        lyre he smote.

IV

And over the cold white body of love and delight
   Orpheus arose in the terrible storm of his grief,
With quivering up-clutched hands, deadly and white,
   And his whole soul wavered and shook like a wind-swept
      leaf:

As a leaf that beats on a mountain, his spirit in vain
   Assaulted his doom and beat on the Gates of Death:
Then prone with his arms o'er the lyre he sobbed out his pain,
   And the tense chords faintly gave voice to the pulse of his
      breath.

And he heard it and rose, once again, with the lyre in his
      hand,
   And smote out the cry that his white-lipped sorrow denied:
And the grief's mad ecstasy swept o'er the summer-sweet land,
   And gathered the tears of all Time in the rush of its tide.

There was never a love forsaken or faith forsworn,
   There was never a cry for the living or moan for the slain,
But was voiced in that great consummation of song; ay, and
      borne
   To storm on the Gates of the land whence none cometh
      again.

Transcending the barriers of earth, comprehending them all
   He followed the soul of his loss with the night in his eyes;
And the portals lay bare to him there; and he heard the faint
      call
   Of his love o'er the rabble that wails by the river of sighs.

Yea, there in the mountains before him, he knew it of old,
   That portal enormous of gloom, he had seen it in dreams,
When the secrets of Time and of Fate through his harmonies
      rolled;
   And behind it he heard the dead moan by their desolate
      streams.

And he passed through the Gates with the light and the cloud
    of his song,
  Dry-shod over Lethe he passed to the chasms of hell;
And the hosts of the dead made mock at him, crying, *How long
  Have we dwelt in the darkness, oh fool, and shall evermore
    dwell ?*

*Did our lovers not love us? the grey skulls hissed in his face;
  Were our lips not red?   Were these cavernous eyes not bright?
Yet us, whom the soft flesh clothed with such roseate grace,
  Our lovers would loathe if we ever returned to their sight!*

Oh then, through the soul of the Singer, a pity so vast
  Mixed with his anguish that, smiting anew on his lyre,
He caught up the sorrows of hell in his utterance at last,
  Comprehending the need of them all in his own great desire.

V

And they that were dead, in his radiant music, remembered
    the dawn with its low deep crimson,
  Heard the murmur of doves in the pine-wood, heard the
    moan of the roaming sea,
Heard and remembered the little kisses, in woods where the
    last of the moon yet swims on
  Fragrant, flower-strewn April nights of young-eyed lovers
    in Arcady;

Saw the soft blue veils of shadow floating over the
    billowy grasses
  Under the crisp white curling clouds that sailed and trailed
    through the melting blue;
Heard once more the quarrel of lovers above them pass, as a
    lark-song passes,
  Light and bright, till it vanished away in an eye-bright
    heaven of silvery dew.

Out of the dark, ah, white as the Huntress, cold and sweet
    as the petals that crowned her,
  Fair and fleet as a fawn that shakes the dew from the fern
      at break of day;
Wreathed with the clouds of her dusky hair that swept in a
    sun-bright glory around her,
  On through the deserts of hell she came, and the brown air
      bloomed with the light of May.

On through the deserts of hell she came; for over the fierce and
    frozen meadows
  Pleaded ever the Voice of voices, calling his love by her
      golden name;
So she arose from her grave in the darkness, and up through
    the wailing fires and shadows,
  On by chasm and cliff and cavern, out of the horrors of death
      she came.

Then had she followed him, then had he won her, striking a
    chord that should echo for ever,
  Had he been steadfast only a little, nor paused in the great
      transcendent song;
But ere they had won to the glory of day, he came to the brink
    of the flaming river
  And ceased, to look on his love a moment, a little moment,
      and overlong.

VI

O'er Phlegethon he stood:
Below him roared and flamed
      The flood
For utmost anguish named.

And lo, across the night,
The shining form he knew
      With light
Swift footsteps upward drew.

Up through the desolate lands
She stole, a ghostly star,
        With hands
Outstretched to him afar.

With arms outstretched, she came
In yearning majesty,
        The same
Royal Eurydice.

Up through the ghastly dead
She came, with shining eyes
        And red
Sweet lips of child-surprise.

Up through the wizened crowds
She stole, as steals the moon
        Through clouds
Of flowery mist in June.

He gazed: he ceased to smite
The golden-chorded lyre:
        Delight
Consumed his heart with fire.

Though in that deadly land
His task was but half-done,
        His hand
Drooped, and the fight half-won.

He saw the breasts that glowed,
The fragrant clouds of hair:
        They flowed
Around him like a snare.

O'er Phlegethon he stood,
For utmost anguish named:
        The flood
Below him roared and flamed.

Out of his hand the lyre
Suddenly slipped and fell,
　　The fire
Acclaimed it into hell.

The night grew dark again:
There came a bitter cry
　　Of pain,
Oh Love, once more I die!

And lo, the earth-dawn broke,
And like a wraith she fled:
　　He woke
Alone: his love was dead.

He woke on earth: the day
Shone coldly: at his side
　　There lay
The body of his bride.

VII

Only now when the purple vintage bubbles and winks in the
　　　　autumn glory,
　Only now when the great white oxen drag the weight of
　　　　the harvest home,
Sunburnt labourers, under the star of the sunset, sing as an
　　　　old-world story
　How two pale and thwarted lovers ever through Arcady still
　　　　must roam.

Faint as the silvery mists of morning over the peaks that the
　　　　noonday parches,
　On through the haunts of the gloaming musk-rose, down
　　　　to the rivers that glisten below,
Ever they wander from meadow to pinewood, under the whis-
　　　　pering woodbine arches,
　Faint as the mists of the dews of the dusk when violets
　　　　dream and the moon-winds blow.

Though the golden lute of Orpheus gathered the splendours of
  earth and heaven,
 All the golden greenwood notes and all the chimes of the
   changing sea,
Old men over the fires of winter murmur again that he was not
  given
 The steadfast heart divine to rule that infinite freedom of
   harmony.

Therefore he failed, say they; but we, that have no wisdom,
  can only remember
 How through the purple perfumed pinewoods white Eurydice
   roamed and sung:
How through the whispering gold of the wheat, where the
  poppy burned like a crimson ember,
 Down to the valley in beauty she came, and under her feet
   the flowers upsprung.

Down to the valley she came, for far and far below in the dreaming
  meadows
 Pleaded ever the Voice of voices, calling his love by her golden
   name;
So she arose from her home in the hills, and down through the
  blossoms that danced with their shadows,
 Out of the blue of the dreaming distance, down to the heart of
   her lover she came.

FROM THE SHORE

Love, so strangely lost and found,
 Love, beyond the seas of death,
Love, immortally re-crowned,
 Love, who swayest this mortal breath,
Sweetlier to thy lover's ear
 Steals the tale that ne'er was told;
Bright-eyes, ah, thine arms are near,
 Nearer now than e'er of old.

When on earth thy hands were mine,
   Mine to hold for evermore,
Oft we watched the sunset shine
   Lonely from this wave-beat shore;
Pent in prison-cells of clay,
   Time had power on thee and me:
Thou and heaven are one to-day,
   One with earth and sky and sea;

Indivisible and one!
   Beauty hath unlocked the Gate,
Oped the portals of the sun,
   Burst the bars of Time and Fate!
Violets in the dawn of Spring
   Hold the secret of thine eyes:
Lilies bare their breasts and fling
   Scents of thee from Paradise.

Brooklets have thy talk by rote;
   Thy farewells array the West;
Fur that clasped thee round the throat
   Leaps—a squirrel—to its nest!
Backward from a sparkling eye
   Half-forgotten jests return
Where the rabbit lollops by
   Hurry-scurry through the fern!

Roses where I lonely pass
   Brush my brow and breathe thy kiss:
Zephyrs, whispering through the grass,
   Lure me on from bliss to bliss:
Here thy robe is rustling close,
   There thy fluttering lace is blown,—
All the tide of beauty flows
   Tributary to thine own.

Birds that sleek their shining throats
   Capture every curve from thee:
All their golden warbled notes,
   Fragments of thy melody,

Crowding, clustering, one by one,
    Build it upward, spray by spray,
Till the lavrock in the sun
    Pours thy rapture down the day.

Silver birch and purple pine,
    Crumpled fern and crimson rose,
Flash to feel their beauty thine,
    Clasp and fold thee, warm and close:
Every beat and gleam of wings
    Holds thee in its bosom furled;
All that chatters, laughs, and sings,
    Darts thy sparkle round the world.

Love, so strangely lost and found,
    Love, beyond the seas of death,
Love, immortally re-crowned,
    Love, who swayest this mortal breath,
Sweetlier to thy lover's ear
    Steals the tale that ne'er was told;
Bright eyes, ah, thine arms are near,
    Nearer now than e'er of old.

THE RETURN

O, HEDGES white with laughing may,
    O, meadows where we met,
This heart of mine will break to-day
    Unless ye, too, forget.

Breathe not so sweet, breathe not so sweet,
    But swiftly let me pass
Across the fields that felt her feet
    In the old time that was.

A year ago, but one brief year,
    O, happy flowering land,
We wandered here and whispered there,
    And hand was warm in hand.

O, crisp white clouds beyond the hill,
   O, lavrock in the skies,
Why do ye all remember still
   Her bright uplifted eyes.

Red heather on the windy moor,
   Wild thyme beside the way,
White jasmine by the cottage door,
   Harden your hearts to-day.

Smile not so kind, smile not so kind,
   Thou happy haunted place,
Or thou wilt strike these poor eyes blind
   With her remembered face.

REMEMBRANCE

O, UNFORGOTTEN lips, grey haunting eyes,
   Soft curving cheeks and heart-remembered brow,
It is all true, the old love never dies;
   And, parted, we must meet for ever now.

We did not think it true!   We did not think
   Love meant this universal cry of pain,
This crown of thorn, this vinegar to drink,
   This lonely crucifixion o'er again.

Yet through the darkness of the sleepless night
   Your tortured face comes meekly answering mine;
Dumb, but I know why those mute lips are white;
   Dark, but I know why those dark lashes shine.

O, love, love, love, what death can set us free
From this implacable ghost of memory?

A PRAYER

ONLY a little, O Father, only to rest
   Or ever the night comes and the eternal sleep,
   Only to rest a little, a little to weep
In the dead love's pitiful arms, on the dead love's breast,

A little to loosen the frozen fountains, to free
   Rivers of blood and tears that should slacken the pulse
   Of this pitiless heart, and appease these pangs that convulse
Body and soul; oh, out of Eternity,

A moment to whisper, only a moment to tell
   My dead, my dead, what words are so helpless to say—
   The dreams unuttered, the prayers no passion could pray
And then—the eternal sleep or the pains of hell,

I could welcome them, Father, gladly as ever a child
   Laying his head on the pillow might turn to his rest
   And remember in dreams, as the hand of the mother is prest
On his hair, how the Pitiful blessed him of old and smiled.

LOVE'S GHOST

I

THY house is dark and still: I stand once more
      Beside the marble door.
It opens as of old: thy pale, pale face
      Peers thro' the narrow space:
Thy hands are mine, thy hands are mine to hold,
      Just as of old.

II

"Hush! hush! or God will hear us!   Ah, speak low
      As Love spake long ago."
"Sweet, sweet, are these thine arms, thy breast, thy hair
      Assuaging my despair,
Assuaging the long thirst, quenching the tears
      Of all these years?

III

"Thy house is deep and still: God cannot hear;
  Sweet, have no fear!
Are not thy cold lips crushed against my kiss?
  Love gives us this,
Not God;" but "Ah," she moans, "God hears us; speak,
  Speak low, hide cheek on cheek."

IV

Oh then what eager whisperings, hoarded long,
  Sweeter than any song,
What treasured news to tell, what hopes, what fears,
  Gleaned from the barren years,
What raptures wrung from out the heart of pain,
  What wild farewells again!

V

Whose pity is this?   Ah, quick, one kiss!   Once more
  Closes the marble door!
I grope here in the darkness all alone.
  Across the cold white stone.
Over thy tomb, a sudden starlight gleams:
  Death gave me this—in dreams.

ON A RAILWAY PLATFORM

 A DRIZZLE of drifting rain
  And a blurred white lamp o'erhead,
 That shines as my love will shine again
  In the world of the dead.

 Round me the wet black night,
  And, afar in the limitless gloom,
 Crimson and green, two blossoms of light,
  Two stars of doom.

15

But the night of death is aflare
  With a torch of back-blown fire,
And the coal-black deeps of the quivering air
  Rend for my soul's desire.

Leap, heart, for the pulse and the roar
  And the lights of the streaming train
That leaps with the heart of thy love once more
  Out of the mist and the rain.

Out of the desolate years
  The thundering pageant flows;
But I see no more than a window of tears
  Which her face has turned to a rose.

OXFORD REVISITED

CHANGED and estranged, like a ghost, I pass the familiar portals
  Echoing now like a tomb, they accept me no more as of old
Yet I go wistfully onward, a shade thro' a kingdom of mortal
  Wanting a face to greet me, a hand to grasp and to hold

Hardly I know as I go if the beautiful City is only
  Mocking me under the moon, with its streams and its wil
    lows agleam,
Whether the City of friends or I that am friendless and lonely
  Whether the boys that go by or the time-worn towers be the
    dream;

Whether the walls that I know, or the unknown fugitive faces
  Faces like those that I loved, faces that haunt and waylay,
Faces so like and unlike, in the dim unforgettable places,
  Startling the heart into sickness that aches with the swee
    of the May,—

Whether all these or the world with its wars be the wandering
    shadows!
  Ah, sweet over green-gloomed waters the may hangs,
    crimson and white;
And quiet canoes creep down by the warm gold dusk of the
    meadows,
  Lapping with little splashes and ripples of silvery light.

Others as I have returned: I shall see the old faces to-morrow,
  Down by the gay-coloured barges, alert for the throb of the
    oars,
Wanting to row once again, or tenderly jesting with sorrow
  Up the old stairways and noting the strange new names on
    the doors.

Is it a dream? And I know not nor care if there be an awaking
  Ever at all any more, for the years that have torn us apart,
Few, so few as they are, will ever be rending and breaking:
  Sooner by far than I knew have they wrought this change
    for my heart!

Well; I grow used to it now! Could the dream but remain
    and for ever,
  With the flowers round the grey quadrangle laughing as time
    grows old!
For the waters go down to the sea, but the sky still gleams on
    the river!
  We plucked them—but there shall be lilies, ivory lilies and
    gold.

And still, in the beautiful City, the river of life is no duller,
  Only a little strange as the eighth hour dreamily chimes,
In the City of friends and echoes, ribbons and music and colour,
  Lilac and blossoming chestnut, willows and whispering limes.

Over the Radcliffe Dome the moon as the ghost of a flower
  Weary and white awakes in the phantom fields of the sky:
The trustful shepherded clouds are asleep over steeple and
    tower,
  Dark under Magdalen walls the Cher like a dream goes by.

Back, we come wandering back, poor ghosts, to the home that
    one misses
  Out in the shelterless world, the world that was heaven to
    us then,
Back from the coil and the vastness, the stars and the boundless
    abysses,
  Like monks from a pilgrimage stealing in bliss to their
    cloisters again.

City of dreams that we lost, accept now the gift we inherit—
  Love, such a love as we knew not of old in the blaze of our
    noon,
We that have found thee at last, half City, half heavenly
    Spirit,
  While over a mist of spires the sunset mellows the moon.

THE THREE SHIPS

(To an old Tune)

I

As I went up the mountain-side,
The sea below me glittered wide,
And, Eastward, far away, I spied
    On Christmas Day, on Christmas Day,
The three great ships that take the tide
    On Christmas Day in the morning.

II

Ye have heard the song, how these must ply
From the harbours of home to the ports o' the sky!
Do ye dream none knoweth the whither and why
    On Christmas Day, on Christmas Day,
The three great ships go sailing by
    On Christmas Day in the morning?

III

Yet, as I live, I never knew
That ever a song could ring so true,
Till I saw them break thro' a haze of blue
  On Christmas Day, on Christmas Day;
And the marvellous ancient flags they flew
  On Christmas Day in the morning!

IV

From the heights above the belfried town
I saw that the sails were patched and brown,
But the flags were a-flame with a great renown
  On Christmas Day, on Christmas Day,
And on every mast was a golden crown
  On Christmas Day in the morning.

V

Most marvellous ancient ships were these!
Were their prows a-plunge to the Chersonese?
For the pomp of Rome or the glory of Greece,
  On Christmas Day, on Christmas Day,
Were they out on a quest for the Golden Fleece
  On Christmas Day in the morning?

VI

And the sun and the wind they told me there
How goodly a load the three ships bear,
For the first is gold and the second is myrrh
  On Christmas Day, on Christmas Day;
And the third is frankincense most rare
  On Christmas Day in the morning.

VII

They have mixed their shrouds with the golden sky,
They have faded away where the last dreams die . . .
Ah yet, will ye watch, when the mist lifts high
     On Christmas Day, on Christmas Day?
Will ye see three ships come sailing by
     On Christmas Day in the morning?

SLUMBER-SONGS OF THE MADONNA

PRELUDE

DANTE saw the great white Rose
    Half unclose;
Dante saw the golden bees
  Gathering from its heart of gold
    Sweets untold,
Love's most honeyed harmonies.

Dante saw the threefold bow
    Strangely glow,
Saw the Rainbow Vision rise,
  And the Flame that wore the crown
    Bending down
O'er the flowers of Paradise.

Something yet remained, it seems;
    In his dreams
Dante missed—as angels may
  In their white and burning bliss—
    Some small kiss
Mortals meet with every day.

Italy in splendour faints
    'Neath her saints!
O, her great Madonnas, too,
  Faces calm as any moon
    Glows in June,
Hooded with the night's deep blue!

What remains?   I pass and hear
                    Everywhere,
Ay, or see in silent eyes
    Just the song she still would sing
                    Thus—a-swing
O'er the cradle where He lies.

I

Sleep, little baby, I love thee.
Sleep, little king, I am bending above thee.
        How should I know what to sing
Here in my arms as I swing thee to sleep?
            Hushaby low,
            Rockaby so,
Kings may have wonderful jewels to bring,
Mother has only a kiss for her king!
Why should my singing so make me to weep?
Only I know that I love thee, I love thee,
        Love thee, my little one, sleep.

II

Is it a dream?   Ah yet, it seems
    Not the same as other dreams!
I can but think that angels sang,
    When thou wast born, in the starry sky,
And that their golden harps out-rang
    While the silver clouds went by!

The morning sun shuts out the stars,
    Which are much loftier than the sun;
But, could we burst our prison-bars
    And find the Light whence light begun,
The dreams that heralded thy birth
Were truer than the truths of earth;
And, by that far immortal Gleam,
Soul of my soul, I still would dream!

A ring of light was round thy head,
The great-eyed oxen nigh thy bed
Their cold and innocent noses bowed!
Their sweet breath rose like an incense cloud
In the blurred and mystic lanthorn light.

About the middle of the night
The black door blazed like some great star
With a glory from afar,
Or like some mighty chrysolite
Wherein an angel stood with white
Blinding arrowy bladed wings
Before the throne of the King of kings;
And, through it, I could dimly see
A great steed tethered to a tree.

Then, with crimson gems aflame
Through the door the three kings came,
And the black Ethiop unrolled
The richly broidered cloth of gold,
And pourèd forth before thee there
Gold and frankincense and myrrh!

III

See, what a wonderful smile!   Does it mean
    That my little one knows of my love?
Was it meant for an angel that passed unseen,
    And smiled at us both from above?
Does it mean that he knows of the birds and the flowers
That are waiting to sweeten his childhood's hours,
And the tales I shall tell and the games he will play,
And the songs we shall sing and the prayers we shall pray
                In his boyhood's May,
                He and I, one day?

IV

For in the warm blue summer weather
We shall laugh and love together:
   I shall watch my baby growing,
I shall guide his feet,
   When the orange trees are blowing
And the winds are heavy and sweet!

   When the orange orchards whiten
   I shall see his great eyes brighten
To watch the long-legged camels going
   Up the twisted street,
When the orange trees are blowing
   And the winds are sweet.

What does it mean?   Indeed, it seems
A dream!   Yet not like other dreams!

We shall walk in pleasant vales,
   Listening to the shepherd's song
I shall tell him lovely tales
   All day long:
He shall laugh while mother sings
Tales of fishermen and kings.

He shall see them come and go
   O'er the wistful sea,
Where rosy oleanders blow
   Round blue Lake Galilee,
Kings with fishers' ragged coats
And silver nets across their boats,
Dipping through the starry glow,
With crowns for him and me!
      Ah, no;
Crowns for him, not me!

Rockaby so!   Indeed, it seems
A dream!   Yet not like other dreams!

V

Ah, see what a wondeful smile again!
  Shall I hide it away in my heart,
To remember one day in a world of pain
  When the years have torn us apart,
      Little babe,
When the years have torn us apart?

Sleep, my little one, sleep,
  Child with the wonderful eyes,
  Wild miraculous eyes,
Deep as the skies are deep!
What star-bright glory of tears
Waits in you now for the years
That shall bid you waken and weep?
Ah, in that day, could I kiss you to sleep
Then, little lips, little eyes,
Little lips that are lovely and wise,
Little lips that are dreadful and wise!

VI

Clenched little hands like crumpled roses
      Dimpled and dear,
Feet like flowers that the dawn uncloses,
      What do I fear?
Little hands, will you ever be clenched in anguish?
White little limbs, will you droop and languish?
      Nay, what do I hear?
I hear a shouting, far away,
You shall ride on a kingly palm-strewn way
      Some day!

But when you are crowned with a golden crown
      And throned on a golden throne,
You'll forget the manger of Bethlehem town
      And your mother that sits alone

Wondering whether the mighty king
Remembers a song she used to sing,
  Long ago,
   "*Rockaby so,*
Kings may have wonderful jewels to bring,
Mother has only a kiss for her king!" . . .

Ah, see what a wonderful smile, once more!
  He opens his great dark eyes!
Little child, little king, nay, hush, it is o'er
  My fear of those deep twin skies,—
   Little child,
  You are all too dreadful and wise!

VII

But now you are mine, all mine,
  And your feet can lie in my hand so small,
And your tiny hands in my heart can twine,
  And you cannot walk, so you never shall fall,
Or be pierced by the thorns beside the door,
Or the nails that lie upon Joseph's floor;
Through sun and rain, through shadow and shine,
  You are mine, all mine!

ENCELADUS

In the Black Country, from a little window,
Before I slept, across the haggard wastes
Of dust and ashes, I saw Titanic shafts
Like shadowy columns of wan-hope arise
To waste, on the blear sky, their slow sad wreaths
Of smoke, their infinitely sad slow prayers.
Then, as night deepened, the blast-furnaces,
Red smears upon the sulphurous blackness, turned
All that sad region to a City of Dis,
Where naked, sweating giants all night long
Bowed their strong necks, melted flesh, blood and bone,
To brim the dry ducts of the gods of gloom
With terrible rivers, branches of living gold.

O, like some tragic gesture of great souls
In agony, those awful columns towered
Against the clouds, that city of ash and slag
Assumed the grandeur of some direr Thebes
Arising to the death-chant of those gods,
A dreadful Order climbing from the dark
Of Chaos and Corruption, threatening to take
Heaven with its vast slow storm.
                                    I slept, and dreamed.
And like the slow beats of some Titan heart
Buried beneath immeasurable woes,
The forging-hammers thudded through the dream:

Huge on a fallen tree,
Lost in the darkness of primeval woods,
Enceladus, earth-born Enceladus,
The naked giant, brooded all alone.
Born of the lower earth, he knew not how,
Born of the mire and clay, he knew not when,
Brought forth in darkness, and he knew not why!

Thus, like a wind, went by a thousand years.

Anhungered, yet no comrade of the wolf,
And cold, but with no power upon the sun,
A master of this world that mastered him!

Thus, like a cloud, went by a thousand years.

Who chained this other giant in his heart
That heaved and burned like Etna?   Heavily
He bent his brows and wondered and was dumb.

And, like one wave, a thousand years went by.

He raised his matted head and scanned the stars.
He stood erect!   He lifted his uncouth arms!
With inarticulate sounds his uncouth lips
Wrestled and strove—*I am full-fed, and yet*
I hunger!
Who set this fiercer famine in my maw?

Can I eat moons, gorge on the Milky Way,
Swill sunsets down, or sup the wash of the dawn
Out of the rolling swine-troughs of the sea?
Can I drink oceans, lie beneath the mountains,
And nuzzle their heavy boulders like a cub
Sucking the dark teats of the tigress?   Who,
Who set this deeper hunger in my heart?
And the dark forest echoed—*Who?   Ah, who?*

"I hunger!"
And the night-wind answered him,
"Hunt, then, for food."

"I hunger!"
And the sleek gorged lioness
Drew nigh him, dripping freshly from the kill,
Redder her lolling tongue, whiter her fangs,
And gazed with ignorant eyes of golden flame.

"I hunger!"
Like a breaking sea his cry
Swept through the night.   Against his swarthy knees
She rubbed the red wet velvet of her ears
With mellow thunders of unweeting bliss,
Purring—*Ah, seek, and you shall find.*
Ah, seek, and you shall slaughter, gorge, ah seek,
Seek, seek, you shall feed full, ah seek, ah seek.

Enceladus, earth-born Enceladus,
Bewildered like a desert-pilgrim, saw
A rosy City, opening in the clouds,
The hunger-born mirage of his own heart,
Far, far above the world, a home of gods,
Where One, a goddess, veiled in the sleek waves
Of her deep hair, yet glimmering golden through,
Lifted, with radiant arms, ambrosial food
For hunger such as this!   Up the dark hills,
He rushed, a thunder-cloud,
Urged by the famine of his heart.   He stood
High on the topmost crags, he hailed the gods
In thunder, and the clouds re-echoed it!

He hailed the gods!
And like a sea of thunder round their thrones
Washing, a midnight sea, his earth-born voice
Besieged the halls of heaven!   He hailed the gods!
They laughed, he heard them laugh!
With echo and re-echo, far and wide,
A golden sea of mockery, they laughed!

Enceladus, earth-born Enceladus,
Laid hold upon the rosy Gates of Heaven,
And shook them with gigantic sooty hands,
Asking he knew not what, but not for alms;
And the Gates, opened as in jest;
And, like a sooty jest, he stumbled in.

Round him the gods, the young and scornful gods,
Clustered and laughed to mark the ravaged face,
The brutal brows, the deep and dog-like eyes,
The blunt black nails, and back with burdens bowed.
And, when they laughed, he snarled with uncouth lips
And made them laugh again.

> *"Whence comest thou?"*

He could not speak!
How should he speak whose heart within him heaved
And burned like Etna?   Through his mouth there came
A sound of ice-bergs in a frozen sea
Of tears, a sullen region of black ice
Rending and breaking, very far away.
They laughed!
He stared at them, bewildered, and they laughed
Again, *"Whence comest thou?"*

He could not speak!
But through his mouth a moan of midnight woods,
Where wild beasts lay in wait to slaughter and gorge,
A moan of forest-caverns where the wolf
Brought forth her litter, a moan of the wild earth
In travail with strange shapes of mire and clay,
Creatures of clay, clay images of the gods,
That hungered like the gods, the most high gods,
But found no food, and perished like the beasts.

And the gods laughed,—
Art thou, then, such a god?   And, like a leaf
Unfolding in dark woods, in his deep brain
A sudden memory woke; and like an ape
He nodded, and all heaven with laughter rocked,
While Artemis cried out with scornful lips,—
Perchance He is the Maker of you all!

Then, piteously outstretching calloused hands,
He sank upon his knees, his huge gnarled knees,
And echoed, falteringly, with slow harsh tongue,—
Perchance, perchance, the Maker of you all.

They wept with laughter!   And Aphrodite, she,
With keener mockery than white Artemis
Who smiled aloof, drew nigh him unabashed
In all her blinding beauty.   Carelessly,
As o'er the brute brows of a stallèd ox
Across that sooty muzzle and brawny breast,
Contemptuously, she swept her golden hair
In one deep wave, a many-millioned scourge
Intolerable and beautiful as fire;
Then turned and left him, reeling, gasping, dumb,
While heaven re-echoed and re-echoed, *See,*
Perchance, perchance, the Maker of us all!

Enceladus, earth-born Enceladus,
Rose to his feet, and with one terrible cry
"*I hunger*," rushed upon the scornful gods
And strove to seize and hold them with his hands,
And still the laughter deepened as they rolled
Their clouds around them, baffling him.   But once,
Once with a shout, in his gigantic arms
He crushed a slippery splendour on his breast
And felt on his harsh skin the cool smooth peaks
Of Aphrodite's bosom.   One black hand
Slid down the naked snow of her long side
And bruised it where he held her.   Then, like snow
Vanishing in a furnace, out of his arms
The splendour suddenly melted, and a roll
Of thunder split the dream, and headlong down

He fell, from heaven to earth; while, overhead
The young and scornful gods—he heard them laugh!—
Toppled the crags down after him.   He lay
Supine.   They plucked up Etna by the roots
And buried him beneath it.   His broad breast
Heaved, like that other giant in his heart,
And through the crater burst his fiery breath,
But could not burst his bonds.   And so he lay
Breathing in agony thrice a thousand years.

Then came a Voice, he knew not whence, "Arise,
Enceladus!"   And from his heart a crag
Fell, and one arm was free, and one thought free,
And suddenly he awoke, and stood upright,
Shaking the mountains from him like a dream;
And the tremendous light and awful truth
Smote, like the dawn, upon his blinded eyes,
That out of his first wonder at the world,
Out of his own heart's deep humility,
And simple worship, he had fashioned gods
Of cloud, and heaven out of a hollow shell.
And groping now no more in the empty space
Outward, but inward in his own deep heart,
He suddenly felt the secret gates of heaven
Open, and from the infinite heavens of hope
Inward, a voice, from the innermost courts of Love,
Rang—*Thou shalt have none other gods but Me.*

Enceladus, the foul Enceladus,
When the clear light out of that inward heaven
Whose gates are only inward in the soul,
Showed him that one true Kingdom, said,
                         "I will stretch
My hands out once again.   And, as the God
That made me is the Heart within my heart,
So shall my heart be to this dust and earth
A god and a creator.   I will strive
With mountains, fires and seas, wrestle and strive,
Fashion and make, and that which I have made
In anguish I shall love as God loves me."

In the Black Country, from a little window,
Waking at dawn, I saw those giant Shafts
—O great dark word out of our elder speech,
Long since the poor man's kingly heritage—
The Shapings, the dim Sceptres of Creation,
The Shafts like columns of wan-hope arise
To waste, on the blear sky, their slow sad wreaths
Of smoke, their infinitely sad slow prayers.
Then, as the dawn crimsoned, the sordid clouds,
The puddling furnaces, the mounds of slag,
The cinders, and the sand-beds and the rows
Of wretched roofs, assumed a majesty
Beyond all majesties of earth or air;
Beauty beyond all beauty, as of a child
In rags, upraised thro' the still gold of heaven,
With wasted arms and hungering eyes, to bring
The armoured seraphim down upon their knees
And teach eternal God humility;
The solemn beauty of the unfulfilled
Moving towards fulfilment on a height
Beyond all heights; the dreadful beauty of hope;
The naked wrestler struggling from the rock
Under the sculptor's chisel; the rough mass
Of clay more glorious for the poor blind face
And bosom that half emerge into the light,
More glorious and august, even in defeat,
Than that too cold dominion God foreswore
To bear this passionate universal load,
This Calvary of Creation, with mankind.

IN THE COOL OF THE EVENING

I

IN the cool of the evening, when the low sweet whispers waken,
When the labourers turn them homeward, and the weary
   have their will,
When the censers of the roses o'er the forest-aisles are shaken,
Is it but the wind that cometh o'er the far green hill?

16

II

For they say 'tis but the sunset winds that wander through
      the heather,
  Rustle all the meadow-grass and bend the dewy fern;
They say 'tis but the winds that bow the reeds in prayer
      together,
  And fill the shaken pools with fire along the shadowy burn.

III

In the beauty of the twilight, in the Garden that He loveth,
  They have veiled His lovely vesture with the darkness of a
      name!
Thro' His Garden, thro' His Garden it is but the wind that
      moveth,
  No more; but O, the miracle, the miracle is the same!

IV

In the cool of the evening, when the sky is an old story
  Slowly dying, but remembered, ay, and loved with passion
      still,
Hush! . . . the fringes of His garment, in the fading golden
      glory,
  Softly rustling as He cometh o'er the far green hill.

A ROUNDHEAD'S RALLYING SONG

I

How beautiful is the battle,
  How splendid are the spears,
When our banner is the sky
And our watchword *Liberty*,
  And our kingdom lifted high above the years.

II

How purple shall our blood be,
　How glorious our scars,
When we lie there in the night
With our faces full of light
　And the death upon them smiling at the stars.

III

How golden is our hauberk,
　And steel, and steel our sword,
And our shield without a stain
As we take the field again,
　We whose armour is the armour of the Lord!

VICISTI, GALILÆE

"The shrines are dust, the gods are dead,"
　They cried in ancient Rome!
"Ah yet, the Idalian rose is red,
　And bright the Paphian foam:
For all your Galilæan tears
　We turn to her," men say . . .
But we, we hasten thro' the years
　To our own yesterday.

Thro' all the thousand years ye need
　To make the lost so fair,
Before ye can award His meed
　Of perfect praise and prayer!
Ye liberated souls, the crown
　Is yours; and yet, some few
Can hail, as this great Cross goes down
　Its distant triumph, too.

Poor scornful Lilliputian souls,
　And are ye still too proud
To risk your little aureoles
　By kneeling with the crowd?

Do ye still dream ye "stand alone"
  So fearless and so strong?
To-day we claim the rebels' throne
  And leave you with the throng.

Yes, He has conquered!   You at least
  The "van-guard" leaves behind
To croon old tales of king and priest
  In the ingles of mankind:
The breast of Aphrodite glows,
  Apollo's face is fair;
But O, the world's wide anguish knows
  No Apollonian prayer.

Not ours to scorn the first white gleam
  Of beauty on this earth,
The clouds of dawn, the nectarous dream,
  The gods of simpler birth;
But, as ye praise them, your own cry
  Is fraught with deeper pain,
And the Compassionate ye deny
  Returns, returns again.

O, worshippers of the beautiful,
  Is this the end then, this,—
That ye can only see the skull
  Beneath the face of bliss?
No monk in the dark years ye scorn
  So barren a pathway trod
As ye who, ceasing not to mourn,
  Deny the mourner's God.

And, while ye scoff, on every side
  Great hints of Him go by,—
Souls that are hourly crucified
  On some new Calvary!
O, tortured faces, white and meek,
  Half seen amidst the crowd,
Grey suffering lips that never speak,
  The Glory in the Cloud!

In flower and dust, in chaff and grain,
  He binds Himself and dies!
We live by His eternal pain,
  His hourly sacrifice;
The limits of our mortal life
  Are His. The whisper thrills
Under the sea's perpetual strife,
  And through the sunburnt hills.

Darkly, as in a glass, our sight
  Still gropes thro' Time and Space:
We cannot see the Light of Light
  With angels, face to face:
Only the tale His martyrs tell
  Around the dark earth rings
He died and He went down to hell
  And lives—the King of Kings!

And, while ye scoff, from shore to shore,
  From sea to moaning sea,
Eloi, Eloi, goes up once more
  Lama sabacthani!
The heavens are like a scroll unfurled,
  The writing flames above—
This is the King of all the world
  Upon His Cross of Love.

DRAKE

DEDICATED TO
RUDOLPH CHAMBERS LEHMANN

PROLOGUE TO AMERICAN EDITION

I

ENGLAND, my mother,
    Lift to my western sweetheart
One full cup of English mead, breathing of the may!
    Pledge the may-flower in her face that you and ah, none other,
      Sent her from the mother-land
        Across the dashing spray.

II

Hers and yours the story:
    Think of it, oh, think of it—
That immortal dream when El Dorado flushed the skies!
    Fill the beaker full and drink to Drake's undying glory,
      Yours and hers (Oh, drink of it!)
        The dream that never dies.

III

Yours and hers the free-men
    Who scanned the stars and westward sung
When a king commanded and the Atlantic thundered "Nay!"
    Hers as yours the pride is, for Drake our first of seamen
      First upon his bow-sprit hung
        That bunch of English may.

IV

Pledge her deep, my mother;
    Through her veins thy life-stream runs!
Spare a thought, too, sweetheart, for my mother o'er the sea!
    Younger eyes are yours; but ah, those old eyes and none
      other
      Once bedewed the may-flower; once,
        As yours, were clear and free.

V

Once!   Nay, now as ever
   Beats within her ancient heart
All the faith that took you forth to seek your heaven alone:
   Shadows come and go; but let no shade of doubt dissever,
     Cloak, or cloud, or keep apart
      Two souls whose prayer is one.

VI

Sweetheart, ah, be tender—
   Tender with her prayer to-night!
Such a goal might yet be ours!—the battle-flags be furled,
   All the wars of earth be crushed, if only now your slender
     Hand should grasp her gnarled old hand
      And federate the world.

VII

Foolish it may seem, sweet!
   Still the battle thunder lours:
Darker look the Dreadnoughts as old Europe goes her way!
   Yet your hand, your hand, has power to crush that evil
     dream, sweet;
     You, with younger eyes than ours
      And brows of English may.

VIII

If a singer cherishes
   Idle dreams or idle words,
You shall judge—and you'll forgive: for, far away or nigh,
   Still abides that Vision without which a people perishes:
     Love will strike the atoning chords!
      Hark—there comes a cry!

IX

Over all this earth, sweet,
    The poor and weak look up to you—
Lift their burdened shoulders, stretch their fettered hands in
        prayer:
    You, with gentle hands, can bring the world-wide dream to
        birth, sweet,
        While I lift this cup to you
            And wonder—will she care?

X

Kindle, eyes, and beat, heart!
    Hold the brimming beaker up!
All the may is burgeoning from East to golden West!
    England, my mother, greet America, my sweetheart:
        —Ah, but ere I drained the cup
            I found her on your breast.

EXORDIUM

When on the highest ridge of that strange land,
Under the cloudless blinding tropic blue,
Drake and his band of swarthy seamen stood
With dazed eyes gazing round them, emerald fans
Of palm that fell like fountains over cliffs
Of gorgeous red anana bloom obscured
Their sight on every side.   Illustrious gleams
Of rose and green and gold streamed from the plumes
That flashed like living rainbows through the glades.
Piratic glints of musketoon and sword,
The scarlet scarves around the tawny throats,
The bright gold ear-rings in the sun-black ears,
And the calm faces of the negro guides
Opposed their barbarous bravery to the noon;
Yet a deep silence dreadfully besieged
Even those mighty hearts upon the verge
Of the undiscovered world.   Behind them lay

The old earth they knew. In front they could not see
What lay beyond the ridge. Only they heard
Cries of the painted birds troubling the heat
And shivering through the woods; till Francis Drake
Plunged through the hush, took hold upon a tree,
The tallest near them, and clomb upward, branch
By branch.
    And there, as he swung clear above
The steep-down forest, on his wondering eyes,
Mile upon mile of rugged shimmering gold,
Burst the unknown immeasurable sea.
Then he descended; and with a new voice
Vowed that, God helping, he would one day plough
Those virgin waters with an English keel.

So here before the unattempted task,
Above the Golden Ocean of my dream
I clomb and saw in splendid pageant pass
The wild adventures and heroic deeds
Of England's epic age, a vision lit
With mighty prophecies, fraught with a doom
Worthy the great Homeric roll of song,
Yet all unsung and unrecorded quite
By those who might have touched with Raphael's hand
The large imperial legend of our race,
Ere it brought forth the braggarts of an hour,
Self-worshippers who love their imaged strength,
And as a symbol for their own proud selves
Misuse the sacred name of this dear land,
While England to the Empire of her soul
Like some great Prophet passes through the crowd
That cannot understand; for he must climb
Up to that sovran thunder-smitten peak
Where he shall grave and trench on adamant
The Law that God shall utter by the still
Small voice, not by the whirlwind or the fire.
There labouring for the Highest in himself
He shall achieve the good of all mankind;
And from that lonely Sinai shall return
Triumphant o'er the little gods of gold
That rule their little hour upon the plain.

Oh, thou blind master of these opened eyes
Be near me, therefore, now; for not in pride
I lift lame hands to this imperious theme;
But yearning to a power above mine own
Even as a man might lift his hands in prayer.
Or as a child, perchance, in those dark days
When London lay beleaguered and the axe
Flashed out for a bigot empire; and the blood
Of martyrs made a purple path for Spain
Up to the throne of Mary; as a child
Gathering with friends upon a winter's morn
For some mock fight between the hateful prince
Philip and Thomas Wyatt, all at once
Might see in gorgeous ruffs embastioned
Popinjay plumes and slouching hats of Spain,
Gay shimmering silks and rich encrusted gems,
Gold collars, rare brocades, and sleek trunk-hose
The Ambassador and peacock courtiers come
Strutting along the white snow-strangled street,
A walking plot of scarlet Spanish flowers,
And with one cry a hundred boyish hands
Put them to flight with snowballs, while the wind
All round their Spanish ears hissed like a flight
Of white-winged geese; so may I wage perchance
A mimic war with all my heart in it,
Munitioned with mere perishable snow
Which mightier hands one day will urge with steel.
Yet may they still remember me as I
Remember, with one little laugh of love,
That child's game, this were wealth enough for me.

Mother and love, fair England, hear my prayer;
Help me that I may tell the enduring tale
Of that great seaman, good at need, who first
Sailed round this globe and made one little isle,
One little isle against that huge Empire
Of Spain whose might was paramount on earth,
O'ertopping Babylon, Nineveh, Greece, and Rome,
Carthage and all huge Empires of the past,
He made this little isle, against the world,

Queen of the earth and sea.   Nor this alone
The theme; for, in a mightier strife engaged
Even than he knew, he fought for the new faiths,
Championing our manhood as it rose
And cast its feudal chains before the seat
Of kings; nay, in a mightier battle yet
He fought for the soul's freedom, fought the fight
Which, though it still rings in our wondering ears,
Was won then and for ever—that great war,
That last Crusade of Christ against His priests,
Wherein Spain fell behind a thunderous roar
Of ocean triumph over burning ships
And shattered fleets, while England, England rose,
Her white cliffs laughing out across the waves,
Victorious over all her enemies.

And while he won the world for her domain,
Her loins brought forth, her fostering bosom fed
Souls that have swept the spiritual seas
From heaven to hell, and justified her crown.
For round the throne of great Elizabeth
Spenser and Burleigh, Sidney and Verulam,
Clustered like stars, rare Jonson like the crown
Of Cassiopeia, Marlowe ruddy as Mars,
And over all those mighty hearts arose
The soul of Shakespeare brooding far and wide
Beyond our small horizons, like a light
Thrown from a vaster sun that still illumes
Tracts which the arc of our increasing day
Must still leave undiscovered, unexplored.

Mother and love, fair England, hear my prayer,
As thou didst touch the heart and light the flame
Of wonder in those eyes which first awoke
To beauty and the sea's adventurous dream
Three hundred years ago, three hundred years,
And five long decades, in the leafy lanes
Of Devon, where the tallest trees that bore
The raven's matted nest had yielded up

Their booty, while the perilous branches swayed
Beneath the boyish privateer, the king
Of many young companions, Francis Drake;
So hear me, and so help, for more than his
My need is, even than when he first set sail
Upon that wild adventure with three ships
And three-score men from grey old Plymouth Sound,
Not knowing if he went to life or death,
Not caring greatly, so that he were true
To his own sleepless and unfaltering soul
Which could not choose but hear the ringing call
Across the splendours of the Spanish Main
From ever fading, ever new horizons,
And shores beyond the sunset and the sea.

Mother and sweetheart, England; from whose breast,
With all the world before them, they went forth,
Thy seamen, o'er the wide uncharted waste,
Wider than that Ulysses roamed of old,
Even as the wine-dark Mediterranean
Is wider than some wave-relinquished pool
Among its rocks, yet none the less explored
To greater ends than all the pride of Greece
And pomp of Rome achieved; if my poor song
Now spread too wide a sail, forgive thy son
And lover, for thy love was ever wont
To lift men up in pride above themselves
To do great deeds which of themselves alone
They could not; thou hast led the unfaltering feet
Of even thy meanest heroes down to death,
Lifted poor knights to many a great emprise,
Taught them high thoughts, and though they kept
                              their souls
Lowly as little children, bidden them lift
Eyes unappalled by all the myriad stars
That wheel around the great white throne of God.

BOOK I

Now through the great doors of the Council-room
Magnificently streamed in rich array
The peers of England, regal of aspèct
And grave.   Their silence waited for the Queen:
And even now she came; and through their midst,
Low as they bowed, she passed without a smile
And took her royal seat.   A bodeful hush
Of huge anticipation gripped all hearts,
Compressed all brows, and loaded the broad noon
With gathering thunder: none knew what the hour
Might yet bring forth; but the dark fire of war
Smouldered in every eye; for every day
The Council met debating how to join
Honour with peace, and every day new tales
Of English wrongs received from the red hands
Of that gigantic Empire, insolent
Spain, spurred fiercer resentments up like steeds
Revolting, on the curb, foaming for battle,
In all men's minds, against whatever odds.
On one side of the throne great Walsingham,
A lion of England, couchant, watchful, calm,
Was now the master of opinion: all
Drew to him.   Even the hunchback Burleigh smiled
With half-ironic admiration now,
As in the presence of the Queen they met
Amid the sweeping splendours of her court,
A cynic smile that seemed to say, "I, too,
Would fain regain that forthright heart of fire;
Yet statesmanship is but a smoother name
For the superior cunning which ensures
Victory."   And the Queen, too, knowing her strength
And weakness, though her woman's heart leaped out
To courage, yet with woman's craft preferred
The subtler strength of Burleigh; for she knew
Mary of Scotland waited for that war
To strike her in the side for Rome; she knew
How many thousands lurked in England still
Remembering Rome and bloody Mary's reign.

France o'er a wall of bleeding Huguenots
Watched for an hour to strike.   Against all these
What shield could England raise, this little isle,—
Out-matched, outnumbered, perilously near
Utter destruction?

                              So the long debate

Proceeded.

                    All at once there came a cry
Along the streets and at the palace-gates
And at the great doors of the Council-room!
Then through the pikes and halberds a voice rose
Imperative for entrance, and the guards
Made way, and a strange whisper surged around,
And through the peers of England thrilled the blood
Of Agincourt as to the foot of the throne
Came Leicester, for behind him as he came
A seaman stumbled, travel-stained and torn,
Crying for justice, and gasped out his tale.
"The Spaniards," he moaned, "the Inquisition!
They have taken all my comrades, all our crew,
And flung them into dungeons: there they lie
Waiting for England, waiting for their Queen!
Will you not free them?   I alone am left!
All London is afire with it, for this
Was one of your chief city merchant's ships—
The *Pride of London*, one of Osborne's ships!
But there is none to help them!   I escaped
With shrieks of torment ringing in these ears,
The glare of torture-chambers in these eyes
That see no faces anywhere but blind
Blind faces, each a bruise of white that smiles
In idiot agony, washed with sweat and blood,
The face of some strange thing that once was man,
And now can only turn from side to side
Babbling like a child, with mouth agape,
And crying for help where there is none to hear
Save those black vizards in the furnace-glow,
Moving like devils at their hellish trade. . . ."
He paused; his memory sickened, his brain swooned
Back into that wild glare of obscene pain!

Once more to his ears and nostrils horribly crept
The hiss and smell of shrivelling human flesh!
His dumb stare told the rest: his head sank down;
He strove in agony
With what all hideous words must leave untold;
While Leicester vouched him, "This man's tale is true!"
But like a gathering storm a low deep moan
Of passion, like a tiger's, slowly crept
From the grey lips of Walsingham.   "My Queen,
Will you not free them?"

                  Then Elizabeth,
Whose name is one for ever with the name
Of England, rose; and in her face the gleam
Of justice that makes anger terrible
Shone, and she stretched her glittering sceptre forth
And spoke, with distant empires in her eyes.

"My lords, this is the last cry they shall wring
From English lips unheeded: we will have
Such remedies for this as all the world
Shall tremble at!"

           And, on that night, while Drake
Close in his London lodging lay concealed
Until he knew if it were peace or war
With Spain (for he had struck on the high seas
At Spain; and well he knew if it were peace
His blood would be made witness to that bond,
And he must die a pirate's death or fly
Westward once more), there all alone, he pored
By a struggling rushlight o'er a well-thumbed chart
Of magic islands in the enchanted seas,
Dreaming, as boys and poets only dream
With those that see God's wonders in the deep,
Perilous visions of those palmy keys,
Cocoa-nut islands, parrot-haunted woods,
Crisp coral reefs and blue shark-finned lagoons
Fringed with the creaming foam, mile upon mile
Of mystery.   Dream after dream went by,
Colouring the brown air of that London night
With many a mad miraculous romance.

There, suddenly, some augury, some flash
Showed him a coming promise, a strange hint,
Which, though he played with it, he scarce believed;
Strange as in some dark cave the first fierce gleam
Of pirate gold to some forlorn maroon
Who tiptoes to the heap and glances round
Askance, and dreads to hear what erst he longed
To hear—some voice to break the hush; but bathes
Both hands with childish laughter in the gold,
And lets it trickle through his fevered palms,
And begins counting half a hundred times
And loses count each time for sheer delight
And wonder in it; meantime, if he knew,
Passing the cave-mouth, far away, beyond
The still lagoon, the coral reef, the foam
And the white fluttering chatter of the birds,
A sail that might have saved him comes and goes
Unseen across the blue Pacific sea.
So Drake, too, played with fancies; but that sail
Passed not unseen, for suddenly there came
A firm and heavy footstep to the door,
Then a loud knocking; and, at first, he thought
"I am a dead man: there is peace with Spain,
And they are come to lead me to my doom."
But, as he looked across one shoulder, pride
Checking the fuller watch for what he feared,
The door opened; and cold as from the sea
The night rushed in, and there against the gloom,
Clad, as it seemed, with wind and cloud and rain,
There loomed a stately form and high grim face
Loaded with deadly thoughts of iron war—
Walsingham,—in one hand he held a map
Marked with red lines; the other hand held down
The rich encrusted hilt of his great sword.
Then Drake rose, and the other cautiously
Closing the door drew near the flickering light
And spread his map out on the table, saying—
"Mark for me here the points whereat the King
Philip of Spain may best be wounded, mark
The joints of his harness;" and Drake looked at him
Thinking, "If he betray me, I am dead."

But the soldier met his eyes and, with a laugh,
Drake, quivering like a bloodhound in the leash,
Stooped, with his finger pointing thus and thus—
"Here would I guard, here would I lie in wait,
Here would I strike him through the breast and throat."
And as he spoke he kindled, and began
To set forth his great dreams, and high romance
Rose like a moon reflecting the true sun
Unseen; and as the full round moon indeed
Rising behind a mighty mountain-chain
Will shadow forth in outline grim and black
Its vast and ragged edges, so that moon
Of high romance rose greatly shadowing forth
The grandeur of his dreams, until their might
Dawned upon Walsingham, and he, too, saw
For a moment of muffled moonlight and wild cloud
The vision of the imperious years to be!
But suddenly Drake paused as one who strays
Beyond the bounds of caution, paused and cursed
His tongue for prating like a moon-struck boy's.
"I am mad," he cried, "I am mad to babble so!"
Then Walsingham drew near him with strange eyes
And muttered slowly, "Write that madness down;
Ay, write it down, that madman's plan of thine;
Sign it, and let me take it to the Queen."
But the weather-wiser seaman warily
Answered him, "If it please Almighty God
To take away our Queen Elizabeth,
Seeing that she is mortal as ourselves,
England might then be leagued with Spain, and I
Should here have sealed my doom.   I will not put
My pen to paper."
                    So, across the charts
With that dim light on each grim countenance
The seaman and the courtier subtly fenced
With words and thoughts, but neither would betray
His whole heart to the other.   At the last
Walsingham gripped the hand of Francis Drake
And left him wondering.

On the third night came
A messenger from Walsingham who bade
Drake to the Palace where, without one word,
The statesman met him in an anteroom
And led him, with flushed cheek and beating heart,
Along a mighty gold-gloomed corridor
Into a high-arched chamber, hung with tall
Curtains of gold-fringed silk and tapestries
From Flanders looms, whereon were flowers and beasts
And forest-work, great knights, with hawk on hand,
Riding for ever on their glimmering steeds
Through bowery glades to some immortal face
Beyond the fairy fringes of the world.
A silver lamp swung softly overhead,
Fed with some perfumed oil that shed abroad
Delicious light and fragrances as rare
As those that stirred faint wings at eventide
Through the King's House in Lebanon of old.
Into a quietness as of fallen bloom
Their feet sank in that chamber; and, all round,
Soft hills of Moorish cushions dimly drowsed
On glimmering crimson couches.   Near the lamp
An ebony chess-board stood inlaid with squares
Of ruby and emerald, garnished with cinquefoils
Of silver, bears and ragged staves: the men,
Likewise of precious stones, were all arrayed—
Bishops and knights and elephants and pawns—
As for a game.   Sixteen of them were set
In silver white, the other sixteen gilt.
Now, as Drake gazed upon an arras, nigh
The farther doors, whereon was richly wrought
The picture of that grave and lovely queen
Penelope, with cold hands weaving still
The unending web, while in an outer court
The broad-limbed wooers basking in the sun
On purple fleeces took from white-armed girls,
Up-kirtled to the knee, the crimson wine;
There, as he gazed and thought, "Is this not like
Our Queen Elizabeth who waits and weaves,
Penelope of England, her dark web
Unendingly till England's Empire come;"

There, as he gazed, for a moment, he could vow
The pictured arras moved. Well had it been
Had he drawn sword and pierced it through and through;
But he suspected nothing and said nought
To Walsingham; for thereupon they heard
The sound of a low lute and a sweet voice
Carolling like a gold-caged nightingale,
Caught by the fowlers ere he found his mate,
And singing all his heart out evermore
To the unknown forest-love he ne'er should see.
And Walsingham smiled sadly to himself,
Knowing the weary queen had bidden some maid
Sing to her, even as David sang to Saul;
Since all her heart was bitter with her love
Or so it was breathed (and there the chess-board stood,
Her love's device upon it), though she still,
For England's sake, must keep great foreign kings
Her suitors, wedding no man till she died.
Nor did she know how, in her happiest hour
Remembered now most sorrowfully, the moon,
Vicegerent of the sky, through summer dews,
As that sweet ballad tells in plaintive rhyme,
Silvering the grey old Cumnor towers and all
The hollow haunted oaks that grew thereby,
Gleamed on a casement whence the pure white face
Of Amy Robsart, wife of Leicester, wife
Unknown of the Queen's lover, a frail bar
To that proud Earl's ambition, quietly gazed
And heard the night-owl hoot a dark presage
Of murder through her timid shuddering heart.
But of that deed Elizabeth knew nought;
Nay, white as Amy Robsart in her dream
Of love she listened to the sobbing lute,
Bitterly happy, proudly desolate;
So heavy are all earth's crowns and sharp with thorns!
But tenderly that high-born maiden sang.

SONG

Now the purple night is past,
  Now the moon more faintly glows,
Dawn has through thy casement cast
  Roses on thy breast, a rose;
Now the kisses are all done,
  Now the world awakes anew,
Now the charmèd hour is gone,
  Let not love go, too.

When old winter, creeping nigh,
  Sprinkles raven hair with white,
Dims the brightly glancing eye,
  Laughs away the dancing light,
Roses may forget their sun,
  Lilies may forget their dew,
Beauties perish, one by one,
  Let not love go, too.

Palaces and towers of pride
  Crumble year by year away;
Creeds like robes are laid aside,
  Even our very tombs decay!
When the all-conquering moth and rust
  Gnaw the goodly garment through,
When the dust returns to dust,
  Let not love go, too.

Kingdoms melt away like snow,
  Gods are spent like wasting flames,
Hardly the new peoples know
  Their divine thrice-worshipped names!
At the last great hour of all,
  When thou makest all things new,
Father, hear Thy children call,
  Let not love go, too.

The song ceased: all was still; and now it seemed
Power brooded on the silence, and Drake saw
A woman come to meet him,—tall and pale
And proud she seemed: behind her head two wings
As of some mighty phantom butterfly
Glimmered with jewel-sparks in the gold gloom.
Her small, pure, grey-eyed face above her ruff
Was chiselled like an agate; and he knew
It was the Queen. Low bent he o'er her hand;
And "Ah," she said, "Sir Francis Walsingham
Hath told me what an English heart beats here!
Know you what injuries the King of Spain
Hath done us?" Drake looked up at her: she smiled,
"We find you apt! Will you not be our knight
For we are helpless"—witchingly she smiled—
"We are not ripe for war; our policy
Must still be to uphold the velvet cloak
Of peace; but I would have it mask the hand
That holds the dagger! Will you not unfold
Your scheme to us?" And then with a low bow
Walsingham, at a signal from the Queen,
Withdrew; and she looked down at Drake and smiled;
And in his great simplicity the man
Spake all his heart out like some youthful knight
Before his Gloriana: his heart burned,
Knowing he talked with England, face to face;
And suddenly the Queen bent down to him,
England bent down to him, and his heart reeled
With the beauty of her presence—for indeed
Women alone have royal power like this
Within their very selves enthroned and shrined
To draw men's hearts out! Royal she bent down
And touched his hand for a moment. "Friend," she said,
Looking into his face with subtle eyes,
"I have searched thy soul to-night and know full well
How I can trust thee! Canst thou think that I,
The daughter of my royal father, lack
The fire which every boor in England feels
Burning within him as the bloody score
Which Spain writes on the flesh of Englishmen
Mounts higher day by day? Am I not Tudor?

I am not deaf or blind; nor yet a king!
I am a woman and a queen, and where
Kings would have plunged into their red revenge
Or set their throne up on this temporal shore,
As flatterers bade that wiser king Canúte,
Thence to command the advancing tides of battle
Till one ensanguined sea whelm throne and king
And kingdom, friend, I take my woman's way,
Smile in mine enemies' faces with a heart
All hell, and undermine them hour by hour!
This island scarce can fend herself from France,
And now Spain holds the keys of all the world,
How should we fight her, save that my poor wit
Hath won the key to Philip?   Oh, I know
His treacherous lecherous heart, and hour by hour
My nets are drawing round him.   I, that starve
My public armies, feed his private foes,
Nourish his rebels in the Netherlands,
Nay, sacrifice mine own poor woman's heart
To keep him mine, and surely now stands Fate
With hand uplifted by the doors of Spain
Ready to knock: the time is close at hand
When I shall strike, once, and no second stroke.
Remember, friend, though kings have fought for her,
This England, with the trident in her grasp,
Was ever woman; and she waits her throne;
And thou canst speed it.   Furnish thee with ships,
Gather thy gentleman adventurers,
And be assured thy parsimonious queen—
Oh ay, she knows that chattering of the world—
Will find thee wealth enough.   Then put to sea,
Fly the black flag of piracy awhile
Against these blackest foes of all mankind.
Nay; what hast thou to do with piracy?
Hostis humani generis indeed
Is Spain: she dwells beyond the bounds of law;
Thine is no piracy, whate'er men say,
Thou art a knight on Gloriana's quest.
Oh, lay that golden unction to thy soul,
This is no piracy, but glorious war,
Waged for thy country and for all mankind,

Therefore put out to sea without one fear,
Ransack their El Dorados of the West,
Pillage their golden galleons, sap their strength
Even at its utmost fountains; let them know
That there is blood, not water, in our veins.
Sail on, my captain, to the glorious end,
And, though at first thou needs must sail alone
And undefended, ere that end be reached,
When I shall give the word, nay, but one word,
All England shall be up and after thee,
The sword of England shall shine over thee,
And round about thee like a guardian fire;
All the great soul of England shall be there;
Her mighty dead shall at that cry of doom
Rise from their graves and in God's panoply
Plunge with our standards through immortal storms
When Drake rides out across the wreck of Rome.
As yet we must be cautious; let no breath
Escape thee, save to thy most trusted friends;
For now, if my lord Burleigh heard one word
Of all thou hast in mind, he is so much
The friend of caution and the beaten road,
He would not rest till he had spilled thy hopes
And sealed thy doom!   Go now, fit out thy ships.
Walsingham is empowered to give thee gold
Immediately, but look to him for more
As thou shalt need it, gold and gold to spare,
My golden-hearted pilot to the shores
Of victory—so farewell;" and through the gloom
She vanished as she came; and Drake groped, dazed,
Out through the doors, and found great Walsingham
Awaiting him with gold.
                    But in the room
Where Drake had held his converse with the Queen
The embroidered arras moved, and a lean face,
White with its long eavesdropping upon death,
Crept out and peered as a venomous adder peers
From out dark ferns, then as the reptile flashes
Along a path between two banks of flowers
Almost too swift for sight, a stealthy form
—One of the fifty spies whom Burleigh paid—

Passed down the gold-gloomed corridor to seek
His master, whom among great books he found,
Calm, like a mountain brooding o'er the sea.
Nor did he break that calm for all these winds
Of rumour that now burst from out the sky.
His brow bent like a cliff over his thoughts,
And the spy watched him half resentfully,
Thinking his news well worth a blacker frown.
At last the statesman smiled and answered, "Go;
Fetch Thomas Doughty, Leicester's secretary."

Few suns had risen and set ere Francis Drake
Had furnished forth his ships with guns and men,
Tried seamen that he knew in storms of old,—
Will Harvest, who could haul the ropes and fight
All day, and sing a foc'sle song to cheer
Sea-weary hearts at night; brave old Tom Moone
The carpenter, whose faithful soul looked up
To Drake's large mastery with a mastiff's eyes;
And three-score trusty mariners, all scarred
And weather-beaten.   After these there came
Some two-score gentleman adventurers,
Gay college lads or lawyers that had grown
Sick of the dusty Temple, and were fired
With tales of the rich Indies and those tall
Enchanted galleons drifting through the West,
Laden with ingots and broad bars of gold.
Already some had bought at a great price
Green birds of Guatemala, which they wore
On their slouched hats, tasting the high romance
And new-found colours of the world like wine.
By night they gathered in a marvellous inn
Beside the black and secret flowing Thames;
And joyously they tossed the magic phrase
"Pieces of eight" from mouth to mouth, and laughed
And held the red wine up, night after night,
Around their tables, toasting Francis Drake.
Among these came a courtier, and none knew
Or asked by whose approval, for each thought
Some other brought him; yet he made his way
Cautiously, being a man with a smooth tongue,

The secretary of Leicester; and his name
Was Thomas Doughty. Most of all with Drake
He won his way to friendship, till at last
There seemed one heart between them and one soul.

BOOK II

So on a misty grey December morn
Five ships put out from calm old Plymouth Sound;
Five little ships, the largest not so large
As many a coasting yacht or fishing-trawl
To-day; yet these must brave uncharted seas
Of unimagined terrors, haunted glooms,
And shadowy horrors of an unknown world
Wild as primeval chaos.   In the first,
The *Golden Hynde*, a ship of eighteen guns,
Drake sailed: John Wynter, a queen's captain, next
Brought out the *Elizabeth*, a stout new ship
Of sixteen guns.   The pinnace *Christopher*
Came next, in staunch command of old Tom Moone
Who, five years back, with reeking powder grimed,
Off Cartagena fought against the stars
All night, and, as the sun arose in blood,
Knee-deep in blood and brine, stood in the dark
Perilous hold and scuttled his own ship
The *Swan*, bidding her down to God's great deep
Rather than yield her up a prize to Spain.
Lastly two gentleman-adventurers
Brought out the new *Swan* and the *Marygold*.
Their crews, all told, were eight score men and boys.
Not only terrors of the deep they braved,
Bodiless witchcrafts of the black abyss,
Red gaping mouths of hell and gulfs of fire
That yawned for all who passed the tropic line;
But death lurked round them from their setting forth.
Mendoza, plenipotentiary of Spain,
By spies informed, had swiftly warned his king,
Who sent out mandates through his huge empire
From Gaudalchiber to the golden West
For the instant sinking of all English ships

And the instant execution of their crews
Who durst appear in the Caribbean sea.
Moreover, in the pith of their emprise
A peril lurked—Burleigh's emissaries,
The smooth-tongued Thomas Doughty, who had brought
His brother—unacquitted of that charge
Of poisoning, raised against him by the friends
Of Essex, but in luckless time released
Lately for lack of proof, on no strong plea.
These two wound through them like two snakes at ease
In Eden, waiting for their venomous hour.
Especially did Thomas Doughty toil
With soft and flowery tongue to win his way;
And Drake, whose rich imagination craved
For something more than simple seaman's talk,
Was marvellously drawn to this new friend
Who with the scholar's mind, the courtier's gloss,
The lawyer's wit, the adventurer's romance,
Gold honey from the blooms of Euphues,
Rare flashes from the *Mermaid* and sweet smiles
Copied from Sidney's self, even to the glance
Of sudden, liquid sympathy, gave Drake
That banquet of the soul he ne'er had known
Nor needed till he knew, but needed now.
So to the light of Doughty's answering eyes
He poured his inmost thoughts out, hour by hour;
And Doughty coiled up in the heart of Drake.

Against such odds the tiny fleet set sail;
Yet gallantly and with heroic pride,
Escutcheoned pavisades, emblazoned poops,
Banners and painted shields and close-fights hung
With scarlet broideries. Every polished gun
Grinned through the jaws of some heraldic beast,
Gilded and carven and gleaming with all hues;
While in the cabin of the *Golden Hynde*
Rich perfumes floated, given by the great Queen
Herself to Drake as Captain-General;
So that it seemed her soul was with the fleet,
A presence to remind him, far away,

Of how he talked with England, face to face,—
No pirate he, but Gloriana's knight.
Silver and gold his table furniture,
Engraved and richly chased, lavishly gleamed
While, fanned by favouring airs, the ships advanced
With streaming flags and ensigns and sweet chords
Of music struck by skilled musicians
Whom Drake brought with him, not from vanity,
But knowing how the pulse of men beats high
To music; and the hearts of men like these
Were open to the high romance of earth,
And they that dwelt so near God's mystery
Were proud of their own manhood.   They went out
To danger, as to a sweetheart, far away.

Light as the sea-birds dipping their white wings
In foam before the gently heaving prows
Each heart beat, while the low soft lapping splash
Of water racing past them ripped and tore
Whiter and faster, and the bellying sails
Filled out, and the chalk cliffs of England sank
Dwindling behind the broad grey plains of sea.
Meekly content and tamely stay-at-home
The sea-birds seemed that piped across the waves·
And Drake, be-mused, leaned smiling to his friend
Doughty and said, "Is it not strange to know
When we return yon speckled herring-gulls
Will still be wheeling, dipping, flashing there?
We shall not find a fairer land afar
Than those thyme-scented hills we leave behind!
Soon the young lambs will bleat across the combes
And breezes will bring puffs of hawthorn scent
Down Devon lanes; over the purple moors
Lavrocks will carol; and on the village greens
Around the May-pole, while the moon hangs low,
The boys and girls of England merrily swing
In country footing through the morrice dance.
But many of us indeed shall not return.
Then the other with a laugh, "Nay, like the man
Who slept a hundred years we shall return

And find our England strange: there are great storms
Brewing; God only knows what we shall find—
Perchance a Spanish king upon the throne!
What then?"   And Drake, "I should put down my helm
And out once more to the unknown golden West
To die, as I have lived, in a free land."
So said he, while the white cliffs dwindled down,
Faded, and vanished; but the prosperous wind
Carried the five ships onward over the swell
Of swinging, sweeping seas, till the sun sank,
And height o'er height the chaos of the skies
Broke out into the miracle of the stars.
Frostily glittering, all the Milky Way
Lay bare like diamond-dust upon the robe
Of some great king.   Orion and the Plough
Glimmered through drifting gulfs of silver fleece,
And, far away, in Italy, that night
Young Galileo, looking upward, heard
The self-same whisper through that wild abyss
Which now called Drake out to the unknown West.
But, after supper, Drake came up on deck
With Doughty, and on the cold poop as they leaned
And gazed across the rolling gleam and gloom
Of mighty muffled seas, began to give
Voices to those lovely captives of the brain
Which, like princesses in some forest-tower,
Still yearn for the delivering prince, the sweet
Far bugle-note that calls from answering minds.
He told him how, in those dark days which now
Seemed like an evil dream, when the Princess
Elizabeth even trembled for her life
And read there, by the gleam of Smithfield fires,
Those cunning lessons of diplomacy
Which saved her then and now for England's sake,
He passed his youth.   'Twas when the power of Spain
Began to light the gloom with that great glare
Of martyrdom which, while the stars endure,
Bears witness how men overcame the world,
Trod the red flames beneath their feet like flowers,
And cast aside the blackening robe of flesh,
While with a crown of joy upon their heads,

Even as into a palace, they passed through
The portals of the tomb to prove their love
Stronger at least than death: and, in those days
A Puritan, with iron in his soul,
Having in earlier manhood occupied
His business in great waters and beheld
The bloody cowls of the Inquisition pass
Before the midnight moon as he kept watch;
And having then forsworn the steely sea
To dwell at home in England with his love
At Tavistock in Devon, Edmund Drake
Began, albeit too near the Abbey walls,
To speak too staunchly for his ancient faith;
And with his young child Francis, had to flee
By night at last for shelter to the coast.
Little the boy remembered of that flight,
Pillioned behind his father, save the clang
And clatter of the hoofs on stony ground
Striking a sharp blue fire, while country tales
Of highwaymen kindled his reckless heart
As the great steed went shouldering through the night
There Francis, laying a little sunburnt hand
On the big holstered pistol at each side,
Dreamed with his wide grey eyes that he himself
Was riding out on some freebooting quest,
And felt himself heroic.   League by league
The magic world rolled past him as they rode,
Leaving him nothing but a memory
Of his own making.   Vaguely he perceived
A thousand meadows darkly streaming by
With clouds of perfume from their secret flowers,
A wayside cottage-window pointing out
A golden finger o'er the purple road;
A puff of garden roses or a waft
Of honeysuckle blown along a wood,
While overhead that silver ship, the moon,
Sailed slowly down the gulfs of glittering stars,
Till, at the last, a buffet of fresh wind
Fierce with sharp savours of the stinging brine
Against his dreaming face brought up a roar
Of mystic welcome from the Channel seas.

And there Drake paused for a moment, as a song
Stole o'er the waters from the *Marygold*
Where some musician, striking luscious chords
Of sweet-stringed music, freed his heart's desire
In symbols of the moment, which the rest,
And Doughty among them, scarce could understand.

SONG

The moon is up: the stars are bright:
  The wind is fresh and free!
We're out to seek for gold to-night
  Across the silver sea!
The world was growing grey and old;
  Break out the sails again!
We're out to seek a Realm of Gold
  Beyond the Spanish Main.

We're sick of all the cringing knees,
  The courtly smiles and lies.
God, let Thy singing Channel breeze
  Lighten our hearts and eyes!
Let love no more be bought and sold
  For earthly loss or gain.
We're out to seek an Age of Gold
  Beyond the Spanish Main.

Beyond the light of far Cathay,
  Beyond all mortal dreams,
Beyond the reach of night and day
  Our El Dorado gleams,
Revealing—as the skies unfold—
  A star without a stain,
The Glory of the Gates of Gold
  Beyond the Spanish Main.

And, as the skilled musician made the words
Of momentary meaning still simply
His own eternal hope and heart' desire,
Without belief, perchance, in Drake's own quest—

To Drake's own greater mind the eternal glory
Seemed to transfigure his immediate hope.
But Doughty only heard a sweet concourse
Of sounds.   They ceased.   And Drake resumed his tale
Of that strange flight in boyhood to the sea.
Next, the red-curtained inn and kindly hands
Of Protestant Plymouth held his memory long;
Often in strange and distant dreams he saw
That scene which now he tenderly portrayed
To Doughty's half-ironic smiling lips,
Half-sympathetic eyes; he saw again
That small inn parlour with the homely fare
Set forth upon the table, saw the gang
Of seamen dripping from the spray come in,
Like great new thoughts to some adventurous brain.
Feeding his wide grey eyes he saw them stand
Around the crimson fire and stamp their feet
And scatter the salt drops from their big sea-boots;
And all that night he lay awake and heard
Mysterious thunderings of eternal tides
Moaning out of a cold and houseless gloom
Beyond the world, that made it seem most sweet
To slumber in a little four-walled inn
Immune from all that vastness.   But at dawn
He woke, he leapt from bed, he ran and lookt,
There, through the tiny high bright casement, there,—
O, fairy vision of that small boy's face
Peeping at daybreak through the diamond pane!—
There first he saw the wondrous new-born world,
And round its princely shoulders wildly flowing,
Gemmed with a myriad clusters of the sun,
The magic azure mantle of the sea.

And, afterwards, there came those marvellous days
When, on that battleship, a disused hulk
Rotting to death in Chatham Reach, they found
Sanctuary and a dwelling-place at last.
For, Hawkins, that great ship-man, being their friend,
A Protestant, with power on Plymouth town,
Nigh half whereof he owned, made Edmund Drake
Reader of prayer to all the ships of war

That lay therein. So there the dreaming boy,
Francis, grew up in that grim nursery
Among the ropes and masts and great dumb mouths
Of idle ordnance. In that hulk he heard
Many a time his father and his friends
Over some wild-eyed troop of refugees
Thunder against the powers of Spain and Rome,
"Idolaters who defiled the House of God
In England;" and all round them, as he heard,
The clang and clatter of shipwright hammers rang,
And hour by hour upon his vision rose,
In solid oak reality, new ships,
As Ilion rose to music, ships of war,
The visible shapes and symbols of his dream,
Unconscious yet, but growing as they grew,
A wondrous incarnation, hour by hour,
Till with their towering masts they stood complete,
Embodied thoughts, in God's own dockyards built,
For Drake ere long to lead against the world.

There, as to round the tale with ringing gold,
Across the waters from the full-plumed *Swan*
The music of a *Mermaid* roundelay—
Our Lady of the Sea, a Dorian theme
Tuned to the soul of England—charmed the moon.

SONG

I

Queen Venus wandered away with a cry,—
　　　N'oserez vous, mon bel ami?—
For the purple wound in Adon's thigh;
　　　Je vous en prie, pity me;
With a bitter farewell from sky to sky,
　　　And a moan, a moan, from sea to sea;
N'oserez vous, mon bel, mon bel,
　　　N'oserez vous, mon bel ami?

II

The soft Ægean heard her sigh,—
    N'oserez vous, mon bel ami?—
Heard the Spartan hills reply,
    Je vous en prie, pity me;
Spain was aware of her drawing nigh
    Foot-gilt from the blossoms of Italy;
N'oserez vous, mon bel, mon bel,
    N'oserez vous, mon bel ami?

III

In France they heard her voice go by,—
    N'oserez vous, mon bel ami?—
And on the May-wind droop and die,
    Je vous en prie, pity me;
Your maidens choose their loves, but I—
    White as I came from the foam-white sea,
N'oserez vous, mon bel, mon bel,
    N'oserez vous, mon bel ami?—

IV

The warm red-meal-winged butterfly,—
    N'oserez vous, mon bel ami?—
Beat on her breast in the golden rye,—
    Je vous en prie, pity me,—
Stained her breast with a dusty dye
    Red as the print of a kiss might be!
N'oserez vous, mon bel, mon bel,
    N'oserez vous, mon bel ami?

V

Is there no land, afar or nigh—
    N'oserez vous, mon bel ami?—
But dreads the kiss o' the sea? Ah, why—
    Je vous en prie, pity me!—

18

Why will ye cling to the loves that die?
    Is earth all Adon to my plea?
N'oserez vous, mon bel, mon bel,
    N'oserez vous, mon bel ami?

VI

Under the warm blue summer sky,—
    N'oserez vous, mon bel ami?
With outstretched arms and a low long sigh,—
    Je vous en prie, pity me;—
Over the Channel they saw her fly
    To the white-cliffed island that crowns the sea,
N'oserez vous, mon bel, mon bel,
    N'oserez vous, mon bel ami?

VII

England laughed as her queen drew nigh,—
    N'oserez vous, mon bel ami?
To the white-walled cottages gleaming high,
    Je vous en prie, pity me!
They drew her in with a joyful cry
    To the hearth where she sits with a babe on her knee,
She has turned her moan to a lullaby,
    She is nursing a son to the kings of the sea,
N'oserez vous, mon bel, mon bel,
    N'oserez vous, mon bel ami?

Such memories, on the plunging *Golden Hynde*,
Under the stars, Drake drew before his friend,
Clomb for a moment to that peak of vision,
That purple peak of Darien, laughing aloud
O'er those wild exploits down to Rio Grande
Which even now had made his fierce renown
Terrible to all lonely ships of Spain.
E'en now, indeed, that poet of Portugal,
Lope de Vega, filled with this new fear
Began to meditate his epic muse
Till, like a cry of panic from his lips,
He shrilled the faint *Dragontea* forth, wherein
Drake is that Dragon of the Apocalypse,
The dread Antagonist of God and Man.

Well had it been for Doughty on that night
Had he not heard what followed; for, indeed,
When two minds clash, not often does the less
Conquer the greater; but, without one thought
Of evil, seeing they now were safe at sea,
Drake told him, only somewhat, yet too much,
Of that close conference with the Queen. And lo,
The face of Doughty blanched with a slow thought
That crept like a cold worm through all his brain,
"Thus much I knew, though secretly, before;
But here he freely tells me as his friend;
If I be false and he be what they say,
His knowledge of my knowledge will mean death."
But Drake looked round at Doughty with a smile
And said, "Forgive me now: thou art not used
To these cold nights at sea! thou tremblest, friend;
Let us go down and drink a cup of sack
To our return!" And at that kindly smile
Doughty shook off his nightmare mood, and thought,
"The yard-arm is for dogs, not gentlemen!
Even Drake would not misuse a man of birth!"
And in the cabin of the *Golden Hynde*
Revolving subtle treacheries he sat.
There with the sugared phrases of the court
Bartering beads for gold, he drew out all
The simple Devon seaman's inmost heart,
And coiled up in the soul of Francis Drake.
There in the solemn night they interchanged
Lies for sweet confidences. From one wall
The picture of Drake's love looked down on him;
And, like a bashful schoolboy's, that bronzed face
Flushed as he blurted out with brightening eyes
And quickening breath how he had seen her first,
Crowned on the village green, a Queen of May.
Her name, too, was Elizabeth, he said,
As if it proved that she, too, was a queen,
Though crowned with milk-white Devon may alone,
And queen but of one plot of meadow-sweet.
As yet, he said, he had only kissed her hand,
Smiled in her eyes and—there Drake also flinched,
Thinking, "I ne'er may see her face again."

And Doughty comforted his own dark heart
Thinking, "I need not fear so soft a soul
As this"; and yet, he wondered how the man,
Seeing his love so gripped him, none the less
Could leave her, thus to follow after dreams;
For faith to Doughty was an unknown word,
And trustfulness the property of fools.
At length they parted, each to his own couch,
Doughty with half a chuckle, Francis Drake
With one old-fashioned richly grateful prayer
Blessing all those he loved, as he had learnt
Beside his mother's knee in Devon days.

So all night long they sailed; but when a rift
Of orchard crimson broke the yellowing gloom
And barred the closely clouded East with dawn,
Behold, a giant galleon overhead,
Lifting its huge black shining sides on high,
Loomed like some misty monster of the deep:
And, sullenly rolling out great gorgeous folds,
Over her rumbled like a thunder-cloud
The heavy flag of Spain.   The splendid poop,
Mistily lustrous as a dragon's hoard
Seen in some magic cave-mouth o'er the sea
Through shimmering April sunlight after rain,
Blazed to the morning; and her port-holes grinned
With row on row of cannon.   There at once
One sharp shrill whistle sounded, and those five
Small ships, mere minnows clinging to the flanks
Of that Leviathan, unseen, unheard,
Undreamt of, grappled her.   She seemed asleep,
Swinging at ease with great half-slackened sails,
Majestically careless of the dawn.
There in the very native seas of Spain,
There with the yeast and foam of her proud cliffs,
Her own blue coasts, in sight across the waves,
Up her Titanic sides without a sound
The naked-footed British seamen swarmed
With knives between their teeth: then on her decks
They dropped like panthers, and the softly fierce
Black-bearded watch of Spaniards, all amazed,

Rubbing their eyes as if at a wild dream,
Upraised a sudden shout, *El Draque! El Draque!*
And flashed their weapons out, but all too late;
For, ere their sleeping comrades reached the deck,
The little watch, out-numbered and out-matched,
Lay bound, and o'er the hatches everywhere
The points of naked cutlasses on guard
Gleamed, and without a struggle those below
Gave up their arms, their poignards jewelled thick
With rubies, and their blades of Spanish steel.

Then onward o'er the great grey gleaming sea
They swept with their rich booty, night and day.
Five other prizes, one for every ship,
Out of the seas of Spain they suddenly caught
And carried with them, laughing as they went—
"Now, now indeed the Rubicon is crossed;
Now have we singed the eyelids and the beard
Of Spain; now have we roused the hornet's nest;
Now shall we sail against a world in arms;
Now we have nought between us and black death
But our own hands, five ships, and three score guns."
So laughed they, plunging through the bay of storms,
Biscay, and past Gibraltar, not yet clothed
With British thunder, though, as one might dream,
Gazing in dim prophetic grandeur out
Across the waves while that small fleet went by,
Or watching them with love's most wistful fear
As they plunged Southward to the lonely coasts
Of Africa, till right in front up-soared,
Tremendous over ocean, Teneriffe,
Cloud-robed, but crowned with colours of the dawn.

Already those two traitors were at work,
Doughty and his false brother, among the crews,
Who knew not yet the vastness of their quest,
Nor dreamed of aught beyond the accustomed world;
For Drake had kept it secret, and the thoughts
Of some that he had shipped before the mast
Set sail scarce farther than for Mogadore

In West Morocco, or at the utmost mark
For northern Egypt, by the midnight woods
And crystal palace roofed with chrysoprase
Where Prester John had reigned five hundred years,
And Sydon, river of jewels, through the dark
Enchanted gorges rolled its rays along!
Some thought of Rio Grande; but scarce to ten
The true intent was known; while to divert
The rest from care the skilled musicians played.
But those two Doughtys cunningly devised
By chance-dropt words to breathe a hint abroad;
And through the foc'sles crept a grisly fear
Of things that lay beyond the bourne of earth,
Till even those hardy seamen almost quailed;
And now, at any whisper, they might turn
With terror in their eyes.   They might refuse
To sail into that fabled burning Void
Or brave that *primum mobile* which drew
O'er-daring ships into the jaws of hell
Beyond the Poie Antarticke, where the sea
Rushed down through fiery mountains, and no sail
Could e'er return against its roaring stream.

Now down the coast of Barbary they cruised
Till Christmas Eve embraced them in the heart
Of summer.   In a bay of mellow calm
They moored, and as the fragrant twilight brought
The stars, the sound of song and dance arose;
And down the shores in stealthy silence crept,
Out of the massy forest's emerald gloom,
The naked, dark-limbed children of the night,
Unseen, to gaze upon the floating glare
Of revelry; unheard, to hear that strange
New music of the gods, where o'er the soft
Ripple and wash of the lanthorn-crimsoned tide
Will Harvest's voice above the chorus rang.

SONG

In Devonshire, now, the Christmas chime
    Is carolling over the lea;
And the sexton shovels away the snow
    From the old church porch, maybe;
And the waits with their lanthorns and noses a-glow
    Come round for their Christmas fee;
But, as in old England it's Christmas-time,
    Why, so is it here at sea,
       My lads,
    Why, so is it here at sea!

When the ship comes home, from turret to poop
    Filled full with Spanish gold,
There'll be many a country dance and joke,
    And many a tale to be told;
Every old woman shall have a red cloak
    To fend her against the cold;
And every old man shall have a big round stoup
    Of jolly good ale and old,
       My lads,
    Jolly good ale and old!

But on the morrow came a prosperous wind
Whereof they took advantage, and shook out
The flashing sails, and held their Christmas feast
Upon the swirling ridges of the sea:
And, sweeping Southward with full many a rouse
And shout of laughter, at the fall of day,
While the black prows drove, leapt, and plunged, and ploughed
Through the broad dazzle of sunset-coloured tides,
Outside the cabin of the *Golden Hynde*,
Where Drake and his chief captains dined in state,
The skilled musicians made a great new song.

SONG

I

Happy by the hearth sit the lasses and the lads, now,
*   Roasting of their chestnuts, toasting of their toes!*
When the door is opened to a blithe new-comer,
*   Stamping like a ploughman to shuffle off the snows;*
Rosy flower-like faces through the soft red firelight
*   Float as if to greet us, far away at sea,*
Sigh as they remember, and turn the sigh to laughter,
*   Kiss beneath the mistletoe and wonder at their glee.*
*   With their "heigh ho, the holly!*
*   This life is most jolly!"*
*   Christmas-time is kissing-time,*
*   Away with melancholy!*

II

Ah, the Yule of England, the happy Yule of England,
*   Yule of berried holly and the merry mistletoe;*
The boar's head, the brown ale, the blue snapdragon,
*   Yule of groaning tables and the crimson log aglow!*
Yule, the golden bugle to the scattered old companions,
*   Ringing as with laughter, shining as through tears!*
Loved of little children, oh guard the holy Yuletide,
*   Guard it, men of England, for the child beyond the years.*
*   With its "heigh ho, the holly!"*
*   Away with melancholy!*
*   Christmas-time is kissing-time,*
*   "This life is most jolly!"*

Now to the Fortunate Islands of old time
They came, and found no glory as of old
Encircling them, no red ineffable calm
Of sunset round crowned faces pale with bliss
Like evening stars. Rugged and desolate
Those isles were when they neared them, though afar
They beautifully smouldered in the sun
Like dusky purple jewels fringed and frayed
With silver foam across that ancient sea

Of wonder. On the largest of the seven
Drake landed Doughty with his musketeers
To exercise their weapons and to seek
Supplies among the matted uncouth huts
Which, as the ships drew round each ragged cliff,
Crept like remembered misery into sight;
Oh, like the strange dull waking from a dream
They blotted out the rosy courts and fair
Imagined marble thresholds of the King
Achilles and the heroes that were gone.
But Drake cared nought for these things. Such a heart
He had, to make each utmost ancient bourne
Of man's imagination but a point
Of new departure for his Golden Dream.
But Doughty with his men ashore, alone,
Among the sparse wind-bitten groves of palm,
Kindled their fears of all they must endure
On that immense adventure. Nay, sometimes
He hinted of a voyage far beyond
All history and fable, far beyond
Even that Void whence only two returned,—
Columbus, with his men in mutiny;
Magellan, who could only hound his crew
Onward by threats of death, until they turned
In horror from the Threat that lay before,
Preferring to be hanged as mutineers
Rather than venture farther. Nor indeed
Did even Magellan at the last return;
But, with all hell around him, in the clutch
Of devils died upon some savage isle
By poisonous black enchantment. Not in vain
Were Doughty's words on that volcanic shore
Among the stunted dark acacia trees,
Whose heads, all bent one way by the trade-wind,
Pointed North-east by North, South-west by West
Ambiguous sibyls that with wizened arms
Mysteriously declared a twofold path,
Homeward or onward. But aboard the ships,
Among the hardier seamen, old Tom Moone,
With one or two stout comrades, overbore
All doubts and questionings with blither tales

Of how they sailed to Darien and heard
Nightingales in November all night long
As down a coast like Paradise they cruised
Through seas of lasting summer, Eden isles,
Where birds like rainbows, butterflies like gems,
And flowers like coloured fires o'er fairy creeks
Floated and flashed beneath the shadowy palms;
While ever and anon a bark canoe
With naked Indian maidens flower-festooned
Put out from shadowy coves, laden with fruit
Ambrosial o'er the silken shimmering sea.
And once a troop of nut-brown maidens came—
So said Tom Moone, a twinkle in his eye—
Swimming to meet them through the warm blue waves
And wantoned through the water, like those nymphs
Which one green April at the Mermaid Inn
Should hear Kit Marlowe mightily portray,
Among his boon companions, in a song
Of Love that swam the sparkling Hellespont
Upheld by nymphs, not lovelier than these,—
Though whiter yet not lovelier than these—
For those like flowers, but these like rounded fruit
Rosily ripening through the clear tides tossed
From nut-brown breast and arm all round the ship
The thousand-coloured spray. Shapely of limb
They were; but as they laid their small brown hands
Upon the ropes we cast them, Captain Drake
Suddenly thundered at them and bade them pack
For a troop of naughty wenches! At that tale
A tempest of fierce laughter rolled around
The foc'sle; but one boy from London town,
A pale-faced prentice, run-away to sea,
Asking why Drake had bidden them pack so soon,
Tom Moone turned to him with his deep-sea growl,
"Because our Captain is no pink-eyed boy
Nor soft-limbed Spaniard, but a staunch-souled Man,
Full-blooded; nerved like iron; with a girl
He loves at home in Devon; and a mind
For ever bent upon some mighty goal,
I know not what—but 'tis enough for me
To know my Captain knows." And then he told

How sometimes o'er the gorgeous forest gloom
Some marble city, rich, mysterious, white,
An ancient treasure-house of Aztec kings,
Or palace of forgotten Incas gleamed;
And in their dim rich lofty cellars gold,
Beyond all wildest dreams, great bars of gold,
Like pillars, tossed in mighty chaos, gold
And precious stones, agate and emerald,
Diamond, sapphire, ruby, and sardonyx.
So said he, as they waited the return
Of Doughty, resting in the foc'sle gloom,
Or idly couched about the sun-swept decks
On sails or coils of rope, while overhead
Some boy would climb the rigging and look out,
Arching his hand to see if Doughty came.
But when he came, he came with a strange face
Of feigned despair; and with a stammering tongue
He vowed he could not find those poor supplies
Which Drake himself in other days had found
Upon that self-same island.   But, perchance,
This was a barren year, he said.   And Drake
Looked at him, suddenly, and at the musketeers.
Their eyes were strained; their faces wore a cloud.
That night he said no more; but on the morn,
Mistrusting nothing, Drake with subtle sense
Of weather-wisdom, through that little fleet
Distributed his crews anew.   And all
The prisoners and the prizes at those isles
They left behind them, taking what they would
From out their carven cabins,—glimmering silks,
Chiselled Toledo blades, and broad doubloons.
And lo, as they weighed anchor, far away
Behind them on the blue horizon line
It seemed a city of towering masts arose;
And from the crow's nest of the *Golden Hynde*
A seaman cried, "By God; the hunt is up!"
And like a tide of triumph through their veins
The red rejoicing blood began to race
As there they saw the avenging ships of Spain,
Eight mighty galleons, nosing out their trail.
And Drake growled,"Oh, my lads of Bideford,

It cuts my heart to show the hounds our heels;
But we must not emperil our great quest!
Such fights as that must wait—as our reward
When we return.   Yet I will not put on
One stitch of sail.   So, lest they are not too slow
To catch us, clear the decks.   God, I would like
To fight them!"   So the little fleet advanced
With decks all cleared and shotted guns and men
Bare-armed beside them, hungering to be caught,
And quite distracted from their former doubts;
For danger, in that kind, they never feared.
But soon the heavy Spaniards dropped behind;
And not in vain had Thomas Doughty sown
The seeds of doubt; for many a brow grew black
With sullen-seeming care that erst was gay.
But happily and in good time there came,
Not from behind them now, but right in front,
On the first sun-down of their quest renewed,
Just as the sea grew dark around their ships,
A chance that loosed heart-gnawing doubt in deeds.
For through a mighty zone of golden haze
Blotting the purple of the gathering night
A galleon like a floating mountain moved
To meet them, clad with sunset and with dreams.
Her masts and spars immense in jewelled mist
Shimmered: her rigging, like an emerald web
Of golden spiders, tangled half the stars!
Embodied sunset, dragging the soft sky
O'er dazzled ocean, through the night she drew
Out of the unknown lands; and round a prow
That jutted like a moving promontory
Over a cloven wilderness of foam,
Upon a lofty blazoned scroll her name
San Salvador challenged obsequious isles
Where'er she rode; who kneeling like dark slaves
Before some great Sultàn must lavish forth
From golden cornucopias, East and West,
Red streams of rubies, cataracts of pearl.
But, at a signal from their admiral, all
Those five small ships lay silent in the gloom
Which, just as if some god were on their side,

Covered them in the dark troughs of the waves,
Letting her pass to leeward.   On she came,
Blazing with lights, a City of the Sea,
Belted with crowding towers and clouds of sail,
And round her bows a long-drawn thunder rolled
Splendid with foam; but ere she passed them by
Drake gave the word, and with one crimson flash
Two hundred yards of black and hidden sea
Leaped into sight between them as the roar
Of twenty British cannon shattered the night.
Then after her they drove, like black sea-wolves
Behind some royal high-branched stag of ten,
Hanging upon those bleeding foam-flecked flanks,
Leaping, snarling, worrying, as they went
In full flight down the wind; for those light ships
Much speedier than their huge antagonist,
Keeping to windward, worked their will with her.
In vain she burnt wild lights and strove to scan
The darkening deep.   Her musketeers in vain
Provoked the crackling night with random fires:
In vain her broadside bellowings burst at large
As if the Gates of Erebus unrolled.
For ever and anon the deep-sea gloom
From some new quarter, like a dragon's mouth
Opened and belched forth crimson flames and tore
Her sides as if with iron claws unseen;
Till, all at once, rough voices close at hand
Out of the darkness thundered, "Grapple her!"
And, falling on their knees, the Spaniards knew
The Dragon of that red Apocalypse.
There with one awful cry, *El Draque! El Draque!*
They cast their weapons from them; for the moon
Rose, eastward, and, against her rising, black
Over the bloody bulwarks, Francis Drake,
Grasping the great hilt of his naked sword,
Towered for a moment to their startled eyes
Through all the zenith like the King of Hell.
Then he leaped down upon their shining decks,
And after him swarmed and towered and leapt in haste
A brawny band of three score Englishmen,
Gigantic as they loomed against the sky

And risen, it seemed, by miracle from the sea.
So small were those five ships below the walls
Of that huge floating mountain.   Royally
Drake, from the swart commander's trembling **hands**
Took the surrendered sword, and bade his men
Gather the fallen weapons on an heap,
And placed a guard about them, while the moon
Silvering the rolling seas for many a mile
Glanced on the huddled Spaniards' rich attire,
As like one picture of despair they grouped
Under the splintered main-mast's creaking shrouds,
And the great swinging shadows of the sails
Mysteriously swept the gleaming decks;
Where many a butt of useless cannon gloomed
Along the accoutred bulwarks or upturned,
As the ship wallowed in the heaving deep,
Dumb mouths of empty menace to the stars.

Then Drake appointed Doughty, with a guard,
To sail the prize on to the next dim isle
Where they might leave her, taking aught they would
From out her carven cabins and rich holds.
And Doughty's heart leaped in him as he thought,
"I have my chance at last"; but Drake, who still
Trusted the man, made surety doubly sure,
And in his wary weather-wisdom sent
—Even as a breathing type of friendship, sent—
His brother, Thomas Drake, aboard the prize;
But set his brother, his own flesh and blood,
Beneath the man, as if to say, "I give
My loyal friend dominion over me."
So courteously he dealt with him; but he,
Seeing his chance once more slipping away,
Raged inwardly and, from his own false heart
Imputing his own evil, he contrived
A cunning charge that night; and when they came
Next day, at noon, upon the destined isle,
He suddenly spat the secret venom forth,
With such fierce wrath in his defeated soul
That he himself almost believed the charge.

For when Drake stepped on the *San Salvador*
To order all things duly about the prize,
What booty they must keep and what let go,
Doughty received him with a blustering voice
Of red mock-righteous wrath, "Is this the way
Englishmen play the pirate, Francis Drake?
While thou wast dreaming of thy hero's crown—
God save the mark!—thy brother, nay, thy spy,
Must play the common pilferer, must convert
The cargo to his uses, rob us all
Of what we risked our necks to win: he wears
The ransom of an emperor round his throat
That might enrich us àll.   Who saw him wear
That chain of rubies ere last night?"
                              And Drake,
"Answer him, brother;" and his brother smiled
And answered, "Nay, I never wore this chain
Before last night; but Doughty knows, indeed,
For he was with me—and none else was there
But Doughty—'tis my word against his word,
That close on midnight we were summoned down
To an English seaman who lay dying below
Unknown to any of us, a prisoner
In chains, that had been captured none knew where,
For all his mind was far from Darien,
And wandering evermore through Devon lanes
At home; whom we released; and from his waist
He took this hidden chain and gave it me,
Begging me that if ever I returned
To Bideford in Devon I would go
With whatsoever wealth it might produce
To his old mother who, with wrinkled hands
In some small white-washed cottage o'er the sea,
Where wall-flowers bloom in April, even now
Is turning pages of the well-worn Book
And praying for her son's return, nor knows
That he lies cold upon the heaving main.
But this he asked; and this in all good faith
I swore to do; and even now he died,
And hurrying hither from his side I clasped
His chain of rubies round my neck awhile,

In full sight of the sun. I have no more
To say." Then up spoke Hatton's trumpeter:
"But I have more to say. Last night I saw
Doughty, but not in full sight of the sun,
Nor once, nor twice, but three times at the least,
Carrying chains of gold, clusters of gems,
And whatsoever wealth he could convey
Into his cabin and smuggle in smallest space."
"Nay," Doughty stammered, mixing sneer and lie,
Yet bolstering up his courage with the thought
That being what courtiers called a gentleman
He ranked above the rude sea-discipline,
"Nay, they were free gifts from the Spanish crew
Because I treated them with courtesy."
Then bluff Will Harvest, "That perchance were true,
For he hath been close closeted for hours
With their chief officers, drinking their health
In our own war-bought wine, while down below
Their captured English seaman groaned his last."
Then Drake, whose utter silence, with a sense
Of infinite power and justice, ruled their hearts,
Suddenly thundered—and the traitor blanched
And quailed before him. "This my flesh and blood
I placed beneath thee as my dearer self!
But thou, in trampling on him, shalt not say
I charged thy brother. Nay, thou chargest me!
Against me only hast thou stirred this strife;
And now, by God, shalt thou learn, once for all,
That I, thy captain for this voyage, hold
The supreme power of judgment in my hands.
Get thee aboard my flagship! When I come
I shall have more to say to thee; but thou,
My brother, take this galleon in thy charge;
For, as I see, she holdeth all the stores
Which Doughty failed to find. She shall return
With us to that New World from which she came.
But now let these our prisoners all embark
In yonder pinnace; let them all go free.
I care not to be cumbered on my way
Through dead Magellan's unattempted dream
With chains and prisoners. In that Golden World

Which means much more to me than I can speak,
Much more, much more than I can speak or breathe.
Being, behind whatever name it bears—
Earthly Paradise, Island of the Saints,
Cathay, or Zipangu, or Hy Brasil—
The eternal symbol of my soul's desire,
A sacred country shining on the sea,
That Vision without which, the wise king said,
A people perishes; in that place of hope,
That Tirn'an Og, that land of lasting youth,
Where whosoever sails with me shall drink
Fountains of immortality and dwell
Beyond the fear of death for evermore,
There shall we see the dust of battle dance
Everywhere in the sunbeam of God's peace!
Oh, in the new Atlantis of my soul
There are no captives: there the wind blows free;
And, as in sleep, I have heard the marching song
Of mighty peoples rising in the West,
Wonderful cities that shall set their foot
Upon the throat of all old tyrannies;
And on the West wind I have heard a cry,
The shoreless cry of the prophetic sea
Heralding through that golden wilderness
The Soul whose path our task is to make straight,
Freedom, the last great Saviour of mankind.
I know not what I know: these are wild words,
Which, as the sun draws out earth's morning mists
Over dim fields where careless cattle sleep,
Some visionary Light, unknown, afar,
Draws from my darkling soul.   Why should we drag
Thither this Old-World weight of utter gloom,
Or with the ballast of these heavy hearts
Make sail in sorrow for Pacific Seas?
Let us leave chains and prisoners to Spain;
But set these free to make their own way home!"
So said he, groping blindly towards the truth,
And heavy with the treason of his friend.
His face was like a king's face as he spake,
For sorrows that strike deep reveal the deep;
And through the gateways of a raggèd wound

19

Sometimes a god will drive his chariot wheels
From some deep heaven within the hearts of men.
Nevertheless, the immediate seamen there
Knowing how great a ransom they might ask
For some among their prisoners, men of wealth
And high degree, scarce liked to free them thus;
And only saw in Drake's conflicting moods
The moment's whim. "For little will he care,"
They muttered, "when we reach those fabled shores,
Whether his cannon break their golden peace."
Yet to his face they murmured not at all;
Because his eyes compelled them like a law.
So there they freed the prisoners and set sail
Across the earth-shaking shoulders of the broad
Atlantic, and the great grey slumbrous waves
Triumphantly swelled up to meet the keels.

BOOK III

Now in the cabin of the *Golden Hynde*
At dusk, Drake sent for Doughty. From one wall
The picture of his love looked down on him;
And on the table lay the magic chart,
Drawn on a buffalo horn, all small peaked isles,
Dwarf promontories, tiny twisted creeks,
And fairy harbours under elfin hills,
With marvellous inscriptions lined in red,—
As *Here is Gold*, or *Many Rubies Here*,
Or *Ware Witch-crafte*, or *Here is Cannibals*.
For in his great simplicity the man
Delighted in it, with the adventurous heart
Of boyhood poring o'er some well-thumbed tale
On blue Twelfth Night beside the crimson fire;
And o'er him, like a vision of a boy
In his first knighthood when, upon some hill
Washed by the silver fringes of the sea,
Amidst the purple heather he lies and reads
Of Arthur and Avilion, like a star
His love's pure face looked down. There Doughty came

Half fearful, half defiant, with a crowd
Of jostling half-excuses on his lips,
And one dark swarm of adders in his heart.
For now what light of chivalry remained
In Doughty's mind was thickening with a plot,
Subtler and deadlier than the serpent's first
Attempt on our first sire in Eden bower.
Drake, with a countenance open as the sun,
Received him, saying: "Forgive me, friend, for I
Was hasty with thee.   I well nigh forgot
Those large and liberal nights we two have passed
In this old cabin, telling all our dreams
And hopes, in friendship, o'er and o'er again.
But Vicary, thy friend hath talked with me,
And now—I understand.   Thou shalt no more
Be vexed with a divided mastership.
Indeed, I trust thee, Doughty.   Wilt thou not
Be friends with me?   For now in ample proof
Thou shalt take charge of this my *Golden Hynde*
In all things, save of seamanship, which rests
With the ship's master under my command.
But I myself will sail upon the prize."
And with the word he gathered up the chart,
Took down his lady's picture with a smile,
Gripped Doughty's hand and left him, staring, sheer
Bewildered with that magnanimity
Of faith, throughout all shadows, in some light
Unseen behind the shadows.   Thus did Drake
Give up his own fair cabin which he loved;
Being, it seemed, a little travelling home,
Fragrant with memories,—gave it, as he thought,
In recompense to one whom he had wronged.
For even as his mind must ever yearn
To shores beyond the sunset, even so
He yearned through all dark shadows to his friend,
And with his greater nature striving still
To comprehend the lesser, as the sky
Embraces our low earth, he would adduce
Justifications, thus: "These men of law
Are trained to plead for any and every cause,
To feign an indignation, or to prove

The worse is better and that black is white!
Small wonder that their passion goes astray:
There is one prayer, one prayer for all of us—
Enter not into judgment with Thy servant!"

Yet as his boat pulled tow'rd the Spanish prize
Leaving the *Golden Hynde,* far off he heard
A voice that chilled him, as the voice of Fate
Crying like some old Bellman through the world.

SONG

Yes; oh, yes; if any seek
    Laughter flown or lost delight,
Glancing eye or rosy cheek,
    Love shall claim his own to-night!
    Say, hath any lost a friend?
        Yes; oh, yes!
        Let his distress
In my ditty find its end.

Yes; oh, yes; here all is found!
    Kingly palaces await
Each its rightful owner, crowned
    King and consecrate,
Under the wet and wintry ground!
        Yes; oh, yes!
        There sure redress
Lies where all is lost and found.

And Doughty, though Drake's deed of kindness flashed
A moment's kind contrition through his heart,
Immediately, with all his lawyer's wit
True to the cause that hired him, laughed it by,
And straight began to weave the treacherous web
Of soft intrigue wherein he meant to snare
The passions of his comrades.   Night and day,
As that small fleet drove onward o'er the deep,
Cleaving the sunset with their bright black prows
Or hunted by the red pursuing Dawn,

He stirred between the high-born gentlemen
(Whose white and jewelled hands, gallant in fight,
And hearts remembering Crécy and Poictiers,
Were of scant use in common seamanship),
Between these and the men whose rough tarred arms
Were good at equal need in storm or war
Yet took a poorer portion of the prize,
He stirred a subtle jealousy and fanned
A fire that swiftly grew almost to hate.
For when the seamen must take precedence
Of loiterers on the deck—through half a word,
Small, with intense device, like some fierce lens,
He magnified their rude and blustering mode;
Or urged some scented fop, whose idle brain
Busied itself with momentary whims,
To bid the master alter here a sail,
Or there a rope; and, if the man refused,
Doughty, at night, across the wine-cups, raved
Against the rising insolence of the mob;
And hinted Drake himself was half to blame,
In words that seemed to say, "I am his friend,
Or I should bid you think him all to blame."
So fierce indeed the strife became that once,
While Chester, Doughty's catspaw, played with fire,
The grim ship-master growled between his teeth,
"Remember, sir, remember, ere too late,
Magellan's mutinous vice-admiral's end."
And Doughty heard, and with a boisterous laugh
Slapped the old sea-dog on the back and said,
"The gallows are for dogs, not gentlemen!"
Meanwhile his brother, sly John Doughty, sought
To fan the seamen's fear of the unknown world
With whispers and conjectures; and, at night,
He brought old books of Greek and Hebrew down
Into the foc'sle, claiming by their aid
A knowledge of Black Art, and power to tell
The future, which he dreadfully displayed
There in the flickering light of the oily lamp,
Bending above their huge and swarthy palms
And tracing them to many a grisly doom.

So many a night and day westward they plunged.
The half-moon ripened to its mellow round,
Dwindled again and ripened yet again.
And there was nought around them but the grey
Ruin and roar of huge Atlantic seas.
And only like a memory of the world
They left behind them rose the same great sun,
And daily rolled his chariot through their sky,
Whereof the skilled musicians made a song.

SONG

The same sun is o'er us,
    The same Love shall find us,
        The same and none other,
            Wherever we be;
With the same goal before us,
    The same home behind us,
        England, our mother,
            Ringed round with the sea.

When the breakers charged thundering
    In thousands all round us
        With a lightning of lances
            Uphurtled on high,
When the stout ships were sundering
    A rapture hath crowned us,
        Like the wild light that dances
            On the crests that flash by.

When the waters lay breathless
    Gazing at Hesper
        Guarding the golden
            Fruit of the tree,
Heard we the deathless
    Wonderful whisper
        Wafting the olden
            Dream of the sea.

No land in the ring of it
  Now, all around us
    Only the splendid
      Resurging unknown!
How should we sing of it?—
  This that hath found us
    By the great sun attended
      In splendour, alone.

Ah! the broad miles of it,
  White with the onset
    Of waves without number
      Warring for glee.
Ah₁ the soft smiles of it
  Down to the sunset,
    Holy for slumber,
      The peace of the sea.

The wave's heart, exalted,
  Leaps forward to meet us,
    The sun on the sea-wave
      Lies white as the moon:
The soft sapphire-vaulted
  Deep heaven smiles to greet us,
    Free sons of the free-wave
      All singing one tune.

The same sun is o'er us,
  The same Love shall find us,
    The same and none other,
      Wherever we be;
With the same goal before us,
  The same home behind us,
    England, our mother,
      Queen of the sea.

At last a faint-flushed April Dawn arose
With milk-white arms up-binding golden clouds
Of fragrant hair behind her lovely head;
And lo, before the bright black plunging prows
The whole sea suddenly shattered into shoals

Of rolling porpoises.   Everywhere they tore
The glittering water.   Like a moving crowd
Of black bright rocks washed smooth by foaming tides,
They thrilled the unconscious fancy of the crews
With subtle, wild, and living hints of land.
And soon Columbus' happy signals came,
The signs that saved him when his mutineers
Despaired at last and clamoured to return,—
And there, with awe triumphant in their eyes,
They saw, lazily tossing on the tide,
A drift of seaweed and a berried branch,
Which silenced them as if they had seen a Hand
Writing with fiery letters on the deep.
Then a black cormorant, vulture of the sea,
With neck outstretched and one long ominous *honk*,
Went hurtling past them to its unknown bourne.
A mighty white-winged albatross came next;
Then flight on flight of clamorous clanging gulls;
And last, a wild and sudden shout of "Land!"
Echoed from crew to crew across the waves.
Then, dumb upon the rigging as they hung
Staring at it, a menace chilled their blood.
For like *Il Gran Nemico* of Dante, dark,
Ay, coloured like a thunder-cloud, from North
To South, in front, there slowly rose to sight
A country like a dragon fast asleep
Along the West, with wrinkled, purple wings
Ending in ragged forests o'er its spine;
And with great craggy claws out-thrust, that turned
(As the dim distances dissolved their veils)
To promontories bounding a huge bay.
There o'er the hushed and ever shallower tide
The staring ships drew nigh and thought, "Is this
The Dragon of our Golden Apple Tree,
The guardian of the fruit of our desire
Which grows in gardens of the Hesperides
Where those three sisters weave a white-armed dance
Around it everlastingly, and sing
Strange songs in a strange tongue that still convey
Warning to heedful souls?"   Nearer they drew,
And now, indeed, from out a soft blue-grey

Mingling of colours on that coast's deep flank
There crept a garden of enchantment, height
O'er height, a garden sloping from the hills,
Wooded as with Aladdin's trees that bore
All-coloured clustering gems instead of fruit;
Now vaster as it grew upon their eyes,
And like some Roman amphitheatre
Cirque above mighty cirque all round the bay,
With jewels and flowers ablaze on women's breasts
Innumerably confounded and confused;
While lovely faces flushed with lust of blood,
Rank above rank upon their tawny thrones
In soft barbaric splendour lapped, and lulled
By the low thunderings of a thousand lions,
Luxuriously smiled as they bent down
Over the scarlet-splashed and steaming sands
To watch the white-limbed gladiators die.

Such fears and dreams for Francis Drake, at least,
Rose and dissolved in his nigh fevered brain
As they drew near that equatorial shore;
For rumours had been borne to him; and now
He knew not whether to impute the wrong
To his untrustful mind or to believe
Doughty a traitorous liar; yet there seemed
Proof and to spare.   A thousand shadows rose
To mock him with their veiled indicative hands.
And each alone he laid and exorcised
But for each doubt he banished, one returned
From darker depths to mock him o'er again.

So, in that bay, the little fleet sank sail
And anchored; and the wild reality
Behind those dreams towered round them on the hills,
Or so it seemed.   And Drake bade lower a boat,
And went ashore with sixteen men to seek
Water; and, as they neared the embowered beach,
Over the green translucent tide there came,
A hundred yards from land, a drowsy sound
Immeasurably repeated and prolonged,

As of innumerable elfin drums
Dreamily mustering in the tropic bloom.
This from without they heard, across the waves;
But when they glided into a flowery creek
Under the sharp black shadows of the trees—
Jaca and Mango and Palm and red festoons
Of garlanded Liana wreaths—it ebbed
Into the murmur of the mighty fronds,
Prodigious leaves whose veinings bore the fresh
Impression of the finger-prints of God.
There humming-birds, like flakes of purple fire
Upon some passing seraph's plumage, beat
And quivered in blinding blots of golden light
Between the embattled cactus and cardoon;
While one huge whisper of primeval awe
Seemed to await the cool green eventide
When God should walk His Garden as of old.

Now as the boats were plying to and fro
Between the ships and that enchanted shore,
Drake bade his comrades tarry a little and went
Apart, alone, into the trackless woods.
Tormented with his thoughts, he saw all round
Once more the battling image of his mind,
Where there was nought of man, only the vast
Unending silent struggle of Titan trees,
Large internecine twistings of the world,
The hushed death-grapple and the still intense
Locked anguish of Laocoons that gripped
Death by the throat for thrice three hundred years.
Once, like a subtle mockery overhead,
Some black-armed chattering ape swung swiftly by,
But he strode onward, thinking—"Was it false,
False all that kind outreaching of the hands?
False?   Was there nothing certain, nothing sure
In those divinest aisles and towers of Time
Wherein we took sweet counsel?   Is there nought
Sure but the solid dust beneath our feet?
Must all those lovelier fabrics of the soul,
Being so divinely bright and delicate,
Waver and shine no longer than some poor

Prismatic aery bubble?   Ay, they burst,
And all their glory shrinks into one tear
No bitterer than some idle love-lorn maid
Sheds for her dead canary.   God, it hurts,
This, this hurts most, to think how we must miss
What might have been, for nothing but a breath,
A babbling of the tongue, an argument,
Or such a poor contention as involves
The thrones and dominations of this earth,—
How many of us, like seed on barren ground,
Must miss the flower and harvest of their prayers,
The living light of friendship and the grasp
Which for its very meaning once implied
Eternities of utterance and the life
Immortal of two souls beyond the grave?"

Now, wandering upward ever, he reached and clomb
The slope side of a fern-fringed precipice,
And, at the summit, found an opening glade,
Whence, looking o'er the forest, he beheld
The sea; and, in the land-locked bay below,
Far, far below, his elfin-tiny ships,
All six at anchor on the crawling tide!
Then onward, upward, through the woods once more
He plunged with bursting heart and burning brow;
And, once again, like madness, the black shapes
Of doubt swung through his brain and chattered and
                laughed,
Till he upstretched his arms in agony
And cursed the name of Doughty, cursed the day
They met, cursed his false face and courtier smiles,
"For oh," he cried, "how easy a thing it were
For truth to wear the garb of truth! This proves
His treachery!"   And there, at once, his thoughts
Tore him another way, as thus, "And yet
If he were false, is he not subtle enough
To hide it? Why, this proves his innocence—
This very courtly carelessness which I,
Black-hearted evil-thinker as I am,
In my own clumsier spirit so misjudge!
These children of the court are butterflies

Fluttering hither and thither, and I—poor fool—
Would fix them to a stem and call them flowers,
Nay, bid them grasp the ground like towering oaks
And shadow all the zenith;" and yet again
The madness of distrustful friendship gleamed
From his fierce eyes, "Oh villain, damnèd villain,
God's murrain on his heart! I know full well
He hides what he can hide! He wears no fault
Upon the gloss and frippery of his breast!
It is not that! It is the hidden things,
Unseizable, the things I do not know,
Ay, it is these, these, these and these alone
That I mistrust."
            And, as he walked, the skies
Grew full of threats, and now enormous clouds
Rose mammoth-like above the ensanguined deep,
Trampling the daylight out; and, with its death
Dyed purple, rushed along as if they meant
To obliterate the world. He took no heed.
Though that strange blackness brimmed the branching aisles
With horror, he strode on till in the gloom,
Just as his winding way came out once more
Over a precipice that o'erlooked the bay,
There, as he went, not gazing down, but up,
He saw what seemed a ponderous granite cliff,
A huge ribbed shell upon a lonely shore
Left by forgotten mountains when they sank
Back to earth's breast like billows on a sea.
A tall and whispering crowd of tree-ferns waved
Mysterious fringes round it. In their midst
He flung himself at its broad base, with one
Sharp shivering cry of pain, "Show me Thy ways,
O God, teach me Thy paths! I am in the dark!
Lighten my darkness!"
            Almost as he spoke
There swept across the forest, far and wide,
Gathering power and volume as it came,
A sound as of a rushing mighty wind;
And, overhead, like great black gouts of blood
Wrung from the awful forehead of the Night
The first drops fell and ceased. Then, suddenly,

Out of the darkness, earth with all her seas,
Her little ships at anchor in the bay
(Five ebony ships upon a sheet of silver,
Drake saw not that, indeed, Drake saw not that!),
Her woods, her boughs, her leaves, her tiniest twigs.
Leapt like a hunted stag through one immense
Lightning of revelation into the murk
Of Erebus: then heaven o'er rending heaven
Shattered and crashed down ruin over the world.
But, in that deeper darkness, Francis Drake
Stood upright now, and with blind outstretched arms
Groped at that strange forgotten cliff and shell
Of mystery; for in that flash of light
Æons had passed; and now the Thing in front
Made his blood freeze with memories that lay
Behind his Memory.   In the gloom he groped,
And with dark hands that knew not what they knew,
As one that shelters in the night, unknowing,
Beneath a stranded shipwreck, with a cry
He touched the enormous rain-washed belted ribs
And bones like battlements of some Mastodon
Embedded there until the trump of doom.

After long years, long centuries, perchance,
Triumphantly some other pioneer
Would stand where Drake now stood and read the tale
Of ages where he only felt the cold
Touch in the dark of some huge mystery;
Yet Drake might still be nearer to the light
Who now was whispering from his great deep heart,
"Show me Thy ways, O God, teach me Thy paths!"
And there by some strange instinct, oh, he felt
God's answer there, as if he grasped a hand
Across a gulf of twice ten thousand years;
And he regained his lost magnificence
Of faith in that great Harmony which resolves
Our discords, faith through all the ruthless laws
Of nature in their lovely pitilessness,
Faith in that Love which outwardly must wear,
Through all the sorrows of eternal change,
The splendour of the indifference of God.

All round him through the heavy purple gloom
Sloped the soft rush of silver-arrowed rain,
Loosening the skies' hard anguish as with tears.
Once more he felt his unity with all
The vast composure of the universe,
And drank deep at the fountains of that peace
Which comprehends the tumult of our days.
But with that peace the power to act returned;
And, with his back against the Mastodon,
He stared through the great darkness tow'rds the sea.
The rain ceased for a moment: only the slow
Drip of the dim droop-feathered palms all round
Deepened the hush.
                        Then, out of the gloom once more
The whole earth leapt to sight with all her woods,
Her boughs, her leaves, her tiniest twigs distinct
For one wild moment; but Drake only saw
The white flash of her seas and there, oh there
That land-locked bay with those five elfin ships,
Five elfin ebony ships upon a sheet
Of wrinkled silver! Then, as the thunder followed,
One thought burst through his brain—

                                    One ship was gone

Over the grim precipitous edge he hung,
An eagle waiting for the lightning now
To swoop upon his prey. One iron hand
Gripped a rough tree-root like a bunch of snakes;
And, as the rain rushed round him, far away
He saw to northward yet another flash,
A scribble of God's finger in the sky
Over a waste of white stampeding waves.
His eye flashed like a falchion as he saw it,
And from his lips there burst the sea-king's laugh;
For there, with a fierce joy he knew, he knew
Doughty, at last—an open mutineer!
An open foe to fight! Ay, there she went,—
His *Golden Hynde*, his little *Golden Hynde*
A wild deserter scudding to the North.
And, almost ere the lightning, Drake had gone
Crashing down the face of the precipice,
By a narrow water-gully, and through the huge

Forest he tore the straight and perilous way
Down to the shore; while, three miles to the North,
Upon the wet poop of the *Golden Hynde*
Doughty stood smiling.   Scarce would he have smiled
Knowing that Drake had seen him from that tower
Amidst the thunders; but, indeed, he thought
He had escaped unseen amidst the storm.
Many a day he had worked upon the crew,
Fanning their fears and doubts until he won
The more part to his side.   And when they reached
That coast, he showed them how Drake meant to sail
Southward, into that unknown Void; but he
Would have them suddenly slip by stealth away
Northward to Darien, showing them what a life
Of roystering glory waited for them there,
If, laying aside this empty quest, they joined
The merry feasters round those island fires
Which over many a dark-blue creek illumed
Buccaneer camps in scarlet logwood groves,
Fringing the Guf of Mexico, till dawn
Summoned the Black Flags out to sweep the sea.

But when Drake reached the flower-embowered boat
And found the men awaiting his return
There, in a sheltering grove of bread-fruit trees
Beneath great eaves of leafage that obscured
Their sight, but kept the storm out, as they tossed
Pieces of eight or rattled the bone dice,
His voice went through them like a thunderbolt,
For none of them had seen the *Golden Hynde*
Steal from the bay; and now the billows burst
Like cannon down the coast; and they had thought
Their boat could not be launched until the storm
Abated.   Under Drake's compelling eyes,
Nevertheless, they poled her down the creek
Without one word, waiting their chance.   Then all
Together with their brandished oars they thrust,
And on the fierce white out-draught of a wave
They shot up, up and over the toppling crest
Of the next, and plunged crashing into the trough
Behind it: then they settled at their thwarts,

And the fierce water boiled before their blades
As, with Drake's iron hand upon the helm,
They soared and crashed across the rolling seas.

Not for the Spanish prize did Drake now steer,
But for that little ship the *Marygold*,
Swiftest of sail, next to the *Golden Hynde*,
And, in the hands of Francis Drake, indeed
Swiftest of all; and ere the seamen knew
What power, as of a wind, bore them along,
Anchor was up, their hands were on the sheets,
The sails were broken out, the *Marygold*
Was flying like a storm-cloud to the North,
And on her poop an iron statue still
As death stood Francis Drake.
                              One hour they rushed
Northward, with green seas washing o'er the deck
And buffeted with splendour; then they saw
The *Golden Hynde* like some wing-broken gull
With torn mismanaged plumes beating the air
In peril of utter shipwreck; saw her fly
Half-mast, a feeble signal of distress
Despite all Doughty's curses; for her crew
Wild with divisions torn amongst themselves
Most gladly now surrendered in their hearts,
As close alongside grandly onward swept
The *Marygold*, with canvas trim and taut
Magnificently drawing the full wind,
Her gunners waiting at their loaded guns
Bare-armed and silent; and that iron soul
Alone, upon her silent quarter-deck.
There they hauled up into the wind and lay
Rocking, while Drake, alone, without a guard,
Boarding the runaway, dismissed his boat
Back to the *Marygold*. Then his voice out-rang
Trumpet-like o'er the trembling mutineers,
And clearly, as if they were but busied still
About the day's routine. They hid their shame,
As men that would propitiate a god,
By flying to fulfil his lightest word;

And ere they knew what power, as of a wind,
Impelled them—that half wreck was trim and taut,
Her sails all drawing and her bows afoam;
And, creeping past the *Marygold* once more,
She led their Southward way!   And not till then
Did Drake vouchsafe one word to the white face
Of Doughty, as he furtively slunk nigh
With some new lie upon his fear-parched lips
Thirsting for utterance in his crackling laugh
Of deprecation; and with one ruffling puff
Of pigeon courage in his blinded soul—
"I am no sea-dog—even Francis Drake
Would scarce misuse a gentleman."
                                   Then Drake turned
And summoned four swart seamen out by name.
His words went like a cold wind through their flesh
As with a passionless voice he slowly said,
"Take ye this fellow: bind him to the mast
Until what time I shall decide his fate."
And Doughty gasped as at the world's blank end,—
"Nay, Francis," cried he, "wilt thou thus misuse
A gentleman?"   But as the seamen gripped
His arms he struggled vainly and furiously
To throw them off; and in his impotence
Let slip the whole of his treacherous cause and hope
In empty wrath,—"Fore God," he foamed and snarled,
"Ye shall all smart for this when we return!
Unhand me, dogs!   I have Lord Burleigh's power
Behind me.   There is nothing I have done
Without his warrant!   Ye shall smart for this!
Unhand me, I say, unhand me!"
                                   And in one flash
Drake saw the truth, and Doughty saw his eyes
Lighten upon him; and his false heart quailed
Once more; and he suddenly suffered himself
Quietly, strangely, to be led away
And bound without a murmur to the mast.
And strangely Drake remembered, as those words,
"Ye shall all smart for this when we return,"
Yelped at his faith, how while the Dover cliffs
Faded from sight he leaned to his new friend
20

Doughty and said: "I blame them not who stay!
I blame them not at all who cling to home,
For many of us, indeed, shall not return,
Nor ever know that sweetness any more."

And when they had reached their anchorage anew,
Drake, having now resolved to bring his fleet
Beneath a more compact control, at once
Took all the men and the chief guns and stores
From out the Spanish prize; and sent Tom Moone
To set the hulk afire.   Also he bade
Unbind the traitor and ordered him aboard
The pinnace *Christopher*.   John Doughty, too,
He ordered thither, into the grim charge
Of old Tom Moone, thinking it best to keep
The poisonous leaven carefully apart
Until they had won well Southward, to a place
Where, finally committed to their quest,
They might arraign the traitor without fear
Or favour, and acquit him or condemn.
But those two brothers, doubting as the false
Are damned to doubt, saw murder in his eyes,
And thought "He means to sink the smack one night."
And they refused to go, till Drake abruptly
Ordered them straightway to be slung on board
With ropes.
        The daylight waned; but ere the sun
Sank, the five ships were plunging to the South;
For Drake would halt no longer, least the crews
Also should halt betwixt two purposes.
He took the tide of fortune at the flood;
And onward through the now subsiding storm,
Ere they could think what power as of a wind
Impelled them, he had swept them on their way.
Far, far into the night they saw the blaze
That leapt in crimson o'er the abandoned hulk
Behind them, like a mighty hecatomb
Marking the path of some Titanic will.
Many a night and day they Southward drove.
Sometimes at midnight round them all the sea
Quivered with witches' oils and water snakes,

Green, blue, and red, with lambent tongues of fire.
Mile upon mile about the blurred black hulls
A cauldron of tempestuous colour coiled.
On every mast mysterious meteors burned,
And from the shores a bellowing rose and fell
As of great bestial gods that walked all night
Through some wild hell unknown, too vast for men;
But when the silver and crimson of the dawn
Broke out, they saw the tropic shores anew,
The fair white foam, and, round about the rocks,
Weird troops of tusked sea-lions; and the world
Mixed with their dreams and made them stranger still.
And, once, so fierce a tempest scattered the fleet
That even the hardiest souls began to think
There was a Jonah with them; for the seas
Rose round them like green mountains, peaked and rigged
With heights of Alpine snow amongst the clouds;
And many a league to Southward, when the ships
Gathered again amidst the sinking waves
Four only met.   The ship of Thomas Drake
Was missing; and some thought it had gone down
With all hands in the storm.   But Francis Drake
Held on his way, learning from hour to hour
To merge himself in immortality;
Learning the secrets of those pitiless laws
Which dwarf all mortal grief, all human pain,
To something less than nothing by the side
Of that eternal travail dimly guessed,
Since first he felt in the miraculous dark
The great bones of the Mastodon, that hulk
Of immemorial death.   He learned to judge
The passing pageant of this outward world
As by the touch-stone of that memory;
Even as in that country which some said
Lay now not far, the great Tezcucan king,
Resting his jewelled hand upon a skull,
And on a smouldering glory of jewels throned
There in his temple of the Unknown God
Over the host of Aztec princes, clad
In golden hauberks gleaming under soft
Surcoats of green or scarlet feather-work,

Could in the presence of a mightier power
Than life or death give up his guilty sons,
His only sons, to the sacrificial sword.
And hour by hour the soul of Francis Drake,
Unconscious as an oak-tree of its growth,
Increased in strength and stature as he drew
Earth, heaven, and hell within him, more and more.
For as the dream we call our world, with all
Its hues is but a picture in the brain,
So did his soul enfold the universe
With gradual sense of superhuman power,
While every visible shape within the vast
Horizon seemed the symbol of some thought
Waiting for utterance.   He had found indeed
God's own Nirvana, not of empty dream,
But of intensest life.   Nor did he think
Aught of all this; but, as the rustic deems
The colours that he carries in his brain
Are somehow all outside him while he peers
Unaltered through two windows in his face,
Drake only knew that as the four ships plunged
Southward, the world mysteriously grew
More like a prophet's vision, hour by hour,
Fraught with dark omens and significances,
A world of hieroglyphs and sacred signs
Wherein he seemed to read the truth that lay
Hid from the Roman augurs when of old
They told the future from the flight of birds.
How vivid with disaster seemed the flight
Of those blood-red flamingoes o'er the dim
Blue steaming forest, like two terrible thoughts
Flashing, unapprehended, through his brain!

And now, as they drove Southward, day and night,
Through storm and calm, the shores that fleeted by
Grew wilder, grander, with his growing soul,
And pregnant with the approaching mystery.
And now along the Patagonian coast
They cruised, and in the solemn midnight saw
Wildernesses of shaggy barren marl,
Petrified seas of lava, league on league,

Craters and bouldered slopes and granite cliffs
With ragged rents, grim gorges, deep ravines,
And precipice on precipice up-piled
Innumerable to those dim distances
Where, over valleys hanging in the clouds,
Gigantic mountains and volcanic peaks
Catching the wefts of cirrus fleece appeared
To smoke against the sky, though all was now
Dead as that frozen chaos of the moon,
Or some huge passion of a slaughtered soul
Prostrate under the marching of the stars.

At last, and in a silver dawn, they came
Suddenly on a broad-winged estuary,
And, in the midst of it, an island lay,
There they found shelter, on its leeward side,
And Drake convened upon the *Golden Hynde*
His dread court-martial.   Two long hours he heard
Defence and accusation, then broke up
The conclave, and, with burning heart and brain,
Feverishly seeking everywhere some sign
To guide him, went ashore upon that isle,
And lo, turning a rugged point of rock,
He rubbed his eyes to find out if he dreamed,
For there—a Crusoe's wonder, a miracle,
A sign—before him stood on that lone strand
Stark, with a stern arm pointing out his way
And jangling still one withered skeleton,
The grim black gallows where Magellan hanged
His mutineers.   Its base was white with bones
Picked by the gulls, and crumbling o'er the sand
A dread sea-salt, dry from the tides of time.
There, on that lonely shore, Death's finger-post
Stood like some old forgotten truth made strange
By the long lapse of many memories,
All starting up in resurrection now
As at the trump of doom, heroic ghosts
Out of the cells and graves of his deep brain
Reproaching him.   *"Were this man not thy friend,*
Ere now he should have died the traitor's death.
What wilt thou say to others if they, too,

Prove false?   Or wilt thou slay the lesser and save
The greater sinner?   Nay, if thy right hand
Offend thee, cut it off!"   And, in one flash,
Drake saw his path and chose it.

                                    With a voice
Low as the passionless anguished voice of Fate
That comprehends all pain, but girds it round
With iron, lest some random cry break out
For man's misguidance, he drew all his men
Around him, saying, "Ye all know how I loved
Doughty, who hath betrayed me twice and thrice,
For I still trusted him: he was no felon
That I should turn my heart away from him.
He is the type and image of man's laws;
While I—am lawless as the soul that still
Must sail and seek a world beyond the worlds,
A law behind earth's laws.   I dare not judge!
But ye—who know the mighty goal we seek,
Who have seen him sap our courage, hour by hour,
Till God Himself almost appeared a dream
Behind his technicalities and doubts
Of aught he could not touch or handle; ye
Who have seen him stir up jealousy and strife
Between our seamen and our gentlemen,
Even as the world stirs up continual strife,
Bidding the man forget he is a man
With God's own patent of nobility;
Ye who have seen him strike this last sharp blow—
Sharper than any enemy hath struck,—
He whom I trusted, he alone could strike—
So sharply, for indeed I loved this man.
Judge ye—for see, I cannot.   Do not doubt
I loved this man!
But now, if ye will let him have his life,
Oh, speak!   But, if ye think it must be death,
Hold up your hands in silence!"   His voice dropped,
And eagerly he whispered forth one word
Beyond the scope of Fate—
"I would not have him die!"   There was no sound
Save the long thunder of eternal seas,—
Drake bowed his head and waited.

Suddenly,
One man upheld his hand; then, all at once,
A brawny forest of brown arms arose
In silence, and the great sea whispered *Death*.

. . . .

There, with one big swift impulse, Francis Drake
Held out his right sun-blackened hand and gripped
The hand that Doughty proffered him; and lo,
Doughty laughed out and said, "Since I must die,
Let us have one more hour of comradeship,
One hour as old companions. Let us make
A feast here, on this island, ere I go
Where there is no more feasting."   So they made
A great and solemn banquet as the day
Decreased; and Doughty bade them all unlock
Their sea-chests and bring out their rich array.
There, by that wondering ocean of the West,
In crimson doublets, lined and slashed with gold,
In broidered lace and double golden chains
Embossed with rubies and great cloudy pearls
They feasted, gentlemen adventurers,
Drinking old malmsey, as the sun sank down.

Now Doughty, fronting the rich death of day,
And flourishing a silver pouncet-box
With many a courtly jest and rare conceit,
There as he sat in rich attire, out-braved
The rest.   Though darker-hued, yet richer far,
His murrey-coloured doublet double-piled
Of Genoa velvet, puffed with ciprus, shone;
For over its grave hues the gems that bossed
His golden collar, wondrously relieved,
Blazed lustrous to the West like stars.   But Drake
Was clad in black, with midnight silver slashed,
And, at his side, a great two-handed sword.
At last they rose, just as the sun's last rays
Rested upon the heaving molten gold
Immeasurable.   The long slow sigh of the waves
That creamed across the lonely time-worn reef
All round the island seemed the very voice

Of the Everlasting: black against the sea
The gallows of Magellan stretched its arm
With the gaunt skeleton and its rusty chain
Creaking and swinging in the solemn breath
Of eventide like some strange pendulum
Measuring out the moments that remained.
There did they take the holy sacrament
Of Jesus' body and blood.   Then Doughty and Drake
Kissed each other, as brothers, on the cheek;
And Doughty knelt.   And Drake, without one word,
Leaning upon the two-edged naked sword
Stood at his side, with iron lips, and eyes
Full of the sunset; while the doomed man bowed
His head upon a rock.   The great sun dropped
Suddenly, and the land and sea were dark;
And as it were a sign, Drake lifted up
The gleaming sword.   It seemed to sweep the heavens
Down in its arc as he smote, once, and no more.

Then, for a moment, silence froze their veins,
Till one fierce seamen stooped with a hoarse cry;
And, like an eagle clutching up its prey,
His arm swooped down and bore the head aloft,
Gorily streaming, by the long dark hair;
And a great shout went up, "So perish all
Traitors to God and England."   Then Drake turned
And bade them to their ships; and, wondering,
They left him.   As the boats thrust out from shore
Brave old Tom Moone looked back with faithful eyes
Like a great mastiff to his master's face.
He, looming larger from his loftier ground
Clad with the slowly gathering night of stars
And gazing seaward o'er his quiet dead,
Seemed like some Titan bronze in grandeur based
Unshakeable until the crash of doom
Shatter the black foundations of the world.

BOOK IV

Dawn, everlasting and almighty Dawn,
Hailed by ten thousand names of death and birth,
Who, chiefly by thy name of Sorrow, seem'st
To half the world a sunset, God's great Dawn,
Fair light of all earth's partings till we meet
Where dawn and sunset, mingling East and West,
Shall make in some deep Orient of the soul
One radiant Rose of Love for evermore;
Teach me, oh teach to bear thy broadening light,
Thy deepening wonder, lest as old dreams fade
With love's unfaith, like wasted hours of youth,
And dim illusions vanish in thy beam,
Their rapture and their anguish break that heart
Which loved them, and must love for ever now.
Let thy great sphere of splendour, ring by ring
For ever widening, draw new seas, new skies,
Within my ken; yet, as I still must bear
This love, help me to grow in spirit with thee.
Dawn on my song which trembles like a cloud
Pierced with thy beauty. Rise, shine, as of old
Across the wondering ocean in the sight
Of those world-wandering mariners, when earth
Rolled flat up to the Gates of Paradise,
And each slow mist that curled its gold away
From each new sea they furrowed into pearl
Might bring before their blinded mortal eyes
God and the Glory. Lighten as on the soul
Of him that all night long in torment dire,
Anguish and thirst unceasing for thy ray
Upon that lonely Patagonian shore
Had lain as on the bitterest coasts of Hell.
For all night long, mocked by the dreadful peace
Of world-wide seas that darkly heaved and sank
With cold recurrence, like the slow sad breath
Of a fallen Titan dying all alone
In lands beyond all human loneliness,
While far and wide glimmers that broken targe
Hurled from tremendous battle with the gods,
And, as he breathes in pain, the chain-mail rings

Round his broad breast a muffled rattling make
For many a league, so seemed the sound of waves
Upon those beaches—there, be-mocked all night,
Beneath Magellan's gallows, Drake had watched
Beside his dead; and over him the stars
Paled as the silver chariot of the moon
Drove, and her white steeds ramped in a fury of foam
On splendid peaks of cloud. The *Golden Hynde*
Slept with those other shadows on the bay.
Between him and his home the Atlantic heaved;
And, on the darker side, across the strait
Of starry sheen that softly rippled and flowed
Betwixt the mainland and his isle, it seemed
Death's Gates indeed burst open. The night yawned
Like a foul wound. Black shapes of the outer dark
Poured out of forests older than the world;
And, just as reptiles that take form and hue,
Speckle and blotch, in strange assimilation
From thorn and scrub and stone and the waste earth
Through which they crawl, so that almost they seem
The incarnate spirits of their wilderness,
Were these most horrible kindred of the night.
Æonian glooms unfathomable, grim aisles,
Grotesque, distorted boughs and dancing shades
Out-belched their dusky brood on the dim shore;
Monsters with sooty limbs, red-raddled eyes,
And faces painted yellow, women and men;
Fierce naked giants howling to the moon,
And loathlier Gorgons with long snaky tresses
Pouring vile purple over pendulous breasts
Like wine-bags. On the mainland beach they lit
A brushwood fire that reddened creek and cove
And lapped their swarthy limbs with hideous tongues
Of flame; so near that by their light Drake saw
The blood upon the dead man's long black hair
Clotting corruption. The fierce funeral pyre
Of all things fair seemed rolling on that shore;
And in that dull red battle of smoke and flame,
While the sea crunched the pebbles, and dark drums
Rumbled out of the gloom as if this earth
Had some Titanic tigress for a soul

Purring in forests of Eternity
Over her own grim dreams, his lonely spirit
Passed through the circles of a world-wide waste
Darker than ever Dante roamed.   No gulf
Was this of fierce harmonious reward,
Where Evil moans in anguish after death,
Where all men reap as they have sown, where gluttons
Gorge upon toads and usurers gulp hot streams
Of molten gold.   This was that Malebolge
Which hath no harmony to mortal ears,
But seems the reeling and tremendous dream
Of some omnipotent madman.   There he saw
The naked giants dragging to the flames
Young captives hideous with a new despair:
He saw great craggy blood-stained stones upheaved
To slaughter, saw through mists of blood and fire
The cannibal feast prepared, saw filthy hands
Rend limb from limb, and almost dreamed he saw
Foul mouths a-drip with quivering human flesh
And horrible laughter in the crimson storm
That clomb and leapt and stabbed at the high heaven
Till the whole night seemed saturate with red.

And all night long upon the *Golden Hynde*,
A cloud upon the waters, brave Tom Moone
Watched o'er the bulwarks for some dusky plunge
To warn him if that savage crew should mark
His captain and swim over to his isle.
Whistle in hand he watched, his boat well ready,
His men low-crouched around him, swarthy faces
Grim-chinned upon the taffrail, muttering oaths
That trampled down the fear i' their bristly throats,
While at their sides a dreadful hint of steel
Sent stray gleams to the stars.   But little heed
Had Drake of all that menaced him, though oft
Some wandering giant, belching from the feast,
All blood-besmeared, would come so near he heard
His heavy breathing o'er the narrow strait.
Yet little care had Drake, for though he sat
Bowed in the body above his quiet dead,
His burning spirit wandered through the wastes,

Wandered through hells behind the apparent hell,
Horrors immeasurable, clutching at dreams
Found fair of old, but now most foul.   The world
Leered at him through its old remembered mask
Of beauty: the green grass that clothed the fields
Of England (shallow, shallow fairy dream!)
What was it but the hair of dead men's graves,
Rooted in death, enriched with all decay?
And like a leprosy the hawthorn bloom
Crawled o'er the whitening bosom of the spring;
And bird and beast and insect, ay and man,
How fat they fed on one another's blood!
And Love, what faith in Love, when spirit and flesh
Are found of such a filthy composition?
And Knowledge, God, his mind went reeling back
To that dark voyage on the deadly coast
Of Panama, where one by one his men
Sickened and died of some unknown disease,
Till Joseph, his own brother, in his arms
Died; and Drake trampled down all tender thought,
All human grief, and sought to find the cause,
For his crew's sake, the ravenous unknown cause
Of that fell scourge.   There, in his own dark cabin,
Lit by the wild light of the swinging lanthorn,
He laid the naked body on that board
Where they had supped together.   He took the knife
From the ague-stricken surgeon's palsied hands,
And while the ship rocked in the eternal seas
And dark waves lapped against the rolling hulk
Making the silence terrible with voices,
He opened his own brother's cold white corse,
That pale deserted mansion of a soul,
Bidding the surgeon mark, with his own eyes,
While yet he had strength to use them, the foul spots,
The swollen liver, the strange sodden heart,
The yellow intestines.   Yea, his dry lips hissed
There in the stark face of Eternity,
"Seëst thou?   Seëst thou?   Knowest thou what it means?"
Then, like a dream up-surged the belfried night
Of Saint Bartholomew, the scented palaces
Whence harlots leered out on the twisted streets

Of Paris, choked with slaughter! Europe flamed
With human torches, living altar candles,
Lighted before the Cross where men had hanged
The Christ of little children. Cirque by cirque
The world-wide hell reeled round him, East and West,
To where the tortured Indians worked the will
Of lordly Spain in golden-famed Peru.
"God, is thy world a madman's dream?" he groaned:
And suddenly, the clamour on the shore
Sank and that savage horde melted away
Into the midnight forest as it came,
Leaving no sign, save where the brushwood fire
Still smouldered like a ruby in the gloom;
And into the inmost caverns of his mind
That other clamour sank, and there was peace.
"A madman's dream," he whispered, "Ay, to me
A madman's dream," but better, better far
Than that which bears upon its awful gates,
Gates of a hell defined, unalterable,
Abandon hope all ye who enter here!
Here, here at least the dawn hath power to bring
New light, new hope, new battles. Men may fight
And sweep away that evil, if no more,
At least from the small circle of their swords;
Then die, content if they have struck one stroke
For freedom, knowledge, brotherhood; one stroke
To hasten that great kingdom God proclaims
Each morning through the trumpets of the Dawn.

And far away, in Italy, that night
Young Galileo, gazing upward, heard
The self-same whisper from the abyss of stars
Which lured the soul of Shakespeare as he lay
Dreaming in may-sweet England, even now,
And with its infinite music called once more
The soul of Drake out to the unknown West.

Now like a wild rose in the fields of heaven
Slipt forth the slender fingers of the Dawn,
And drew the great grey Eastern curtains back
From the ivory saffroned couch. Rosily slid

One shining foot and one warm rounded knee
From silken coverlets of the tossed-back clouds.
Then, like the meeting after desolate years,
Face to remembered face, Drake saw the Dawn
Step forth in naked splendour o'er the sea;
Dawn, bearing still her rich divine increase
Of beauty, love, and wisdom round the world;
The same, yet not the same.   So strangely gleamed
Her pearl and rose across the sapphire waves
That scarce he knew the dead man at his feet.
His world was made anew.   Strangely his voice
Rang through that solemn Eden of the morn
Calling his men, and stranger than a dream
Their boats black-blurred against the crimson East,
Or flashing misty sheen where'er the light
Smote on their smooth wet sides, like seraph ships
Moved in a dewy glory towards the land;
Their oars of glittering diamond broke the sea
As by enchantment into burning jewels
And scattered rainbows from their flaming blades.
The clear green water lapping round their prows,
The words of sharp command as now the keels
Crunched on his lonely shore, and the following wave
Leapt slapping o'er the sterns, in that new light
Were more than any miracle.   At last
Drake, as they grouped a little way below
The crumbling sandy cliff whereon he stood,
Seeming to overshadow them as he loomed
A cloud of black against the crimson sky,
Spoke, as a man may hardly speak but once:
"My seamen, oh my friends, companions, kings;
For I am least among you, being your captain;
And ye are men, and all men born are kings,
By right divine, and I the least of these
Because I must usurp the throne of God
And sit in judgment, even till I have set
My seal upon the red wax of this blood,
This blood of my dead friend, ere it grow cold.
Not all the waters of that mighty sea
Could wash my hands of sin if I should now
Falter upon my path.   But look to it, you,

Whose word was doom last night to this dead man;
Look to it, I say, look to it!   Brave men might shrink
From this great voyage; but the heart of him
Who dares turn backward now must be so hardy
That God might make a thousand millstones of it
To hang about the necks of those that hurt
Some little child, and cast them in the sea.
Yet if ye will be found so more than bold,
Speak now, and I will hear you; God will judge.
But ye shall take four ships of these my five,
Tear out the lions from their painted shields,
And speed you homeward.   Leave me but one ship,
My *Golden Hynde*, and five good friends, nay one,
To watch when I must sleep, and I will prove
This judgment just against all winds that blow.
Now ye that will return, speak, let me know you,
Or be for ever silent, for I swear
Over this butchered body, if any swerve
Hereafter from the straight and perilous way,
He shall not die alone.   What?   Will none speak?
My comrades and my friends!   Yet ye must learn,
Mark me, my friends, I'd have you all to know
That ye are kings.   I'll have no jealousies
Aboard my fleet.   I'll have the gentleman
To pull and haul wi' the seaman.   I'll not have
That canker of the Spaniards in my fleet.
Ye that were captains, I cashier you all.
I'll have no captains; I'll have nought but seamen,
Obedient to my will, because I serve
England.   What, will ye murmur?   Have a care,
Lest I should bid you homeward all alone,
You whose white hands are found too delicate
For aught but dallying with your jewelled swords!
And thou, too, master Fletcher, my ship's chaplain,
Mark me, I'll have no priest-craft.   I have heard
Overmuch talk of judgment from thy lips,
God's judgment here, God's judgment there, upon us!
Whene'er the winds are contrary, thou takest
Their powers upon thee for thy moment's end.
Thou art God's minister, not God's oracle:
Chain up thy tongue a little, or, by His wounds,

If thou canst read this wide world like a book,
Thou hast so little to fear, I'll set thee adrift
On God's great sea to find thine own way home.
Why, 'tis these very tyrannies o' the soul
We strike at when we strike at Spain for England;
And shall we here, in this great wilderness,
Ungrappled and unchallenged, out of sight,
Alone, without one struggle, sink that flag
Which, when the cannon thundered, could but stream
Triumphant over all the storms of death.
Nay, master Wynter and my gallant captains,
I see ye are tamed.   Take up your ranks again
In humbleness, remembering ye are kings,
Kings for the sake and by the will of England,
Therefore her servants till your lives' last end.
Comrades, mistake not this, our little fleet
Is freighted with the golden heart of England,
And, if we fail, that golden heart will break.
The world's wide eyes are on us, and our souls
Are woven together into one great flag
Of England.   Shall we strike it?   Shall it be rent
Asunder with small discord, party strife,
Ephemeral conflict of contemptible tongues,
Or shall it be blazoned, blazoned evermore
On the most heaven-wide page of history?
This is that hour, I know it in my soul,
When we must choose for England.   Ye are kings,
And sons of Vikings, exiled from your throne.
Have ye forgotten?   Nay, your blood remembers!
There is your kingdom, Vikings, that great ocean
Whose tang is in your nostrils.   Ye must choose
Whether to re-assume it now for England,
To claim its thunders for her panoply,
To lay its lightnings in her sovereign hands,
Win her the great commandment of the sea
And let its glory roll with her dominion
Round the wide world for ever, sweeping back
All evil deeds and dreams, or whether to yield
For evermore that kinghood.   Ye must learn
Here in this golden dawn our great emprise

Is greater than we knew.   Eye hath not seen,
Ear hath not heard what came across the dark
Last night, as there anointed with that blood
I knelt and saw the wonder that should be.
I saw new heavens of freedom, a new earth
Released from all old tyrannies.   I saw
The brotherhood of man, for which we rode,
Most ignorant of the splendour of our spears,
Against the crimson dynasties of Spain.
Mother of freedom, home and hope and love,
Our little island, far, how far away,
I saw thee shatter the whole world of hate,
I saw the sunrise on thy helmet flame
With new-born hope for all the world in thee!
Come now, to sea, to sea!"

                              And ere they knew
What power impelled them, with one mighty cry
They lifted up their hearts to the new dawn
And hastened down the shores and launched the boats,
And in the fierce white out-draught of the waves
Thrust with their brandished oars and the boats leapt
Out, and they settled at the groaning thwarts,
And the white water boiled before their blades,
As, with Drake's iron hand upon the helm,
His own boat led the way; and ere they knew
What power as of a wind bore them along,
Anchor was up, their hands were on the sheets,
The sails were broken out and that small squadron
Was flying like a sea-bird to the South.
Now to the strait Magellanus they came,
And entered in with ringing shouts of joy.
Nor did they think there was a fairer strait
In all the world than this which lay so calm
Between great silent mountains crowned with snow,
Unutterably lonely.   Marvellous
The pomp of dawn and sunset on those heights,
And like a strange new sacrilege the advance
Of prows that ploughed that time-forgotten tide.
But soon rude flaws, cross currents, tortuous channels

Bewildered them, and many a league they drove
As down some vaster Acheron, while the coasts
With wailing voices cursed them all night long,
And once again the hideous fires leapt red
By many a grim wrenched crag and gaunt ravine.
So for a hundred leagues of whirling spume
They groped, till suddenly, far away, they saw
Full of the sunset, like a cup of gold,
The purple Westward portals of the strait.
Onward o'er roughening waves they plunged and reached
Capo Desiderato, where they saw
What seemed stupendous in that lonely place,—
Gaunt, black, and sharp as death against the sky
The Cross, the great black Cross on Cape Desire,
Which dead Magellan raised upon the height
To guide, or so he thought, his wandering ships,
Not knowing they had left him to his doom,
Not knowing how with tears, with tears of joy,
Rapture, and terrible triumph, and deep awe,
Another should come voyaging and read
Unutterable glories in that sign;
While his rough seamen raised their mighty shout
And, once again, before his wondering eyes,
League upon league of awful burnished gold,
Rolled the unknown immeasurable sea.

Now, in those days, as even Magellan held,
Men thought that Southward of the strait there swept
Firm land up to the white Antarticke Pole,
Which now not far they deemed.   But when Drake passed
From out the strait to take his Northward way
Up the Pacific coast, a great head-wind
Suddenly smote them; and the heaving seas
Bulged all around them into billowy hills,
Dark rolling mountains, whose majestic crests
Like wild white flames far-blown and savagely flickering
Swept through the clouds; and on their sullen slopes
Like wind-whipt withered leaves those little ships,
Now hurtled to the Zenith and now plunged
Down into bottomless gulfs, were suddenly scattered
And whirled away.   Drake, on the *Golden Hynde*,

One moment saw them near him, soaring up
Above him on the huge o'erhanging billows
As if to crash down on his poop; the next,
A mile of howling sea had swept between
Each of those wind-whipt straws, and they were gone
Through roaring deserts of embattled death,
Where, like a hundred thousand chariots charged
With lightnings and with thunders, one great wave
Leading the unleashed ocean down the storm
Hurled them away to Southward.

                                        One last glimpse
Drake caught o' the *Marygold*, when some mighty vortex
Wide as the circle of the wide sea-line
Swept them together again.   He saw her staggering
With mast snapt short and wreckage-tangled deck
Where men like insects clung.   He saw the waves
Leap over her mangled hulk, like wild white wolves,
Volleying out of the clouds down dismal steeps
Of green-black water.   Like a wounded steed
Quivering upon its haunches, up she heaved
Her head to throw them off.   Then, in one mass
Of fury crashed the great deep over her,
Trampling her down, down into the nethermost pit,
As with a madman's wrath.   She rose no more,
And in the stream of the ocean's hurricane laughter
The *Golden Hynde* went hurtling to the South,
With sails rent into ribbons and her mast
Snapt like a twig.   Yea, where Magellan thought
Firm land had been, the little *Golden Hynde*
Whirled like an autumn leaf through league on league
Of bursting seas, chaos on crashing chaos,
A rolling wilderness of charging Alps
That shook the world with their tremendous war;
Grim beetling cliffs that grappled with clamorous gulfs,
Valleys that yawned to swallow the wide heaven;
Immense white-flowering fluctuant precipices,
And hills that swooped down at the throat of hell;
From Pole to Pole, one blanching bursting storm
Of world-wide oceans, where the huge Pacific
Roared greetings to the Atlantic and both swept

In broad white cataracts, league on struggling league,
Pursuing and pursued, immeasurable,
With Titan hands grasping the rent black sky
East, West, North, South.   Then, then was battle indeed
Of midget men upon that wisp of grass
The *Golden Hynde*, who, as her masts crashed, hung
Clearing the tiny wreckage from small decks
With ant-like weapons.   Not their captain's voice
Availed them now amidst the deafening thunder
Of seas that felt the heavy hand of God,
Only they saw across the blinding spume
In steely flashes, grand and grim, a face,
Like the last glimmer of faith among mankind,
Calm in this warring universe, where Drake
Stood, lashed to his post, beside the helm.   Black seas
Buffeted him.   Half-stunned he dashed away
The sharp brine from his eagle eyes and turned
To watch some mountain-range come rushing down
As if to o'erwhelm them utterly.   Once, indeed,
Welkin and sea were one black wave, white-fanged,
White-crested, and up-heaped so mightily
That, though it coursed more swiftly than a herd
Of Titan steeds upon some terrible plain
Nigh the huge City of Ombos, yet it seemed
Most strangely slow, with all those crumbling crests
Each like a cataract on a mountain-side,
And moved with the steady majesty of doom
High over him.   One moment's flash of fear,
And yet not fear, but rather life's regret,
Felt Drake, then laughed a low deep laugh of joy
Such as men taste in battle; yea, 'twas good
To grapple thus with death; one low deep laugh,
One mutter as of a lion about to spring,
Then burst that thunder o'er him.   Height o'er height
The heavens rolled down, and waves were all the world.

Meanwhile, in England, dreaming of her sailor,
Far off, his heart's bride waited, of a proud
And stubborn house the bright and gracious flower.
Whom oft her father urged with scanty grace
That Drake was dead and she had best forget

The fellow, he grunted. For her father's heart
Was fettered with small memories, mocked by all
The greater world's traditions and the trace
Of earth's low pedigree among the suns,
Ringed with the terrible twilight of the Gods,
Ringed with the blood-red dusk of dying nations,
His faith was in his grandam's mighty skirt,
And, in that awful consciousness of power,
Had it not been that even in this he feared
To sully her silken flounce or farthingale
Wi' the white dust on his hands, he would have chalked
To his own shame, thinking it shame, the word
Nearest to God in its divine embrace
Of agonies and glories, the dread word
Demos across that door in Nazareth
Whence came the prentice carpenter whose voice
Hath shaken kingdoms down, whose menial gibbet
Rises triumphant o'er the wreck of Empires
And stretches out its arms amongst the Stars.
But she, his daughter, only let her heart
Loveably forge a charter for her love,
Cheat her false creed with faithful faery dreams
That wrapt her love in mystery; thought, perchance,
He came of some unhappy noble race
Ruined in battle for some lost high cause.
And, in the general mixture of men's blood,
Her dream was truer than his whose bloodless pride
Urged her to wed the chinless moon-struck fool
Sprung from five hundred years of idiocy
Who now besought her hand; would force her bear
Some heir to a calf's tongue and a coronet,
Whose cherished taints of blood will please his friends
With "Yea, Sir William's first-born hath the freak,
The family freak, being embryonic. Yea,
And with a fine half-wittedness, forsooth.
Praise God, our children's children yet shall see
The lord o' the manor muttering to himself
At midnight by the gryphon-guarded gates,
Or gnawing his nails in desolate corridors,
Or pacing moonlit halls, dagger in hand,
Waiting to stab his father's pitiless ghost."

So she—the girl—Sweet Bess of Sydenham,
Most innocently proud, was prouder yet
Than thus to let her heart stoop to the lure
Of lording lovers, though her unstained soul
Slumbered amidst those dreams as in old tales
The princess in the enchanted forest sleeps
Till the prince wakes her with a kiss and draws
The far-flung hues o' the gleaming magic web
Into one heart of flame.   And now, for Drake,
She slept like Brynhild in a ring of fire
Which he must pass to win her.   For the wrath
Of Spain now flamed, awaiting his return,
All round the seas of home; and even the Queen
Elizabeth flinched, as that tremendous Power
Menaced the heart of England, flinched and vowed
Drake's head to Spain's ambassadors, though still
By subtlety she hoped to find some way
Later to save or warn him ere he came.
Perchance too, nay, most like, he will be slain
Or even now lies dead, out in the West,
She thought, and then the promise works no harm.
But, day by day, there came as on the wings
Of startled winds from o'er the Spanish Main,
Strange echoes as of sacked and clamouring ports
And battered gates of fabulous golden cities,
A murmur out of the sunset of Peru,
A sea-bird's wail from Lima.   While no less
The wrathful menace gathered up its might
All round our little isle; till now the King
Philip of Spain half secretly decreed
The building of huge docks from which to launch
A Fleet Invincible that should sweep the seas
Of all the world, throttle with one broad grasp
All Protestant rebellion, having stablished
His red feet in the Netherlands, thence to hurl
His whole World-Empire at this little isle,
England, our mother, home and hope and love,
And bend her neck beneath his yoke.   For now
No half surrender sought he.   At his back,
Robed with the scarlet of a thousand martyrs,
Admonishing him, stood Rome, and, in her hand,

Grasping the Cross of Christ by its great hilt,
She pointed it, like a dagger, tow'rds the throat
Of England.

               One long year, two years had passed
Since Drake set sail from grey old Plymouth Sound;
And in those woods of faery wonder still
Slumbered his love in steadfast faith. But now
With louder lungs her father urged—"He is dead:
Forget him. There is one that loves you, seeks
Your hand in marriage, and he is a goodly match
E'en for my daughter. You shall wed him, Bess!"
But when the new-found lover came to woo,
Glancing in summer silks and radiant hose,
Whipt doublet and enormous pointed shoon,
She played him like a fish and sent him home
Spluttering with dismay, a stickleback
Discoloured, a male minnow of dimpled streams
With all his rainbows paling in the prime,
To hide amongst his lilies, while once more
She took her casement seat that overlooked
The sea and read in Master Spenser's book,
Which Francis gave "To my dear lady and queen
Bess," that most rare processional of love—
"*Sweet Thames, run softly till I end my song!*"
Yet did her father urge her day by day,
And day by day her mother dinned her ears
With petty saws, as—"When *I* was a girl,"
And "I remember what *my* father said,"
And "Love, oh feather-fancies plucked from geese
You call your poets!" Yet she hardly meant
To slight true love, save in her daughter's heart;
For the old folk ever find it hard to see
The passion of their children. When it wakes,
The child becomes a stranger. So with Bess;
But since her soul still slumbered, and the moons
Rolled on and blurred her soul's particular love
With the vague unknown impulse of her youth,
Her brave resistance often melted now
In tears, and her will weakened day by day;
Till on a dreadful summer morn there came,

Borne by a wintry flaw, home to the Thames,
A bruised and battered ship, all that was left,
So said her crew, of Drake's ill-fated fleet.
John Wynter, her commander, told the tale
Of how the *Golden Hynde* and *Marygold*
Had by the wind Euroclydon been driven
Sheer o'er the howling edges of the world;
Of how himself by God's good providence
Was hurled into the strait Magellanus;
Of how on the horrible frontiers of the Void
He had watched in vain, lit red with beacon-fires
The desperate coasts o' the black abyss, whence none
Ever returned, though many a week he watched
Beneath the Cross; and only saw God's wrath
Burn through the heavens and devastate the mountains,
And hurl unheard of oceans roaring down
After the lost ships in one cataract
Of thunder and splendour and fury and rolling doom.

Then, with a bitter triumph in his face,
As if this were the natural end of all
Such vile plebeians, as if he had foreseen it,
As if himself had breathed a tactful hint
Into the aristocratic ears of God,
Her father broke the last frail barriers down,
Broke the poor listless will o' the lonely girl,
Who careless now of aught but misery
Promised to wed their lordling.   Mighty speed
They made to press that loveless marriage on;
And ere the May had mellowed into June
Her marriage eve had come.   Her cold hands held
Drake's gift.   She scarce could see her name, writ broad
By that strong hand as it was, *To my queen Bess.*
She looked out through her casement o'er the sea,
Listening its old enchanted moan, which seemed
Striving to speak, she knew not what.   Its breath
Fluttered the roses round the grey old walls,
And shook the ghostly jasmine.   A great moon
Hung like a red lamp in the sycamore.
A corn-crake in the hay-fields far away
Chirped like a cricket, and the night-jar churred

His passionate love-song. Soft-winged moths besieged
Her lantern. Under many a star-stabbed elm
The nightingale began his golden song,
Whose warm thick notes are each a drop of blood
From that small throbbing breast against the thorn
Pressed close to turn the white rose into red;
Even as her lawn-clad may-white bosom pressed
Quivering against the bars, while her dark hair
Streamed round her shoulders and her small bare feet
Gleamed in the dusk. Then spake she to her maid—
"I cannot sleep, I cannot sleep to-night.
Bring thy lute hither and sing. Alison, think you
The dead can watch us from their distant world?
Can our dead friends be near us when we weep?
I wish 'twere so! for then my love would come,
No matter then how far, my love would come,
And he'd forgive me."

Then Bess bowed down her lovely head: her breast
Heaved with short sobs , sickening at the heart,
She grasped the casement moaning, "Love, Love, Love,
Come quickly, come, before it is too late,
Come quickly, oh come quickly."
                              Then her maid
Slipped a soft arm around her and gently drew
The supple quivering body, shaken with sobs,
And all that firm young, sweetness to her breast,
And led her to her couch, and all night long
She watched beside her, till the marriage morn
Blushed in the heartless East. Then swiftly flew
The pitiless moments, till—as in a dream—
And borne along by dreams, or like a lily
Cut from its anchorage in the stream to glide
Down the smooth bosom of an unknown world
Through fields of unknown blossom, so moved Bess
Amongst her maids, as the procession passed
Forth to the little church upon the cliffs,
And, as in those days was the bridal mode,
Her lustrous hair in billowing beauty streamed
Dishevelled o'er her shoulders, while the sun
Caressed her bent and glossy head, and shone

Over the deep blue, white-flaked, wrinkled sea,
On full-blown rosy-petalled sails that flashed
Like flying blossoms fallen from her crown.

BOOK V

I

With the fruit of Aladdin's garden clustering thick in her hold,
With rubies awash in her scuppers and her bilge ablaze with
        gold,
A world in arms behind her to sever her heart from home,
The Golden Hynde *drove onward over the glittering foam.*

II

If we go as we came, by the Southward, we meet wi' the fleets o'
        Spain!
'Tis a thousand to one against us: we'll turn to the West again.
We have captured a China pilot, his charts and his golden keys
We'll sail to the golden Gateway, over the golden seas.

OVER the immeasurable molten gold
Wrapped in a golden haze, onward they drew;
And now they saw the tiny purple quay
Grow larger and darker and brighten into brown
Across the swelling sparkle of the waves.
Brown on the quay, a train of tethered mules
Munched at the nose-bags, while a Spaniard drowsed
On guard beside what seemed at first a heap
Of fish, then slowly turned to silver bars
Up-piled and glistering in the enchanted sun.
Nor did that sentry wake as, like a dream,
The *Golden Hynde* divided the soft sleep
Of warm green lapping water, sidled up,
Sank sail, and moored beside the quay.   But Drake,
Lightly leaping ashore and stealing nigh,
Picked up the Spaniard's long gay-ribboned gun
Close to his ear.   At once, without a sound,
The watchman opened his dark eyes and stared

As at strange men who suddenly had come,
Borne by some magic carpet, from the stars;
Then, with a courtly bow, his right hand thrust
Within the lace embroideries of his breast.
Politely Drake, with pained apologies
For this disturbance of a cavalier
Napping on guard, straightway resolved to make
Complete amends, by now relieving him
Of these—which doubtless troubled his repose—
These anxious bars of silver.   With that word
Two seamen leaped ashore and, gathering up
The bars in a stout old patch of tawny sail,
Slung them aboard.   No sooner this was done
Than out o' the valley, like a foolish jest
Out of the mouth of some great John-a-dreams,
In soft procession of buffoonery
A woolly train of llamas proudly came
Stepping by two and two along the quay,
Laden with pack on pack of silver bars
And driven by a Spaniard.   His amaze
The seamen greeted with profuser thanks
For his most punctual thought and opportune
Courtesy.   None the less they must avouch
It pained them much to see a cavalier
Turned carrier; and, at once, they must insist
On easing him of that too sordid care.

  .   .   .   .

Then out from Tarapaca once again
They sailed, their hold a glimmering mine of wealth,
Towards Arica and Lima, where they deemed
The prize of prizes waited unaware.
For every year a gorgeous galleon sailed
With all the harvest of Potosi's mines
And precious stones from dead king's diadems,
Aztecs' and Incas' gem-encrusted crowns,
Pearls from the glimmering Temples of the Moon,
Rich opals with their milky rainbow-clouds,
White diamonds from the Temples of the Sun,
Carbuncles flaming scarlet, amethysts,

Rubies, and sapphires; these to Spain she brought
To glut her priestly coffers.   Now not far
Ahead they deemed she lay upon that coast,
Crammed with the lustrous Indies, wrung with threat
And torture from the naked Indian slaves.
To him that spied her top-sails first a prize
Drake offered of the wondrous chain he wore;
And every seaman, every ship-boy, watched
Not only for the prize, but for their friends,
If haply these had weathered through the storm.
Nor did they know their friends had homeward turned,
Bearing to England and to England's Queen,
And his heart's queen, the tale that Drake was dead.

Northward they cruised along a warm wild coast
That like a most luxurious goddess drowsed
Supine to heaven, her arms behind her head,
One knee up-thrust to make a mountain-peak,
Her rosy breasts up-heaving their soft snow
In distant Andes, and her naked side
With one rich curve for half a hundred leagues
Bathed by the creaming foam; her heavy hair
Fraught with the perfume of a thousand forests
Tossed round about her beauty; and her mouth
A scarlet mystery of distant flower
Up-turned to take the kisses of the sun.
But like a troop of boys let loose from school
The adventurers went by, startling the stillness
Of that voluptuous dream-encumbered shore
With echoing shouts of laughter and alien song.

But as they came to Arica, from afar
They heard the clash of bells upon the breeze,
And knew that Rumour with her thousand wings
Had rushed before them.   Horsemen in the night
Had galloped through the white coast-villages
And spread the dreadful cry "El Draque!" abroad,
And when the gay adventurers drew nigh
They found the quays deserted, and the ships
All flown, except one little fishing-boat
Wherein an old man like a tortoise moved

A wrinkled head above the rusty net
His crawling hands repaired.   He seemed to dwell
Outside the world of war and peace, outside
Everything save his daily task, and cared
No whit who else might win or lose; for all
The pilot asked of him without demur
He answered, scarcely looking from his work.
A galleon laden with eight hundred bars
Of silver, not three hours ago had flown
Northward, he muttered.   Ere the words were out,
The will of Drake thrilled through the *Golden Hynde*
Like one sharp trumpet-call, and ere they knew
What power impelled them, crowding on all sail
Northward they surged, and roaring down the wind
At Chiuli, port of Arequipa, saw
The chase at anchor.   Wondering they came
With all the gunners waiting at their guns
Bare-armed and silent—nearer, nearer yet,—
Close to the enemy.   But no sight or sound
Of living creature stirred upon her decks.
Only a great grey cat lay in the sun
Upon a warm smooth cannon-butt.   A chill
Ran through the veins of even the boldest there
At that too peaceful silence.   Cautiously
Drake neared her in his pinnace: cautiously,
Cutlass in hand, up that mysterious hull
He clomb, and wondered, as he climbed, to breathe
The friendly smell o' the pitch and hear the waves
With their incessant old familiar sound
Crackling and slapping against her windward flank.
A ship of dreams was that; for when they reached
The silent deck, they saw no crouching forms,
They heard no sound of life.   Only the hot
Creak of the cordage whispered in the sun.
The cat stood up and yawned, and slunk away
Slowly, with furtive glances.   The great hold
Was empty, and the rich cabin stripped and bare.
Suddenly one of the seamen with a cry
Pointed where, close inshore, a little boat
Stole towards the town; and, with a louder cry,
Drake bade his men aboard the *Golden Hynde*.

Scarce had they pulled two hundred yards away
When, with a roar that seemed to buffet the heavens
And rip the heart of the sea out, one red flame
Blackened with fragments, the great galleon burst
Asunder!   All the startled waves were strewn
With wreckage; and Drake laughed—"My lads, we have
          diced
With death to-day, and won!   My merry lads,
It seems that Spain is bolting with the stakes!
Now, if I have to stretch the skies for sails
And summon the blasts of God up from the South
To fill my canvas, I will overhaul
Those dusky devils with the treasure-ship
That holds our hard-earned booty.   Pull hard all,
Hard for the *Golden Hynde*."

  .   .   .   .

                                    And so they came
At dead of night on Callao de Lima!
They saw the harbour lights across the waves
Glittering, and the shadowy hulks of ships
Gathered together like a flock of sheep
Within the port.   With shouts and clink of chains
A shadowy ship was entering from the North,
And like the shadow of that shadow slipped
The *Golden Hynde* beside her thro' the gloom;
And side by side they anchored in the port
Amidst the shipping!   Over the dark tide
A small boat from the customs-house drew near.
A sleepy, yawning, gold-laced officer
Boarded the *Golden Hynde*, and with a cry,
Stumbling against a cannon-butt, he saw
The bare-armed British seamen in the gloom
All waiting by their guns.   Wildly he plunged
Over the side and urged his boat away,
Crying, "El Draque! El Draque!"   At that dread word
The darkness filled with clamour, and the ships,
Cutting their cables, drifted here and there
In mad attempts to seek the open sea.
Wild lights burnt hither and thither, and all the port,

One furnace of confusion, heaved and seethed
In terror; for each shadow of the night,
Nay, the great night itself, was all *El Draque*.
The Dragon's wings were spread from quay to quay,
The very lights that burnt from mast to mast
And flared across the tide kindled his breath
To fire; while here and there a British pinnace
Slipped softly thro' the roaring gloom and glare,
Ransacking ship by ship; for each one thought
A fleet had come upon them. Each gave up
The struggle as each was boarded; while, elsewhere,
Cannon to cannon, friends bombarded friends.

Yet not one ounce of treasure in Callao
They found; for, fourteen days before they came,
That greatest treasure-ship of Spain, with all
The gorgeous harvest of that year, had sailed
For Panama: her ballast—silver bars;
Her cargo—rubies, emeralds, and gold.

Out through the clamour and the darkness, out,
Out to the harbour mouth, the *Golden Hynde*,
Steered by the iron soul of Drake, returned:
And where the way was blocked, her cannon clove
A crimson highway to the midnight sea.
Then Northward, Northward, o'er the jewelled main,
Under the white moon like a storm they drove
In quest of the *Cacafuego*. Fourteen days
Her start was; and at dawn the fair wind sank,
And chafing lay the *Golden Hynde*, becalmed;
While, on the hills, the Viceroy of Peru
Marched down from Lima with two thousand men,
And sent out four huge ships of war to sink
Or capture the fierce Dragon. Loud laughed Drake
To see them creeping nigh, urged with great oars,
Then suddenly pause; for none would be the first
To close with him. And, ere they had steeled their hearts
To battle, a fair breeze broke out anew,
And Northward sped the little *Golden Hynde*
In quest of the lordliest treasure-ship of Spain.

. . . .

Behind her lay a world in arms; for now
Wrath and confusion clamoured for revenge
From sea to sea.   Spain claimed the pirate's head
From England, and awaited his return
With all her tortures.   And where'er he passed
He sowed the dragon's teeth, and everywhere
Cadmean broods of armèd men arose
And followed, followed on his fiery trail.
Men toiled at Lima to fit out a fleet
Grim enough to destroy him.   All night long
The flare went up from cities on the coast
Where men like naked devils toiled to cast
Cannon that might have overwhelmed the powers
Of Michael when he drave that hideous rout
Through livid chaos to the black abyss.
Small hope indeed there seemed of safe return;
But Northward sped the little *Golden Hynde*,
The world-watched midget ship of eighteen guns,
Undaunted; and upon the second dawn
Sighted a galleon, not indeed the chase,
Yet worth a pause; for out of her they took—
Embossed with emeralds large as pigeon's eggs—
A golden crucifix, with eighty pounds
In weight of gold.   The rest they left behind;
And onward, onward, to the North they flew—
A score of golden miles, a score of green,
An hundred miles, eight hundred miles of foam,
Rainbows and fire, ransacking as they went
Ship after ship for news o' the chase and gold:
Learning from every capture that they drew
Nearer and nearer.   At Truxillo, dim
And dreaming city, a-drowse with purple flowers,
She had paused, ay, paused to take a freight of gold!
At Paita—she had passed two days in front,
Only two days, two days ahead; nay, one!
At Quito, close inshore, a youthful page,
Bright-eyed, ran up the rigging and cried, "A sail!
A sail!   The *Cacafuego*!   And the chain
Is mine!"   And by the strange cut of her sails,
Whereof they had been told in Callao,
They knew her!

Heavily laden with her gems,
Lazily drifting with her golden fruitage,
Over the magic seas they saw her hull
Loom as they onward drew; but Drake, for fear
The prey might take alarm and run ashore,
Trailed wine-skins, filled with water, over the side
To hold his ship back, till the darkness fell,
And with the night the off-shore wind arose.
At last the sun sank down, the rosy light
Faded from Andes' peaked and bosomed snow:
The night-wind rose: the wine-skins were up-hauled;
And, like a hound unleashed, the *Golden Hynde*
Leapt forward thro' the gloom.

A cable's length
Divided them.   The *Cacafuego* heard
A rough voice in the darkness bidding her
Heave to!   She held her course.   Drake gave the word.
A broadside shattered the night, and over her side
Her main-yard clattered like a broken wing!
On to her decks the British sea-dogs swarmed,
Cutlass in hand: that fight was at an end.

The ship was cleared, a prize crew placed a-board,
Then both ships turned their heads to the open sea.
At dawn, being out of sight of land, they 'gan
Examine the great prize.   None ever knew
Save Drake and Gloriana what wild wealth
They had captured there.   Thus much at least was known:
An hundredweight of gold, and twenty tons
Of silver bullion; thirteen chests of coins;
Nuggets of gold unnumbered; countless pearls,
Diamonds, emeralds; but the worth of these
Was past all reckoning.   In the crimson dawn,
Ringed with the lonely pomp of sea and sky,
The naked-footed seamen bathed knee-deep
In gold and gathered up Aladdin's fruit—
All-colored gems—and tossed them in the sun.
The hold like one great elfin orchard gleamed
With dusky globes and tawny glories piled,
Hesperian apples, heap on mellow heap,
Rich with the hues of sunset, rich and ripe
22

And ready for the enchanted cider-press;
An Emperor's ransom in each burning orb;
A kingdom's purchase in each clustered bough;
The freedom of all slaves in every chain.

BOOK VI

Now like the soul of Ophir on the sea
Glittered the *Golden Hynde*, and all her heart
Turned home to England.   As a child that finds
A ruby ring upon the highway, straight
Homeward desires to run with it, so she
Yearned for her home and country.   Yet the world
Was all in arms behind her.   Fleet on fleet
Awaited her return.   Along the coast
The very churches melted down their chimes
And cast them into cannon.   To the South
A thousand cannon watched Magellan's straits,
And fleets were scouring all the sea like hounds,
With orders that where'er they came on Drake,
Although he were the Dragon of their dreams,
They should out-blast his thunders and convey,
Dead or alive, his body back to Spain.

And Drake laughed out and said, "My trusty lads
Of Devon, you have made the wide world ring
With England's name; you have swept one half the seas
From sky to sky; and in our oaken hold
You have packed the gorgeous Indies.   We shall sail
But slowly with such wealth.   If we return,
We are one against ten thousand!   We will seek
The fabled Northern passage, take our gold
Safe home; then out to sea again and try
Our guns against their guns."

                .   .   .   .

                              And as they sailed
Northward, they swooped on warm blue Guatulco
For food and water.   Nigh the dreaming port

The grand alcaldes in high conclave sat,
Blazing with gold and scarlet, as they tried
A batch of negro slaves upon the charge
Of idleness in Spanish mines; dumb slaves,
With bare scarred backs and labour-broken knees,
And sorrowful eyes like those of wearied kine
Spent from the ploughing. Even as the judge
Rose to condemn them to the knotted lash
The British boat's crew, quiet and compact,
Entered the court. The grim judicial glare
Grew wider with amazement, and the judge
Staggered against his gilded throne.
        "I thank
Almighty God," cried Drake, "who hath given me this
—That I who once, in ignorance, procured
Slaves for the golden bawdy-house of Spain,
May now, in England's name, help to requite
That wrong. For now I say in England's name,
Where'er her standard flies, the slave shall stand
Upright, the shackles fall from off his limbs.
Unyoke the prisoners: tell them they are men
Once more, not beasts of burden. Set them free;
But take these gold and scarlet popinjays
Aboard my *Golden Hynde;* and let them write
An order that their town shall now provide
My boats with food and water."
        This being done,
The slaves being placed in safety on the prize,
The *Golden Hynde* revictualled and the casks
Replenished with fresh water, Drake set free
The judges and swept Northward once again;
And, off the coast of Nicaragua, found
A sudden treasure better than all gold;
For on the track of the China trade they caught
A ship whereon two China pilots sailed,
And in their cabin lay the secret charts,
Red hieroglyphs of Empire, unknown charts
Of silken sea-roads down the golden West
Where all roads meet and East and West are one.
And, with that mystery stirring in their hearts
Like a strange cry from home, Northward they swept

And Northward, till the soft luxurious coasts
Hardened, the winds grew bleak, the great green waves
Loomed high like mountains round them, and the spray
Froze on their spars and yards.   Fresh from the warmth
Of tropic seas the men could hardly brook
That cold; and when the floating hills of ice
Like huge green shadows crowned with ghostly snow
Went past them with strange whispers in the gloom,
Or took mysterious colours in the dawn,
Their hearts misgave them, and they found no way;
But all was iron shore and icy sea.
And one by one the crew fell sick to death
In that fierce winter, and the land still ran
Westward and showed no passage.   Tossed with storms,
Onward they plunged, or furrowed gentler tides
Of ice-lit emerald that made the prow
A faery beak of some enchanted ship
Flinging wild rainbows round her as she drove
Thro' seas unsailed by mortal mariners,
Past isles unhailed of any human voice,
Where sound and silence mingled in one song
Of utter solitude.   Ever as they went
The flag of England blazoned the broad breeze,
Northward, where never ship had sailed before,
Northward, till lost in helpless wonderment,
Dazed as a soul awakening from the dream
Of death to some wild dawn in Paradise
(Yet burnt with cold as they whose very tears
Freeze on their faces where Cocytus wails)
All world-worn, bruised, wing-broken, wracked, and wrenched,
Blackened with lightning, scarred as with evil deeds,
But all embalmed in beauty by that sun
Which never sets, bosomed in peace at last
The *Golden Hynde* rocked on a glittering calm.
Seas that no ship had ever sailed, from sky
To glistening sky, swept round them.   Glory and gleam,
Glamour and lucid rapture and diamond air
Embraced her broken spars, begrimed with gold
Her gloomy hull, rocking upon a sphere
New made, it seemed, mysterious with the first
Mystery of the world, where holy sky

And sacred sea shone like the primal Light
Of God, a-stir with whispering sea-bird's wings
And glorious with clouds. Only, all day,
All night, the rhythmic utterance of His will
In the deep sigh of seas that washed His throne,
Rose and relapsed across Eternity,
Timed to the pulse of æons. All their world
Seemed strange as unto us the great new heavens
And glittering shores, if on some aery bark
To Saturn's coasts we came and traced no more
The tiny gleam of our familiar earth
Far off, but heard tremendous oceans roll
Round unimagined continents, and saw
Terrible mountains unto which our Alps
Were less than mole-hills, and such gaunt ravines
Cleaving them and such cataracts roaring down
As burst the gates of our earth-moulded senses,
Pour the eternal glory on our souls,
And, while ten thousand chariots bring the dawn,
Hurl us poor midgets trembling to our knees.
Glory and glamour and rapture of lucid air,
Ice cold, with subtle colours of the sky
Embraced her broken spars, belted her hulk
With brilliance, while she dipped her jacinth beak
In waves of mounded splendour, and sometimes
A great ice-mountain flashed and floated by
Throned on the waters, pinnacled and crowned
With all the smouldering jewels in the world;
Or in the darkness, glimmering berg on berg,
All emerald to the moon, went by like ghosts
Whispering to the South.

      There, as they lay,
Waiting a wind to fill the stiffened sails,
Their hearts remembered that in England now
The Spring was nigh, and in that lonely sea
The skilled musicians filled their eyes with home.

SONG

I

It is the Spring-tide now!
Under the hawthorn-bough
  The milkmaid goes:
Her eyes are violets blue
Washed with the morning dew,
  Her mouth a rose.
    It is the Spring-tide now.

II

The lanes are growing sweet,
The lambkins frisk and bleat
  In all the meadows:
The glossy dappled kine
Blink in the warm sunshine,
  Cooling their shadows.
    It is the Spring-tide now.

III

Soon hand in sunburnt hand
Thro' God's green fairyland,
  England, our home,
Whispering as they stray
Adown the primrose way,
  Lovers will roam.
    It is the Spring-tide now.

And then, with many a chain of linkèd sweetness,
Harmonious gold, they drew their hearts and souls
Back, back to England, thoughts of wife and child
Mother and sweetheart and the old companions,
The twisted streets of London and the deep
Delight of Devon lanes, all softly voiced
In words or cadences, made them breathe hard
And gaze across the everlasting sea,
Craving for that small isle so far away.

SONG

I

O, you beautiful land,
  Deep-bosomed with beeches and bright
    With the flowery largesse of May
Sweet from the palm of her hand
  Out-flung, till the hedges grew white
    As the green-arched billows with spray.

II

White from the fall of her feet
  The daisies awake in the sun!
    Cliff-side and valley and plain
With the breath of the thyme growing sweet
  Laugh, for the Spring is begun;
    And Love hath turned homeward again.

  O, you beautiful land!

III

Where should the home be of Love,
  But there, where the hawthorn-tree blows,
    And the milkmaid trips out with her pail,
And the skylark in heaven above
  Sings, till the West is a rose
    And the East is a nightingale?

  O, you beautiful land!

IV

There where the sycamore trees
  Are shading the satin-skinned kine,
    And oaks, whose brethren of old
Conquered the strength of the seas,
  Grow broad in the sunlight and shine
    Crowned with their cressets of gold;

  O, you beautiful land!

V

Deep-bosomed with beeches and bright
  With rose-coloured cloudlets above;
    Billowing broad and grand
Where the meadows with blossom are white
  For the foot-fall, the foot-fall of Love.
    O, you beautiful land!

VI

How should we sing of thy beauty,
  England, mother of men,
    We that can look in thine eyes
And see there the splendour of duty
  Deep as the depth of their ken,
    Wide as the ring of thy skies.

VII

O, you beautiful land,
  Deep-bosomed with beeches and bright
    With the flowery largesse of May
Sweet from the palm of her hand
  Out-flung, till the hedges grew white
    As the green-arched billows with spray.

    O, you beautiful land!

And when a fair wind rose again, there seemed
No hope of passage by that fabled way
Northward, and suddenly Drake put down his helm
And, with some wondrous purpose in his eyes,
Turned Southward once again, until he found
A lonely natural harbour on the coast
Near San Francisco, where the cliffs were white
Like those of England, and the soft soil teemed
With gold.   There they careened the *Golden Hynde*—

Her keel being thick with barnacles and weeds—
And built a fort and dockyard to refit
Their little wandering home, not half so large
As many a coasting barque to-day that scarce
Would cross the Channel, yet she had swept the seas
Of half the world, and even now prepared
For new adventures greater than them all.
And as the sound of chisel and hammer broke
The stillness of that shore, shy figures came,
Keen-faced and grave-eyed Indians, from the woods
To bow before the strange white-faced newcomers
As gods. Whereat the chaplain all aghast
Persuaded them with signs and broken words
And grunts that even Drake was but a man,
Whom none the less the savages would crown
With woven flowers and barbarous ritual
King of New Albion—so the seamen called
That land, remembering the white cliffs of home.
Much they implored, with many a sign and cry,
Which by the rescued slaves upon the prize
Were part interpreted, that Drake would stay
And rule them; and the vision of the great
Empire of Englishmen arose and flashed
A moment round them, on that lonely shore.
A small and weather-beaten band they stood,
Bronzed seamen by the laughing rescued slaves,
Ringed with gigantic loneliness and saw
An Empire that should liberate the world;
A Power before the lightning of whose arms
Darkness should die and all oppression cease;
A Federation of the strong and weak,
Whereby the weak were strengthened and the strong
Made stronger in the increasing good of all;
A gathering up of one another's loads;
A turning of the wasteful rage of war
To accomplish large and fruitful tasks of peace,
Even as the strength of some great stream is turned
To grind the corn for bread. E'en thus on England
That splendour dawned which those in dreams foresaw
And saw not with their living eyes, but thou,
England, mayst lift up eyes at last and see,

Who, like that angel of the Apocalypse
Hast set one foot upon thy sea-girt isle,
The other upon the waters, and canst raise
Now, if thou wilt, above the assembled nations,
The trumpet of deliverance to thy lips.

.   .   .   .

At last their task was done, the *Golden Hynde*
Undocked, her white wings hoisted; and away
Westward they swiftly glided from the shore
Where, with a wild lament, their Indian friends,
Knee-deep i' the creaming foam, all stood at gaze,
Like men that for one moment in their lives
Have seen a mighty drama cross their path
And played upon the stage of vast events
Knowing, henceforward, all their life is nought.
But Westward sped the little *Golden Hynde*
Across the uncharted ocean, with no guide
But that great homing cry of all their hearts.
Far out of sight of land they steered, straight out
Across the great Pacific, in those days
When even the compass proved no trusty guide,
Straight out they struck in that small bark, straight out
Week after week, without one glimpse of aught
But heaving seas, across the uncharted waste
Straight to the sunset.   Laughingly they sailed,
With all that gorgeous booty in their holds,
A splendour dragging deep through seas of doom,
A prey to the first great hurricane that blew
Except their God averted it.   And still
Their skilled musicians cheered the way along
To shores beyond the sunset and the sea.
And oft at nights, the yellow fo'c'sle lanthorn
Swung over swarthy singing faces grouped
Within the four small wooden walls that made
Their home and shut them from the unfathomable
Depths of mysterious gloom without that rolled
All around them; or Tom Moone would heartily troll
A simple stave that struggled oft with thoughts
Beyond its reach, yet reached their hearts no less.

SONG

I

Good luck befall you, mariners all
That sail this world so wide!
Whither we go, not yet we know:
We steer by wind and tide.
Be it right or wrong, I sing this song;
For now it seems to me
Men steer their souls thr.' rocks and shoals
As mariners use by sea.

Chorus: *As mariners use by sea,*
My lads,
As mariners use by sea!

II

And now they plough to windward, now
They drive before the gale!
Now are they hurled across the world
With torn and tattered sail;
Yet, as they will, they steer and still
Defy the world's rude glee:
Till death o'erwhelm them, mast and helm,
They ride and rule the sea.

Chorus: *They ride and rule the sea,*
My lads,
They ride and rule the sea!

. . . .

Meantime, in England, Bess of Sydenham,
Drake's love and queen, being told that Drake was dead,
And numbed with grief, obeying her father's will
That dreadful summer morn in bridal robes
Had passed to wed her father's choice.   The sun
Streamed smiling on her as she went, half-dazed,
Amidst her smiling maids.   Nigh to the sea

The church was, and the mellow marriage bells
Mixed with its music.   Far away, white sails
Spangled the sapphire, white as flying blossoms
New-fallen from her crown; but as the glad
And sad procession neared the little church,
From some strange ship-of-war, far out at sea,
There came a sudden tiny puff of smoke—
And then a dull strange throb, a whistling hiss,
And scarce a score of yards away a shot
Ploughed up the turf.   None knew, none ever knew
From whence it came, whether a perilous jest
Of English seamen, or a wanton deed
Of Spaniards, or mere accident; but all
Her maids in flight were scattered.   Bess awoke
As from a dream, crying aloud—" 'Tis he,
'Tis he that sends this message.   He is not dead.
I will not pass the porch.   Come home with me.
'Twas he that sent that message."
                                        Nought availed,
Her father's wrath, her mother's tears, her maids'
Cunning persuasions, nought; home she returned,
And waited for the dead to come to life;
Nor waited long; for ere that month was out,
Rumour on rumour reached the coasts of England,
Borne as it seemed on sea-birds' wings, that Drake
Was on his homeward way.

BOOK VII

THE imperial wrath of Spain, one world-wide sea
Of furious pomp and flouted power, now surged
All round this little isle, with one harsh roar
Deepening for Drake's return—"The *Golden Hynde*
Ye swore had foundered, Drake ye swore was drowned;
They are on their homeward way!   The head of Drake!
What answer, what account, what recompense
Now can ye yield our might invincible
Except the head of Drake, whose bloody deeds
Have reddened the Pacific, who hath sacked
Cities of gold, burnt fleets, and ruined realms,
What answer but his life?"

                        To which the Queen
Who saw the storm of Europe slowly rising
In awful menace o'er her wave-beat throne,
And midmost of the storm, the ensanguined robes
Of Rome and murderous hand, grasping the Cross
By its great hilt, pointing it like a brand
Blood-blackened at the throat of England, saw
Like skeleton castles wrapt in rolling mist
The monstrous engines and designs of war,
The secret fleets and brooding panoplies
Philip prepared, growing from day to day
In dusk armipotent and embattled gloom
Surrounding her, replied: "The life of Drake,
If, on our strict enquiry, in due order
We find that Drake have hurt our friends, mark well,
If Drake have hurt our friends, the life of Drake."

     .   .   .   .   .   .

And while the world awaited him, as men
Might wait an earthquake, quietly one grey morn,
One grey October morn of mist and rain
When all the window-panes in Plymouth dripped
With listless drizzle, and only through her streets
Rumbled the death-cart with its dreary bell
Monotonously plangent (for the plague
Had lately like a vampire sucked the veins
Of Plymouth town), a little weed-clogged ship,
Grey as a ghost, glided into the Sound
And anchored, scarce a soul to see her come,
And not an eye to read the faded scroll
Around her battered prow—the *Golden Hynde*.
Then, thro' the dumb grey misty listless port,
A rumour like the colours of the dawn
Streamed o'er the shining quays, up the wet streets,
In at the tavern doors, flashed from the panes
And turned them into diamonds, fired the pools
In every muddy lane with Spanish gold,
Flushed in a thousand faces, Drake is come!
Down every crowding alley the urchins leaped
Tossing their caps, the *Golden Hynde* is come!

Fisherman, citizen, prentice, dame and maid,
Fat justice, floury baker, bloated butcher,
Fishwife, minister and apothecary,
Yea, even the driver of the death-cart, leaving
His ghastly load, using his dreary bell
To merrier purpose, down the seething streets,
Panting, tumbling, jostling, helter-skelter
To the water-side, to the water-side they rushed,
And some knee-deep beyond it, all one wild
Welcome to Francis Drake!
Wild kerchiefs fluttering, thunderous hurrahs
Rolling from quay to quay, a thousand arms
Outstretched to that grey ghostly little ship
At whose masthead the British flag still flew;
Then, over all, in one tumultuous tide
Of pealing joy, the Plymouth bells outclashed
A nation's welcome home to Francis Drake.

The very *Golden Hynde*, no idle dream,
The little ship that swept the Spanish Main,
Carelessly lying there, in Plymouth Sound,
The *Golden Hynde*, the wonder of the world,
A glory wrapt her greyness, and no boat
Dared yet approach, save one, with Drake's close friends,
Who came to warn him: "England stands alone
And Drake is made the price of England's peace.
The Queen, perforce, must temporise with Spain,
The Invincible! She hath forfeited thy life
To Spain, against her will. Only by this
Rejection of thee as a privateer
She averted instant war; for now the menace
Of Spain draws nigher, looms darker every hour.
The world is made Spain's footstool. Philip, the King,
E'en now hath added to her boundless power
Without a blow, the vast domains and wealth
Of Portugal, and deadlier yet, a coast
That crouches over against us. Cadiz holds
A huge Armada, none knows where to strike;
And even this day a flying horseman brought
Rumours that Spain hath landed a great force
In Ireland. Mary of Scotland only waits

The word to stab us in the side for Rome.
The Queen, weighed down by Burleigh and the friends
Of peace at any cost, may yet be driven
To make thy life our ransom, which indeed
She hath already sworn, or seemed to swear."

To whom Drake answered, "Gloriana lives;
And in her life mine only fear lies dead,
Mine only fear, for England, not myself.
Willing am I and glad, as I have lived,
To die for England's sake.
Yet, lest the Queen be driven now to restore
This cargo that I bring her—a world's wealth,
The golden springs of all the power of Spain,
The jewelled hearts of all those cruel realms
(For I have plucked them out) beyond the sea;
Lest she be driven to yield them up again
For Spain and Spain's delight, I will warp out
Behind St. Nicholas' Island.   The fierce plague
In Plymouth shall be colour and excuse,
Until my courier return from court
With Gloriana's will.   If it be death,
I'll out again to sea, strew its rough floor
With costlier largesses than kings can throw,
And, ere I die, will singe the Spaniard's beard
And set the fringe of his imperial robe
Blazing along his coasts.   Then let him roll
His galleons round the little *Golden Hynde*,
Bring her to bay, if he can, on the high seas,
Ring us about with thousands, we'll not yield,
I and my *Golden Hynde*, we will go down,
With flag still flying on the last stump left us
And all my cannon spitting out the fires
Of everlasting scorn into his face."

So Drake warped out the *Golden Hynde* anew
Behind St. Nicholas' Island.   She lay there,
The small grey-golden centre of the world
That raged all round her, the last hope, the star
Of Protestant freedom, she, the outlawed ship
Holding within her the great head and heart

Of England's ocean power; and all the fleets
That have enfranchised earth, in that small ship,
Lay waiting for their doom.

                              Past her at night
Fisher-boats glided, wondering as they heard
In the thick darkness the great songs they deemed
Must oft have risen from many a lonely sea;
For oft had Spaniards brought a rumour back
Of that strange pirate who in royal state
Sailed to a sound of violins, and dined
With skilled musicians round him, turning all
Battle and storm and death into a song.

SONG

The same Sun is o'er us,
    The same Love shall find us,
        The same and none other
            Wherever we be;
With the same hope before us,
    The same home behind us,
        England, our mother,
            Ringed round with the sea.

No land in the ring of it
    Now, all around us
        Only the splendid
            Re-surging unknown;
How should we sing of it,
    This that hath found us
        By the great stars attended
            At midnight, alone?

Our highway none knoweth,
    Yet our blood hath discerned it!
        Clear, clear is our path now
            Whose foreheads are free
Where the hurricane bloweth
    Our spirits have learned it,
        'Tis the highway of wrath, now,
            The storm's way, the sea.

When the waters lay breathless
   Gazing at Hesper
     Guarding that glorious
      Fruitage of gold,
Heard we the deathless
   Wonderful whisper
     We follow, victorious
      To-night, as of old.

Ah, the broad miles of it
   White with the onset
     Of waves without number
      Warring for glee;
Ah, the soft smiles of it
   Down to the sunset,
     Sacred for slumber
      The swan's bath, the sea!

When the breakers charged thundering
   In thousands all round us
     With a lightning of lances
      Up-hurtled on high,
When the stout ships were sundering
   A rapture hath crowned us
     Like the wild light that dances
      On the crests that flash by.

Our highway none knoweth,
   Yet our blood hath discerned it!
     Clear, clear is our path now
      Whose foreheads are free,
Where Euroclydon bloweth
   Our spirits have learned it,
     'Tis the highway of wrath, now,
      The storm's way, the sea!

Who now will follow us
   Where England's flag leadeth us,
     Where gold not inveigles,
      Nor statesmen betray?

Tho' the deep midnight swallow us
Let her cry when she needeth us,
We return, her sea-eagles,
The hurricane's way.

For the same Sun is o'er us,
The same Love shall find us,
The same and none other
Wherever we be;
With the same hope before us,
The same home behind us,
England, our mother,
Ringed round with the sea.

So six days passed, and on the seventh returned
The courier, with a message from the Queen
Summoning Drake to court, bidding him bring
Also such curious trifles of his voyage
As might amuse her, also be of good cheer
She bade him, and rest well content his life
In Gloriana's hands were safe: so Drake
Laughingly landed with his war-bronzed crew
Amid the wide-eyed throng on Plymouth beach
And loaded twelve big pack-horses with pearls
Beyond all price, diamonds, crosses of gold,
Rubies that smouldered once for Aztec kings,
And great dead Incas' gem-encrusted crowns.
Also, he said, we'll add a sack or twain
Of gold doubloons, pieces of eight, moidores,
And such-like Spanish trash, for those poor lords
At court, lilies that toil not neither spin,
Wherefore, methinks their purses oft grow lean
In these harsh times. 'Twere even as well their tongues
Wagged in our favour, now, as in our blame.

.   .   .   .

Six days thereafter a fearful whisper reached
Mendoza, plenipotentiary of Spain
In London, that the pirate Drake was now
In secret conference with the Queen, nay more,

That he, the Master-thief of the golden world,
Drake, even he, that bloody buccaneer,
Had six hours' audience with her Majesty
Daily, nay more, walked with her in her garden
Alone, among the fiery Autumn leaves,
Talking of God knows what, and suddenly
The temporizing diplomatic voice
Of caution he was wont to expect from England
And blandly accept as his imperial due
Changed to a ringing key of firm resolve,
Resistance, nay, defiance. For when he came
Demanding audience of the Queen, behold,
Her officers of state with mouths awry
Informed the high ambassador of Spain,
Despite his pomp and circumstance, the Queen
Could not receive him, being in conference
With some rough seaman, pirate, what you will,
A fellow made of bronze, a buccaneer,
Maned like a lion, bearded like a pard,
With hammered head, clamped jaws, and great deep eyes
That burned with fierce blue colours of the brine,
And liked not Spain—Drake! 'Twas the very name,
One Francis Drake! a Titan that had stood,
Thundering commands against the thundering heavens,
On lightning-shattered, storm-swept decks and drunk
Great draughts of glory from the rolling sea,
El Draque! El Draque! Nor could she promise aught
To Spain's ambassador, nor see his face
Again, while yet one Spanish musketeer
Remained in Ireland.
                        Vainly the Spaniard raged
Of restitution, recompense; for now
Had Drake brought up the little *Golden Hynde*
To London, and the rumor of her wealth
Out-topped the wild reality.   The crew
Were princes as they swaggered down the streets
In weather-beaten splendour.   Out of their doors
To wonder and stare the jostling citizens ran
When They went by; and through the length and breadth
Of England, now, the gathering glory of life
Shone like the dawn.   O'er hill and dale it streamed,

Dawn, everlasting and almighty dawn,
Making a golden pomp of every oak—
Had not its British brethren swept the seas?—
In each remotest hamlet, by the hearth,
The cart, the grey church-porch, the village pump
By meadow and mill and old manorial hall,
By turnpike and by tavern, farm and forge,
Men staved the crimson vintage of romance
And held it up against the light and drank it,
And with it drank confusion to the wrath
That menaced England, but eternal honour,
While blood ran in their veins, to Francis Drake.

BOOK VIII

MEANWHILE, young Bess of Sydenham, the queen
Of Drake's deep heart, emprisoned in her home,
Fenced by her father's angry watch and ward
Lest he—the poor plebeian dread of Spain,
Shaker of nations, king of the untamed seas—
Might win some word with her, sweet Bess, the flower
Triumphant o'er their rusty heraldries,
Waited her lover, as in ancient tales
The pale princess from some grey wizard's tower
Midmost the deep sigh of enchanted woods
Looks for the starry flash of her knight's shield;
Or on the further side o' the magic West
Sees pushing through the ethereal golden gloom
Some blurred black prow, with loaded colours coarse,
Clouded with sunsets of a mortal sea,
And rich with earthly crimson.   She, with lips
Apart, still waits the shattering golden thrill
When it shall grate the coasts of Fairyland.

Only, to Bess of Sydenham, there came
No sight or sound to break that frozen spell
And lonely watch, no message from her love,
Or none that reached her restless helpless hands.
Only the general rumour of the world
Borne to her by the gossip of her maid

Kept the swift pictures passing through her brain
Of how the *Golden Hynde* was hauled ashore
At Deptford through a sea of exultation,
And by the Queen's command was now set up
For an everlasting memory!
Of how the Queen with subtle statecraft still
Kept Spain at arm's-length, dangling, while she played
At fast and loose with France, whose embassy,
Arriving with the marriage-treaty, found
(And trembled at her daring, since the wrath
Of Spain seemed, in their eyes, to flake with foam
The storm-beat hulk) a gorgeous banquet spread
To greet them on that very *Golden Hynde*
Which sacked the Spanish main, a gorgeous feast,
The like of which old England had not seen
Since the bluff days of boisterous king Hal,
Great shields of brawn with mustard, roasted swans,
Haunches of venison, roasted chines of beef,
And chewets baked, big olive-pyes thereto,
And sallets mixed with sugar and cinnamon,
White wine, rose-water, and candied eringoes.
There, on the outlawed ship, whose very name
Rang like a blasphemy in the imperial ears
Of Spain (its every old worm-eaten plank
Being scored with scorn and courage that not storm
Nor death, nor all their Inquisition racks,
The white-hot irons and bloody branding whips
That scarred the backs of Rome's pale galley-slaves,
Her captured English seamen, ever could daunt),
There with huge Empires waiting for one word,
One breath of colour and excuse, to leap
Like wolves at the naked throat of her small isle,
There in the eyes of the staggered world she stood,
Great Gloriana, while the live decks reeled
With flash of jewels and flush of rustling silks,
She stood with Drake, the corsair, and her people
Surged like a sea around. There did she give
Open defiance with her agate smile
To Spain. "Behold this pirate, now," she cried,
"Whose head my Lord, the Invincible, Philip of Spain
Demands from England. Kneel down, Master Drake,

Kneel down; for now have I this gilded sword
Wherewith to strike it off.   Nay, thou my lord
Ambassador of France, since I be woman,
And squeamish at the sight of blood, give thou
The accolade."   With that jest she gave the hilt
(Thus, even in boldness, playing a crafty part,
And dangling France before the adventurous deed)
To Marchaumont; and in the face of Europe,
With that huge fleet in Cadiz and the whole
World-power of Spain crouching around her isle,
Knighted the master-thief of the unknown world,
Sir Francis Drake.

                 And then the rumour came
Of vaster privateerings planned by Drake
Against the coasts of Philip; but held in check
And fretting at the leash, as ever the Queen
Clung to her statecraft, while Drake's enemies
Worked in the dark against him.   Spain had set
An emperor's ransom on his life.   At home
John Doughty, treacherous brother of that traitor
Who met his doom by Drake's own hand, intrigued
With Spain abroad and Spain's dark emissaries
At home to avenge his brother.   Burleigh still
Beset Drake's path with pitfalls: treacherous greed
For Spain's blood-money daggered all the dark
Around him, and John Doughty without cease
Sought to make use of all; until, by chance,
Drake gat the proof of treasonable intrigue
With Spain, against him, up to the deadly hilt,
And hurled him into the Tower.

                      Many a night
She sat by that old casement nigh the sea
And heard its ebb and flow.   With soul erect
And splendid now she waited, yet there came
No message; and, she thought, he hath seen at last
My little worth.   And when her maiden sang,
With white throat throbbing softly in the dusk
And fingers gently straying o'er the lute,
As was her wont at twilight, some old song
Of high disdainful queens and lovers pale
Pining a thousand years before their feet.

She thought, "O, if my lover loved me yet
My heart would break for joy to welcome him:
Perchance his true pride will not let him come
Since false pride barred him out"; and yet again
She burned with shame, thinking, "to him such pride
Were matter for a jest. Ah no, he hath seen
My little worth."   Even so, one night she sat,
One dark rich summer night, thinking him far
Away, wrapped in the multitudinous cares
Of one that seemed the steersman of the State
Now, thro' the storm of Europe; while her maid
Sang to the lute, and soft sea-breezes brought
Wreathed scents and sighs of secret waves and flowers
Warm through the casement's muffling jasmine bloom.

SONG

I

Nymphs and naiads, come away,
Love lies dead!
Cover the cast-back golden head,
Cover the lovely limbs with may,
And with fairest boughs of green,
And many a rose-wreathed briar spray;
But let no hateful yew be seen
Where Love lies dead.

II

Let not the queen that would not hear,
(Love lies dead!)
Or beauty that refused to save.
Exult in one dejected tear;
But gather the glory of the year,
The pomp and glory of the year,
The triumphing glory of the year,
And softly, softly, softly shed
Its light and fragrance round the grave
Where Love lies dead.

The song ceased.   Far away the great sea slept,
And all was very still.   Only hard by
One bird-throat poured its passion through the gloom,
And the whole night breathlessly listened.

                                        A twig
Snapped, the song ceased, the intense dumb night was all
One passion of expectation—as if that song
Were prelude, and ere long the heavens and earth
Would burst into one great triumphant psalm.
The song ceased only as if that small bird-throat
Availed no further.   Would the next great chord
Ring out from harps in flaming seraph hands
Ranged through the sky?   The night watched, breathless,
      dumb.
Bess listened.   Once again a dry twig snapped
Beneath her casement, and a face looked up,
Draining her face of blood, of sight, of life,
Whispering, a voice from far beyond the stars,
Whispering, unutterable joy, the whole
Glory of life and death in one small word—
Sweetheart!
                    The jasmine at her casement shook,
She knew no more than he was at her side,
His arms were round her, and his breath beat warm
Against her cheek.

   .   .   .   .

                    Suddenly, nigh the house,
A deep-mouthed mastiff bayed and a foot crunched
The gravel.   "Hark! they are watching for thee," she cried.
He laughed: "There's half of Europe on the watch
Outside for my poor head.   'Tis cosier here
With thee; but now"—his face grew grave, he drew
A silken ladder from his doublet—"quick,
Before yon good gamekeeper rounds the house
We must be down."   And ere the words were out
Bess reached the path, and Drake was at her side.
Then into the star-stabbed shadow of the woods
They sped, his arm around her.   Suddenly
She drew back with a cry, as four grim faces,
With hand to forelock, glimmered in their way.

Laughing she saw their storm-beat friendly smile
Welcome their doughty captain in this new
Adventure.   Far away, once more they heard
The mastiff bay; then nearer, as if his nose
Were down upon the trail; and then a cry
As of a hot pursuit.   They reached the brook,
Hurrying to the deep.   Drake lifted Bess
In his arms, and down the watery bed they splashed
To baffle the clamouring hunt.   Then out of the woods
They came, on the seaward side, and Bess, with a shiver,
Saw starlight flashing from bare cutlasses,
As the mastiff bayed still nearer.   Swiftlier now
They passed along the bare blunt cliffs and saw
The furrow ploughed by that strange cannon-shot
Which saved this hour for Bess; down to the beach
And starry foam that churned the silver gravel
Around an old black lurching boat, a strange
Grim Charon's wherry for two lovers' flight,
Guarded by old Tom Moone.   Drake took her hand,
And with one arm around her waist, her breath
Warm on his cheek for a moment, in she stepped
Daintily o'er the gunwale, and took her seat,
His throned princess, beside him at the helm,
Backed by the glittering waves, his throned princess,
With jewelled throat and glorious hair that seemed
Flashing back scents and colours to a sea
Which lived but to reflect her loveliness.

Then, all together, with their brandished oars
The seamen thrust as a heavy mounded wave
Lifted the boat; and up the flowering breast
Of the next they soared, then settled at the thwarts,
And the fierce water boiled before their blades
While with Drake's iron hand upon the helm
They plunged and ploughed across the starlit seas
To where a small black lugger at anchor swung,
Dipping her rakish brow i' the liquid moon.
Small was she, but not fangless; for Bess saw,
With half a tremor, the dumb protective grin
Of four grim guns above the tossing boat.

But ere his seamen or his sweetheart knew
What power, as of a wind, bore them along,
Anchor was up, the sails were broken out,
And as they scudded down the dim grey coast
Of a new enchanted world (for now had Love
Made all things new and strange) the skilled musicians
Upraised, at Drake's command, a song to cheer
Their midnight path across that faery sea.

SONG

I

Sweet, what is love?   'Tis not the crown of kings,
Nay, nor the fire of white seraphic wings!
Is it a child's heart leaping while he sings?
    Even so say I;
    Even so say I.

II

Love like a child around our world doth run,
Happy, happy, happy for all that God hath done,
Glad of all the little leaves dancing in the sun,
    Even so say I;
    Even so say I.

III

Sweet, what is love?   'Tis not the burning bliss
Angels know in heaven!   God blows the world a kiss
Wakes on earth a wild-rose!   Ah, who knows not this
    Even so say I;
    Even so say I.

IV

Love, love is kind!   Can it be far away,
Lost in a light that blinds our little day?
Seems it a great thing?   Sweetheart, answer nay;
    Even so say I;
    Even so say I.

V

Sweet, what is love?   The dust beneath our feet,
Whence breaks the rose and all the flowers that greet
April and May with lips and heart so sweet;
     Even so say I;
     Even so say I.

VI

Love is the dust whence Eden grew so fair,
Dust of the dust that set my lover there,
Ay, and wrought the gloriole of Eve's gold hair,
     Even so say I;
     Even so say I.

VII

Also the springing spray, the little topmost flower
Swung by the bird that sings a little hour,
Earth's climbing spray into the heaven's blue bower,
     Even so say I;
     Even so say I.

And stranger, ever stranger, grew the night
Around those twain, for whom the fleecy moon
Was but a mightier Cleopatra's pearl
Dissolving in the rich dark wine of night,
While 'mid the tenderer talk of eyes and hands
And whispered nothings, his great ocean realm
Rolled round their gloomy barge, robing its hulk
With splendours Rome and Egypt never knew.
Old ocean was his Nile, his mighty queen
An English maiden purer than the dawn,
His cause the cause of Freedom, his reward
The glory of England.   Strangely simple, then,
Simple as life and death, anguish and love,
To Bess appeared those mighty dawning dreams,
Whereby he shaped the pageant of the world
To a new purpose, strangely simple all
Those great new waking tides i' the world's great soul

That set towards the fall of tyranny
Behind a thunderous roar of ocean triumph
O'er burning ships and shattered fleets, while England
Grasped with sure hands the sceptre of the sea,
That untamed realm of Liberty which none
Had looked upon as aught but wilderness
Ere this, or even dreamed of as the seat
Of power and judgment and high sovereignty
Whereby all nations at the last should make
One brotherhood, and war should be no more.
And ever, as the vision broadened out,
The sense of some tremendous change at hand,
The approach of vast Armadas and the dawn
Of battle, reddening the diviner dawn
With clouds, confused it, till once more the song
Rang out triumphant o'er the glittering sea.

SONG

I

Ye that follow the vision
 Of the world's weal afar,
Have ye met with derision
 And the red laugh of war;
Yet the thunder shall not hurt you,
 Nor the battle-storms dismay;
Tho' the sun in heaven desert you,
 "Love will find out the way."

II

When the pulse of hope falters,
 When the fire flickers low
On your faith's crumbling altars,
 And the faithless gods go;
When the fond hope ye cherished
 Cometh, kissing, to betray;
When the last star hath perished,
 "Love will find out the way."

III

When the last dream bereaveth you,
   And the heart turns to stone,
When the last comrade leaveth you
   In the desert, alone;
With the whole world before you
   Clad in battle-array,
And the starless night o'er you,
   "Love will find out the way."

IV

Your dreamers may dream it
   The shadow of a dream,
Your sages may deem it
   A bubble on the stream;
Yet our kingdom draweth nigher
   With each dawn and every day,
Through the earthquake and the fire
   "Love will find out the way."

V

Love will find it, tho' the nations
   Rise up blind, as of old,
And the new generations
   Wage their warfares of gold;
Tho' they trample child and mother
   As red clay into the clay,
Where brother wars with brother,
   "Love will find out the way."

Dawn, ever bearing some divine increase
Of beauty, love, and wisdom round the world,
Dawn, like a wild-rose in the fields of heaven
Washed grey with dew, awoke, and found the barque
At anchor in a little land-locked bay.
A crisp breeze blew, and all the living sea
Beneath the flower-soft colours of the sky,

Now like a myriad-petalled rose and now
Innumerably scalloped into shells
Of rosy fire, with dwindling wrinkles edged
Fainter and fainter to the unruffled glow
And soft white pallor of the distant deep,
Shone with a mystic beauty for those twain
Who watched the gathering glory; and, in an hour,
Drake and sweet Bess, attended by a guard
Of four swart seamen, with bare cutlasses,
And by the faithful eyes of old Tom Moone,
Went up the rough rock-steps and twisted street
O' the small white sparkling seaport, tow'rds the church
Where, hand in hand, before God's altar they,
With steadfast eyes, did plight eternal troth,
And so were wedded.   Never a chime of bells
Had they; but as they passed from out the porch
Between the sleeping graves, a skylark soared
Above the world in an ecstasy of song,
And quivering heavenwards, lost himself in light.

BOOK IX

Now like a white-cliffed fortress England shone
Amid the mirk of chaos; for the huge
Empire of Spain was but the dusky van
Of that dread night beyond all nights and days,
Night of the last corruption of a world
Fast-bound in misery and iron, with chains
Of priest and king and feudal servitude,
Night of the fettered flesh and ravaged soul,
Night of anarchic chaos, darkening the deep,
Swallowing up cities, kingdoms, empires, gods,
With vaster gloom approaching, till the sun
Of love was blackened, the moon of faith was blood.
All round our England, our small struggling star,
Fortress of freedom, rock o' the world's desire,
Bearing at last the hope of all mankind,
The thickening darkness surged, and close at hand
Those first fierce cloudy fringes of the storm,

The Armada sails, gathered their might; and Spain
Crouched close behind them with her screaming fires
And steaming shambles, Spain, the hell-hag, crouched,
Still grasping with red hand the cross of Christ
By its great hilt, pointing it like a dagger,
Spear-head of the ultimate darkness, at the throat
Of England.   Under Philip's feet at last
Writhed all the Protestant Netherlands, dim coasts
Right over against us, whence his panoplies
Might suddenly whelm our isle.   But all night long,
On many a mountain, many a guardian height,
From Beachy Head to Skiddaw, little groups
Of seamen, torch and battle-lanthorn nigh,
Watched by the brooding unlit beacons, piled
Of sun-dried gorse, funereal peat, rough logs,
Reeking with oil, 'mid sharp scents of the sea,
Waste trampled grass and heather and close-cropped thyme,
High o'er the thundering coast, among whose rocks
Far, far below, the pacing coastguards gazed
Steadfastly seaward through the loaded dusk.
And through that deepening gloom when, as it seemed,
All England held her breath in one grim doubt,
Swift rumours flashed from North to South as runs
The lightning round a silent thunder-cloud;
And there were muttering crowds in the London streets,
And hurrying feet in the brooding Eastern ports.
All night, dark inns, gathering the country-side,
Reddened with clashing auguries of war.
All night, in the ships of Plymouth Sound, the soul
Of Francis Drake was England, and all night
Her singing seamen by the silver quays
Polished their guns and waited for the dawn.

But hour by hour that night grew deeper.   Spain
Watched, cloud by cloud, her huge Armadas grow,
Watched, tower by tower, and zone by zone, her fleets
Grapple the sky with a hundred hands and drag
Whole sea-horizons into her menacing ranks,
Joining her powers to the fierce night, while Philip
Still strove, with many a crafty word, to lull
The fears of Gloriana, till his plots

Were ripe, his armaments complete; and still
Great Gloriana took her woman's way,
Preferring ever tortuous intrigue
To battle, since the stakes had grown so great;
Now, more than ever, hoping against hope
To find some subtler means of victory;
Yet not without swift impulses to strike,
Swiftly recalled.   Blind, yet not blind, she smiled
On Mary of Scotland waiting for her throne,
A throne with many a strange dark tremor thrilled
Now as the rumoured murderous mines below
Converged towards it, mine and countermine,
Till the live earth was honeycombed with death.
Still with her agate smile, still she delayed,
Holding her pirate admiral in the leash
Till Walsingham, nay, even the hunchback Burleigh,
That crafty king of statesmen, seeing at last
The inevitable thunder-crash at hand,
Grew heart-sick with delay and ached to shatter
The tense tremendous hush that seemed to oppress
All hearts, compress all brows, load the broad night
With more than mortal menace.

                              Only once
The night was traversed with one lightning flash,
One rapier stroke from England, at the heart
Of Spain, as swiftly parried, yet no less
A fiery challenge; for Philip's hate and scorn
Growing with his Armada's growth, he lured
With promises of just and friendly trade
A fleet of English corn-ships to relieve
His famine-stricken coast.   There as they lay
Within his ports he seized them, one and all,
To fill the Armada's maw.

                              Whereat the Queen,
Passive so long, summoned great Walsingham,
And, still averse from open war, despite
The battle-hunger burning in his eyes,
With one strange swift sharp agate smile she hissed,
"Unchain *El Draque!*"

                              A lightning flash indeed
Was this; for he whose little *Golden Hynde*
With scarce a score of seamen late had scourged
The Spanish Main; he whose piratic neck
Scarcely the Queen's most wily statecraft saved
From Spain's revenge: he, privateer to the eyes
Of Spain, but England to all English hearts,
Gathered together, in all good jollity,
All help and furtherance himself could wish,
Before that moon was out, a pirate fleet
Whereof the like old ocean had not seen—
Eighteen swift cruisers, two great battleships,
With pinnaces and store-ships and a force
Of nigh three thousand men, wherewith to singe
The beard o' the King of Spain.
                                    By night they gathered
In marvellous wind-whipt inns nigh Plymouth Sound,
Not secretly as, ere the *Golden Hynde*
Burst thro' the West, that small adventurous crew
Gathered beside the Thames, tossing the phrase
"Pieces of eight" from mouth to mouth, and singing
Great songs of the rich Indies, and those tall
Enchanted galleons, red with blood and gold,
Superb with rubies, glorious as clouds,
Clouds in the sun, with mighty press of sail
Dragging the sunset out of the unknown world,
And staining all the grey old seas of Time
With rich romance; but these, though privateers,
Or secret knights on Gloriana's quest,
Recked not if round the glowing magic door
Of every inn the townsfolk grouped to hear
The storm-scarred seamen toasting Francis Drake,
Nor heeded what blithe urchin faces pressed
On each red-curtained magic casement, bright
With wild reflection of the fires within,
The fires, the glasses, and the singing lips
Lifting defiance to the powers of Spain.

SONG

Sing we the Rose,
   The flower of flowers most glorious!
Never a storm that blows
   Across our English sea,
But its heart breaks out wi' the Rose
   On England's flag victorious,
The triumphing flag that flows
   Thro' the heavens of Liberty.

Sing we the Rose,
   The flower of flowers most beautiful!
Until the world shall end
   She blossometh year by year,
Red with the blood that flows
   For England's sake, most dutiful,
Wherefore now we bend
   Our hearts and knees to her.

Sing we the Rose,
   The flower, the flower of war it is,
Where deep i' the midnight gloom
   Its waves are the waves of the sea,
And the glare of battle grows,
   And red over hulk and spar it is,
Till the grim black broadsides bloom
   With our Rose of Victory.

Sing we the Rose,
   The flower, the flower of love it is,
Which lovers aye shall sing
   And nightingales proclaim;
For O, the heaven that glows,
   That glows and burns above it is
Freedom's perpetual Spring,
   Our England's faithful fame.

Sing we the Rose,
    That Eastward still shall spread for us
Upon the dawn's bright breast,
    Red leaves wi' the foam impearled;
And onward ever flows
    Till eventide make red for us
A Rose that sinks i' the West
    And surges round the world;
        Sing we the Rose!

One night as, with his great vice-admiral,
Frobisher, his rear-admiral, Francis Knollys,
And Thomas Fenner, his flag-captain, Drake
Took counsel at his tavern, there came a knock,
The door opened, and cold as from the sea
The gloom rushed in, and there against the night,
Clad as it seemed with wind and cloud and rain,
Glittered a courtier whom by face and form
All knew for the age's brilliant paladin,
Sidney, the king of courtesy, a star
Of chivalry. The seamen stared at him,
Each with a hand upon the red-lined chart
Outspread before them. Then all stared at Drake,
Who crouched like a great bloodhound o'er the table,
And rose with a strange light burning in his eyes;
For he remembered how, three years agone,
That other courtier came, with words and smiles
Copied from Sidney's self; and in his ears
Rang once again the sound of the two-edged sword
Upon the desolate Patagonian shore
Beneath Magellan's gallows. With a voice
So harsh himself scarce knew it, he desired
This fair new courtier's errand. With grim eyes
He scanned the silken knight from head to foot,
While Sidney, smiling graciously, besought
Some place in their adventure. Drake's clenched fist
Crashed down on the old oak table like a rock,
Splintering the wood and dashing his rough wrist
With blood, as he thundered, "By the living God,
No! We've no room for courtiers, now! We leave
All that to Spain."

                    Whereat, seeing Sidney stood

Amazed, Drake, drawing nearer, said, "You ask
More than you dream: I know you for a knight
Most perfect and most gentle, yea, a man
Ready to die on any battle-field
To save a wounded friend" (even so said Drake,
Not knowing how indeed this knight would die),
Then fiercely he outstretched his bleeding hand
And pointed through the door to where the gloom
Glimmered with bursting spray, and the thick night
Was all one wandering thunder of hidden seas
Rolling out of Eternity: "You'll find
No purple fields of Arcady out there,
No shepherds piping in those boisterous valleys,
No sheep among those roaring mountain-tops,
No lists of feudal chivalry. I've heard
That voice cry death to courtiers. 'Tis God's voice.
Take you the word of one who has occupied
His business in great waters. There's no room,
Meaning, or reason, office, or place, or name
For courtiers on the sea. Does the sea flatter?
You cannot bribe it, torture it, or tame it!
Its laws are those of the Juggernaut universe,
Remorseless—listen to that!"—a mighty wave
Broke thundering down the coast; "your hands are white,
Your rapier jewelled, can you grapple that?
What part have you in all its flaming ways?
What share in its fierce gloom? Has your heart broken
As those waves break out there? Can you lie down
And sleep, as a lion-cub by the old lion,
When it shakes its mane out over you to hide you,
And leap out with the dawn as I have done?
These are big words; but, see, my hand is red:
You cannot torture me, I have borne all that;
And so I have some kinship with the sea,
Some sort of wild alliance with its storms,
Its exultations, ay, and its great wrath
At last, and power upon them. 'Tis the worse
For Spain. Be counselled well: come not between
My sea and its rich vengeance."
                              Silently,
Bowing his head, Sidney withdrew. But Drake,
So fiercely the old grief rankled in his heart,

Summoned his swiftest horseman, bidding him ride,
Ride like the wind through the night, straight to the Queen,
Praying she would most instantly recall
Her truant courtier.   Nay, to make all sure,
Drake sent a gang of seamen out to crouch
Ambushed in woody hollows nigh the road,
Under the sailing moon, there to waylay
The Queen's reply, that she might never know
It reached him, if it proved against his will.

And swiftly came that truant's stern recall;
But Drake, in hourly dread of some new change
In Gloriana's mood, slept not by night
Or day, till out of roaring Plymouth Sound
The pirate fleet swept to the wind-swept main,
And took the wind and shook out all its sails.
Then with the unfettered sea he mixed his soul
In great rejoicing union, while the ships
Crashing and soaring o'er the heart-free waves
Drave ever straight for Spain.
                              Water and food
They lacked; but the fierce fever of his mind
To sail from Plymouth ere the Queen's will changed
Had left no time for these.   Right on he drave,
Determining, though the Queen's old officers
Beneath him stood appalled, to take in stores
Of all he needed, water, powder, food,
By plunder of Spain herself.   In Vigo bay,
Close to Bayona town, under the cliffs
Of Spain's world-wide and thunder-fraught prestige
He anchored, with the old sea-touch that wakes
Our England still.   There, in the tingling ears
Of the world he cried, *En garde!* to the King of Spain.
There, ordering out his pinnaces in force,
While a great storm, as if he held indeed
Heaven's batteries in reserve, growled o'er the sea,
He landed.   Ere one cumbrous limb of all
The monstrous armaments of Spain could move
His ships were stored; and ere the sword of Spain
Stirred in its crusted sheath, Bayona town

Beheld an empty sea; for like a dream
The pirate fleet had vanished, none knew whither.
But, in its visible stead, invisible fear
Filled the vast rondure of the sea and sky
As with the omnipresent soul of Drake.
For when Spain saw the small black anchored fleet
Ride in her bays, the sight set bounds to fear.
She knew at least the ships were oak, the guns
Of common range: nor did she dream e'en Drake
Could sail two seas at once. Now all her coasts
Heard him all night in every bursting wave,
His topsails gleamed in every moonlit cloud;
His battle-lanthorn glittered in the stars
That hung the low horizon. He became
A universal menace; yet there followed
No sight or sound of him, unless the sea
Were that grim soul incarnate. Did it not roar
His great commands? The very spray that lashed
The cheeks of Spanish seamen lashed their hearts
To helpless hatred of him. The wind sang
El Draque across the rattling blocks and sheets
When storms perplexed them; and when ships went down,
As under the fury of his onsetting battle,
The drowning sailors cursed him while they sank.

Suddenly a rumour shook the Spanish Court,
He has gone once more to the Indies. Santa Cruz,
High Admiral of Spain, the most renowned
Captain in Europe, clamoured for a fleet
Of forty sail instantly to pursue.
For unto him whose little *Golden Hynde*
Was weapon enough, now leading such a squadron,
The West Indies, the whole Pacific coast,
And the whole Spanish Main, lay at his mercy.

And onward over the great grey gleaming sea
Swept like a thunder-cloud the pirate fleet
With vengeance in its heart. Five years agone,
Young Hawkins, in the Cape Verde Islands, met—
At Santiago—with such treachery
As Drake burned to requite, and from that hour

Was Santiago doomed. His chance had come;
Drake swooped upon it, plundered it, and was gone,
Leaving the treacherous isle a desolate heap
Of smoking ashes in the leaden sea,
While onward all those pirate bowsprits plunged
Into the golden West, across the broad
Atlantic once again; "For I will show,"
Said Drake, "that Englishmen henceforth will sail
Old ocean where they will." Onward they surged,
And the great glittering crested majestic waves
Jubilantly rushed up to meet the keels,
And there was nought around them but the grey
Ruin and roar of the huge Atlantic seas,
Grey mounded seas, pursuing and pursued,
That fly, hounded and hounding on for ever,
From empty marge to marge of the grey sky.
Over the wandering wilderness of foam,
Onward, through storm and death, Drake swept; for now
Once more a fell plague gripped the tossing ships,
And not by twos and threes as heretofore
His crews were minished; but in three black days
Three hundred seamen in their shotted shrouds
Were cast into the deep. Onward he swept,
Implacably, having in mind to strike
Spain in the throat at St. Domingo, port
Of Hispaniola, a city of far renown,
A jewel on the shores of old romance,
Palm-shadowed, gated with immortal gold,
Queen city of Spain's dominions over sea,
And guarded by great guns. Out of the dawn
The pirate ships came leaping, grim and black,
And ere the Spaniards were awake, the flag
Of England floated from their topmost tower.
But since he had not troops enough to hold
So great a city, Drake entrenched his men
Within the Plaza and held the batteries.
Thence he demanded ransom, and sent out
A boy with flag of truce. The boy's return
Drake waited long. Under a sheltering palm
He stood, watching the enemies' camp, and lo,
Along the hot white purple-shadowed road

Tow'rds him, a crawling shape writhed through the dust
Up to his feet, a shape besmeared with blood,
A shape that held the stumps up of its wrists
And moaned, an eyeless thing, a naked rag
Of flesh obscenely mangled, a small face
Hideously puckered, shrivelled like a monkey's
With lips drawn backward from its teeth.

> "Speak, speak,
In God's name, speak, what art thou?" whispered Drake,
And a sharp cry came, answering his dread,
A cry as of a sea-bird in the wind
Desolately astray from all earth's shores,
"Captain, I am thy boy, only thy boy!
See, see, my captain, see what they have done!
Captain, I only bore the flag; I only——"

"O, lad, lad, lad," moaned Drake, and, stooping, strove
To pillow the mangled head upon his arm.
"What have they done to thee, what have they done?"
And at the touch the boy screamed, once, and died.

Then like a savage sea with arms uplift
To heaven the wrath of Drake blazed thundering,
"Eternal God, be this the doom of Spain!
Henceforward have no pity. Send the strength
Of Thy great seas into my soul that I
May devastate this empire, this red hell
They make of Thy good earth."

> His men drew round,
Staring in horror at the silent shape
That daubed his feet. Like a cold wind
His words went through their flesh:

> "This is the lad
That bore our flag of truce. This hath Spain done.
Look well upon it, draw the smoke of the blood
Up into your nostrils, my companions,
And down into your souls. This makes an end
For Spain! Bring forth the Spanish prisoners
And let me look on them."

Forth they were brought,
A swarthy gorgeous band of soldiers, priests,
And sailors, hedged between two sturdy files
Of British tars with naked cutlasses.
Close up to Drake they halted, under the palm,
Gay smiling prisoners, for they thought their friends
Had ransomed them. Then they looked up and met
A glance that swept athwart them like a sword,
Making the blood strain back from their blanched faces
Into their quivering hearts, with unknown dread,
As that accuser pointed to the shape
Before his feet.

"Dogs, will ye lap his blood
Before ye die? Make haste; for it grows cold!
Ye will not, will not even dabble your hands
In that red puddle of flesh, what? Are ye Spaniards?
Come, come, I'll look at you, perchance there's one
That's but a demi-devil and holds you back."
And with the word Drake stepped among their ranks
And read each face among the swarthy crew—
The gorgeous soldiers, ringleted sailors, priests
With rosary and cross, a slender page
In scarlet with a cloud of golden hair,
And two rope-girdled friars.

The slim page
Drake drew before the throng. "You are young," he said,
"Go; take this message to the camp of Spain:
Tell them I have a hunger in my soul
To look upon the murderers of this boy,
To see what eyes they have, what manner of mouths,
To touch them and to take their hands in mine,
And draw them close to me and smile upon them
Until they know my soul as I know theirs,
And they grovel in the dust and grope for mercy.
Say that, until I get them, every day
I'll hang two Spaniards though I dispeople
The Spanish Main. Tell them that, every day,
I'll burn a portion of their city down,
Then find another city and burn that,
And then burn others till I burn away
Their empire from the world, ay, till I reach

The imperial throne of Philip with my fires,
And send it shrieking down to burn in hell
For ever.   Go!"
                            Then Drake turned once again
To face the Spanish prisoners.   With a voice
Cold as the passionless utterance of Fate
His grim command went forth.   "Now, provost-marshal,
Begin with yon two friars, in whose faces
Chined like singed swine, and eyed with the spent coals
Of filthy living, sweats the glory of Spain.
Strip off their leprous rags
And twist their ropes around their throats and hang them
High over the Spanish camp for all to see.
At dawn I'll choose two more."

BOOK X

                                        Across the Atlantic

Great rumours rushed as of a mighty wind,
The wind of the spirit of Drake.   But who shall tell
In this cold age the power that he became
Who drew the universe within his soul
And moved with cosmic forces?   Though the deep
Divided it from Drake, the gorgeous court
Of Philip shuddered away from the streaming coasts
As a wind-cuffed field of golden wheat.   The King,
Bidding his guests to a feast in his own ship
On that wind-darkened sea, was made a mock,
As one by one his ladies proffered excuse
For fear of That beyond.   Round Europe now
Ballad and story told how in the cabin
Of Francis Drake there hung a magic glass
Wherein he saw the fleets of every foe
And all that passed aboard them.   Rome herself,
Perplexed that this proud heretic should prevail,
Fostered a darker dream, that Drake had bought,
Like old Norse wizards, power to loose or bind
The winds at will.

                    And now a wilder tale
Flashed o'er the deep—of a distant blood-red dawn
O'er San Domingo, where the embattled troops
Of Spain and Drake were met—but not in war—
Met in the dawn, by his compelling will,
To offer up a sacrifice.   Yea, there
Between the hosts, the hands of Spain herself
Slaughtered the Spanish murderers of the boy
Who had borne Drake's flag of truce; offered them up
As a blood-offering and an expiation
Lest Drake, with that dread alchemy of his soul,
Should e'en transmute the dust beneath their feet
To one same substance with the place of pain
And whelm them suddenly in the eternal fires.
Rumour on rumour rushed across the sea,
Large mockeries, and one most bitter of all,
Wormwood to Philip, of how Drake had stood
I' the governor's house at San Domingo, and seen
A mighty scutcheon of the King of Spain
Whereon was painted the terrestrial globe,
And on the globe a mighty steed in act
To spring into the heavens, and from its mouth
Streaming like smoke a scroll, and on the scroll
Three words of flame and fury—*Non sufficit
Orbis*—of how Drake and his seamen stood
Gazing upon it, and could not forbear
From summoning the Spaniards to expound
Its meaning, whereupon a hurricane roar
Of mirth burst from those bearded British lips,
And that immortal laughter shook the world.

So, while the imperial warrior eyes of Spain
Watched, every hour, her vast Armada grow
Readier to launch and shatter with one stroke
Our island's frail defence, fear gripped her still,
For there came sounds across the heaving sea
Of secret springs unsealed, forces unchained,
A mustering of deep elemental powers,
A sound as of the burgeoning of boughs
In universal April and dead hearts

Uprising from their tombs; a mighty cry
Of resurrection, surging through the souls
Of all mankind.   For now the last wild tale
Swept like another dawn across the deep;
And, in that dawn, men saw the slaves of Spain,
The mutilated negroes of the mines,
With gaunt backs wealed and branded, scarred and seared
By whip and iron, in Spain's brute lust for gold,
Saw them, at Drake's great liberating word,
Burst from their chains, erect, uplifting hands
Of rapture to the glad new light that then,
Then first, began to struggle thro' the clouds
And crown all manhood with a sacred crown
August—a light which, though from age to age
Clouds may obscure it, grows and still shall grow,
Until that Kingdom come, that grand Communion,
That Commonweal, that Empire, which still draws
Nigher with every hour, that Federation,
That turning of the wasteful strength of war
To accomplish large and fruitful tasks of peace,
That gathering up of one another's loads
Whereby the weak are strengthened and the strong
Made stronger in the increasing good of all.
Then, suddenly, it seemed, as he had gone,
A ship came stealing into Plymouth Sound
And Drake was home again, but not to rest;
For scarce had he cast anchor ere the road
To London rang beneath the flying hoofs
That bore his brief despatch to Burleigh, saying—
"We have missed the Plate Fleet by but twelve hours' sail
The reason being best known to God.   No less
We have given a cooling to the King of Spain.
There is a great gap opened which, methinks,
Is little to his liking.   We have sacked
The towns of his chief Indies, burnt their ships,
Captured great store of gold and precious stones,
Three hundred pieces of artillery,
The more part brass.   Our loss is heavy indeed,
Under the hand of God, eight hundred men,
Three parts of them by sickness.   Captain Moone.
My trusty old companion, he that struck

The first blow in the South Seas at a Spaniard,
Died of a grievous wound at Cartagena.
My fleet and I are ready to strike again
At once, where'er the Queen and England please.
I pray for her commands, and those with speed,
That I may strike again."   Outside the scroll
These words were writ once more—"My Queen's commands
I much desire, your servant, Francis Drake."

This terse despatch the hunchback Burleigh read
Thrice over, with the broad cliff of his brow
Bending among his books.   Thrice he assayed
To steel himself with caution as of old;
And thrice, as a glorious lightning running along
And flashing between those simple words, he saw
The great new power that lay at England's hand,
An ocean-sovereignty, a power unknown
Before, but dawning now; a power that swept
All earth's old plots and counterplots away
Like straws; the germ of an unmeasured force
New-born, that laid the source of Spanish might
At England's mercy!   Could that force but grow
Ere Spain should nip it, ere the mighty host
That waited in the Netherlands even now,
That host of thirty thousand men encamped
Round Antwerp, under Parma, should embark
Convoyed by that Invincible Armada
To leap at England's throat!   Thrice he assayed
To think of England's helplessness, her ships
Little and few.   Thrice he assayed to quench
With caution the high furnace of his soul
Which Drake had kindled.   As he read the last
Rough simple plea, *I wait my Queen's commands*,
His deep eyes flashed with glorious tears.

                                        He leapt
To his feet and cried aloud, "Before my God,
I am proud, I am very proud for England's sake!
This Drake is a terrible man to the King of Spain."

And still, still, Gloriana, brooding darkly
On Mary of Scotland's doom, who now at last

Was plucked from out her bosom like a snake
Hissing of war with France, a queenly snake,
A Lilith in whose lovely gleaming folds
And sexual bonds the judgment of mankind
Writhes even yet half-strangled, meting out
Wild execrations on the maiden Queen
Who quenched those jewelled eyes and mixt with dust
That white and crimson, who with cold sharp steel
In substance and in spirit, severed the neck
And straightened out those glittering supple coils
For ever; though for evermore will men
Lie subject to the unforgotten gleam
Of diamond eyes and cruel crimson mouth,
And curse the sword-bright intellect that struck
Like lightning far through Europe and the world
For England, when amid the embattled fury
Of world-wide empires, England stood alone.
Still she held back from war, still disavowed
The deeds of Drake to Spain; and yet once more
Philip, resolved at last never to swerve
By one digressive stroke, one ell or inch
From his own patient, sure, laborious path,
Accepted her suave plea, and with all speed
Pressed on his huge emprise until it seemed
His coasts groaned with grim bulks of cannonry,
Thick loaded hulks of thunder and towers of doom;
And, all round Antwerp, Parma still prepared
To hurl such armies o'er the rolling sea
As in all history hardly the earth herself
Felt shake with terror her own green hills and plains.
I wait my Queen's commands! Despite the plea
Urged every hour upon her with the fire
That burned for action in the soul of Drake,
Still she delayed, till on one darkling eve
She gave him audience in that glimmering room
Where first he saw her. Strangely sounded there
The seaman's rough strong passion as he poured
His heart before her, pleading—"Every hour
Is one more victory lost," and only heard
The bitter answer—"Nay, but every hour
Is a breath snatched from the unconquerable

Doom, that awaits us if we are forced to war.
Yea, and who knows?—though Spain may forge a sword,
Its point is not inevitably bared
Against the breast of England!"   As she spake,
The winds without clamoured with clash of bells,
There was a gleam of torches and a roar—
Mary, the traitress of the North, is dead,
God save the Queen!
                    Her head bent down: she wept.
"Pity me, friend, though I be queen, O yet
My heart is woman, and I am sore pressed
On every side,—Scotland and France and Spain
Beset me, and I know not where to turn."
Even as she spake, there came a hurried step
Into that dim rich chamber.   Walsingham
Stood there, before her, without ceremony
Thrusting a letter forth: "At last," he cried,
"Your Majesty may read the full intent
Of priestly Spain.   Here, plainly written out
Upon this paper, worth your kingdom's crown,
This letter, stolen by a trusty spy,
Out of the inmost chamber of the Pope
Sixtus himself, here is your murder planned:
Blame not your Ministers who with such haste
Plucked out this viper, Mary, from your breast!
Read here—how, with his thirty thousand men,
The pick of Europe, Parma joins the Scots,
While Ireland, grasped in their Armada's clutch,
And the Isle of Wight, against our west and south
Become their base."
                    "Rome, Rome, and Rome again,
And always Rome," she muttered; "even here
In England hath she thousands yet.   She hath struck
Her curse out with pontific finger at me,
Cursed me down and away to the bottomless pit.
Her shadow like the shadow of clouds or sails,
The shadow of that huge event at hand,
Darkens the seas already, and the wind
Is on my cheek that shakes my kingdom down.
She hath thousands here in England, born and bred
Englishmen.   They will stand by Rome!"

"'Fore God,"
Cried Walsingham, "my Queen, you do them wrong!
There is another Rome—not this of Spain
Which lurks to pluck the world back into darkness
And stab it there for gold.   There is a City
Whose eyes are tow'rd the morning; on whose heights
Blazes the Cross of Christ above the world;
A Rome that shall wage warfare yet for God
In the dark days to come, a Rome whose thought
Shall march with our humanity and be proud
To cast old creeds like seed into the ground,
Watch the strange shoots and foster the new flower
Of faiths we know not yet.   Is this a dream?
I speak as one by knighthood bound to speak;
For even this day—and my heart burns with it—
I heard the Catholic gentlemen of England
Speaking in grave assembly.   At one breath
Of peril to our island, why, their swords
Leapt from their scabbards, and their cry went up
To split the heavens—*God save our English Queen!*"
Even as he spake there passed the rushing gleam
Of torches once again, and as they stood
Silently listening, all the winds ran wild
With clamouring bells, and a great cry went up—
God save Elizabeth, our English Queen!

"I'll vouch for some two hundred Catholic throats
Among that thousand," whispered Walsingham
Eagerly, with his eyes on the Queen's face.
Then, seeing it brighten, fervently he cried,
Pressing the swift advantage home, "O, Madam,
The heart of England now is all on fire!
We are one people, as we have not been
In all our history, all prepared to die
Around your throne.   Madam, you are beloved
As never yet was English king or queen!"
She looked at him, the tears in her keen eyes
Glittered—"And I am very proud," she said,
"But if our enemies command the world,
And we have one small island and no more . . ."
She ceased; and Drake, in a strange voice, hoarse and low,

Trembling with passion deeper than all speech,
Cried out—"No more than the great ocean-sea
Which makes the enemies' coast our frontier now;
No more than that great Empire of the deep
Which rolls from Pole to Pole, washing the world
With thunder, that great Empire whose command
This day is yours to take.   Hear me, my Queen,
This is a dream, a new dream, but a true;
For mightier days are dawning on the world
Than heart of man hath known.   If England hold
The sea, she holds the hundred thousand gates
That open to futurity.   She holds
The highway of all ages.   Argosies
Of unknown glory set their sails this day
For England out of ports beyond the stars.
Ay, on the sacred seas we ne'er shall know
They hoist their sails this day by peaceful quays,
Great gleaming wharves in the perfect Cityof God,
If she but claim her heritage."
                                    He ceased;
And the deep dream of that new realm the sea,
Through all the soul of Gloriana surged,
A moment, then with splendid eyes that filled
With fire of sunsets far away, she cried
(Faith making her a child, yet queenlier still)
"Yea, claim it thou for me!"
                                    A moment there
Trembling she stood.   Then, once again, there passed
A rush of torches through the gloom without,
And a great cry *"God save Elizabeth,*
God save our English Queen!"
                                    "Yea go, then, go, "
She said, "God speed you now, Sir Francis Drake,
Not as a privateer, but with full powers,
My Admiral-at-the-Seas!"
                                    Without a word
Drake bent above her hand and, ere she knew it,
His eyes from the dark doorway flashed farewell
And he was gone.   But ere he leapt to saddle
Walsingham stood at his stirrup, muttering "Ride,
Ride now like hell to Plymouth; for the Queen
25

Is hard beset, and ere ye are out at sea
Her mood will change. The friends of Spain will move
Earth and the heavens for your recall. They'll tempt her
With their false baits of peace, though I shall stand
Here at your back through thick and thin; farewell!"
Fire flashed beneath the hoofs and Drake was gone.

Scarce had he vanished in the night than doubt
Once more assailed the Queen. The death of Mary
Had brought e'en France against her. Walsingham,
And Burleigh himself, prime mover of that death,
Being held in much disfavour for it, stood
As helpless. Long ere Drake or human power,
They thought, could put to sea, a courier sped
To Plymouth bidding Drake forbear to strike
At Spain, but keep to the high seas, and lo,
The roadstead glittered empty. Drake was gone!

Gone! Though the friends of Spain had poured their gold
To thin his ranks, and every hour his crews
Deserted, he had laughed—"Let Spain buy scum!
Next to an honest seaman I love best
An honest landsman. What more goodly task
Than teaching brave men seamanship?" He had filled
His ships with soldiers! Out in the teeth of the gale
That raged against him he had driven. In vain,
Amid the boisterous laughter of the quays,
A pinnace dashed in hot pursuit and met
A roaring breaker and came hurtling back
With oars and spars all trailing in the foam,
A tangled mass of wreckage and despair.
Sky swept to stormy sky: no sail could live
In that great yeast of waves; but Drake was gone!

Then, once again, across the rolling sea
Great rumours rushed of how he had sacked the port
Of Cadiz and had swept along the coast
To Lisbon, where the whole Armada lay.
Had snapped up prizes under its very nose,
And taunted Santa Cruz, High Admiral
Of Spain, striving to draw him out for fight,
And offering, if his course should lie that way,

To convoy him to Britain, taunted him
So bitterly that for once, in the world's eyes,
A jest had power to kill; for Santa Cruz
Died with the spleen of it, since he could not move
Before the appointed season.   Then there came
Flying back home, the Queen's old Admiral
Borough, deserting Drake and all aghast
At Drake's temerity: "For," he said, "this man,
Thrust o'er my head, against all precedent,
Bade me follow him into harbour mouths
A-flame with cannon like the jaws of death,
Whereat I much demurred; and straightway Drake
Clapped me in irons, me—an officer
And Admiral of the Queen; and, though my voice
Was all against it, plunged into the pit
Without me, left me with some word that burns
And rankles in me still, making me fear
The man was mad, some word of lonely seas,
A desert island and a mutineer
And dead Magellan's gallows.   Sirs, my life
Was hardly safe with him.   Why, he resolved
To storm the Castle of St. Vincent, sirs,
A castle on a cliff, grinning with guns,
Well known impregnable!   The Spaniards fear
Drake; but to see him land below it and bid
Surrender, sirs, the strongest fort of Spain
Without a blow, they laughed!   And straightway he,
With all the fury of Satan, turned that cliff
To hell itself.   He sent down to the ships
For faggots, broken oars, beams, bowsprits, masts,
And piled them up against the outer gates,
Higher and higher, and fired them.   There he stood
Amid the smoke and flame and cannon-shot,
This Admiral, like a common seamen, black
With soot, besmeared with blood, his naked arms
Full of great faggots, labouring like a giant
And roaring like Apollyon.   Sirs, he is mad!
But did he take it, say you?   Yea, he took it,
The mightiest stronghold on the coast of Spain,
Took it and tumbled all its big brass guns
Clattering over the cliffs into the sea.

But, sirs, ye need not raise a cheer so loud!
It is not warfare.   'Twas a madman's trick,
A devil's!"
                        Then the rumour of a storm
That scattered the fleet of Drake to the four winds
Disturbed the heart of England, as his ships
Came straggling into harbour, one by one,
Saying they could not find him.   Then, at last,
When the storm burst in its earth-shaking might
Along our coasts, one night of rolling gloom
His cannon woke old Plymouth.   In he came
Across the thunder and lightning of the sea
With his grim ship of war and, close behind,
A shadow like a mountain or a cloud
Torn from the heaven-high panoplies of Spain,
A captured galleon loomed, and round her prow
A blazoned scroll, whence (as she neared the quays
Which many a lanthorn swung from brawny fist
Yellowed) the sudden crimson of her name
San Filippe flashed o'er the white sea of faces,
And a rending shout went skyward that outroared
The blanching breakers—" 'Tis the heart of Spain!
The great *San Filippe!*"   Overhead she towered,
The mightiest ship afloat; and in her hold
The riches of a continent, a prize
Greater than earth had ever known; for there
Not only ruby and pearl like ocean-beaches
Heaped on some wizard coast in that dim hull
Blazed to the lanthorn-light; not only gold
Gleamed, though of gold a million would not buy
Her store; but in her cabin lay the charts
And secrets of the wild unwhispered wealth
Of India, secrets that splashed London wharves
With coloured dreams and made her misty streets
Flame like an Eastern City when the sun
Shatters itself on jewelled domes and spills
Its crimson wreckage thro' the silvery palms.
And of those dreams the far East India quest
Began: the first foundation-stone was laid
Of our great Indian Empire, and a star
Began to tremble on the brows of England
That time can never darken.

                              But now the seas
Darkened indeed with menace; now at last
The cold wind of the black approaching wings
Of Azrael crept across the deep: the storm
Throbbed with their thunderous pulse, and ere that moon
Waned, a swift gunboat foamed into the Sound
With word that all the Invincible Armada
Was hoisting sail for England.

                              Even now,
Elizabeth, torn a thousand ways, withheld
The word for which Drake pleaded as for life,
That he might meet them ere they left their coasts,
Meet them or ever they reached the Channel, meet them
Now, or—"Too late!   Too late!"   At last his voice
Beat down e'en those that blindly dinned her ears
With chatter of meeting Spain on British soil;
And swiftly she commanded (seeing once more
The light that burned amid the approaching gloom
In Drake's deep eyes) Lord Howard of Effingham,
High Admiral of England, straight to join him
At Plymouth Sound.   "How many ships are wanted?"
She asked him, thinking "we are few, indeed!"
"Give me but sixteen merchantmen," he said,
"And but four battleships, by the mercy of God,
I'll answer for the Armada!"   Out to sea
They swept, in the teeth of a gale; but vainly Drake
Strove to impart the thought wherewith his mind
Travailed—to win command of the ocean-sea
By bursting on the fleets of Spain at once
Even as they left their ports, not as of old
To hover in a vain dream of defence
Round fifty threatened points of British coast,
But Howard, clinging to his old-world order,
Flung out his ships in a loose, long, straggling line
Across the Channel, waiting, wary, alert,
But powerless thus as a string of scattered sea-gulls
Beating against the storm.   Then, flying to meet them,
A merchantman brought terror down the wind,
With news that she had seen that monstrous host
Stretching from sky to sky, great hulks of doom,
Dragging death's midnight with them o'er the sea

Tow'rds England.   Up to Howard's flag-ship Drake
In his immortal battle-ship—*Revenge*,
Rushed thro' the foam, and thro' the swirling seas
His pinnace dashed alongside.   On to the decks
O' the tossing flag-ship, like a very Viking
Shaking the surf and rainbows of the spray
From sun-smit lion-like mane and beard he stood
Before Lord Howard in the escutcheoned poop
And poured his heart out like the rending sea
In passionate wave on wave:
                              "If yonder fleet
Once reach the Channel, hardly the mercy of God
Saves England!   I would pray with my last breath,
Let us beat up to windward of them now,
And handle them before they reach the Channel."
"Nay; but we cannot bare the coast," cried Howard,
"Nor have we stores of powder or food enough!"
"My lord," said Drake, with his great arm outstretched,
"There is food enough in yonder enemy's ships,
And powder enough and cannon-shot enough!
We must re-victual there.   Look! look!" he cried,
And pointed to the heavens.   As for a soul
That by sheer force of will compels the world
To work his bidding, so it seemed the wind
That blew against them slowly veered.   The sails
Quivered, the skies revolved.   A northerly breeze
Awoke and now, behind the British ships,
Blew steadily tow'rds the unseen host of Spain.
"It is the breath of God," cried Drake; "they lie
Wind-bound, and we may work our will with them.
Signal the word, Lord Howard, and drive down!"
And as a man convinced by heaven itself
Lord Howard ordered, straightway, the whole fleet
To advance.
                 And now, indeed, as Drake foresaw,
The Armada lay, beyond the dim horizon,
Wind-bound and helpless in Corunna bay,
At England's mercy, could her fleet but draw
Nigh enough, with its fire-ships and great guns
To windward.   Nearer, nearer, league by league
The ships of England came; till Ushant lay

Some seventy leagues behind.   Then, yet once more
The wind veered, straight against them.   To remain
Beating against it idly was to starve:
And, as a man whose power upon the world
Fails for one moment of exhausted will,
Drake, gathering up his forces as he went
For one more supreme effort, turned his ship
Tow'rds Plymouth, and retreated with the rest.

There, while the ships refitted with all haste
And axe and hammer rang, one golden eve
Just as the setting sun began to fringe
The clouds with crimson, and the creaming waves
Were one wild riot of fairy rainbows, Drake
Stood with old comrades on the close-cropped green
Of Plymouth Hoe, playing a game of bowls.
Far off unseen, a little barque, full-sail,
Struggled and leapt and strove tow'rds Plymouth Sound,
Noteless as any speckled herring-gull
Flickering between the white flakes of the waves.
A group of schoolboys with their satchels lay
Stretched on the green, gazing with great wide eyes
Upon their seamen heroes, as like gods
Disporting with the battles of the world
They loomed, tossing black bowls like cannon-balls
Against the rosy West, or lounged at ease
With faces olive-dark against that sky
Laughing, while from the neighboring inn mine host,
White aproned and blue-jerkined, hurried out
With foaming cups of sack, and they drank deep,
Tossing their heads back under the golden clouds
And burying their bearded lips.   The hues
That slashed their doublets, for the boy's bright eyes
(Even as the gleams of Grecian cloud or moon
Revealed the old gods) were here rich dusky streaks
Of splendour from the Spanish Main, that shone
But to proclaim these heroes.   There a boy
More bold crept nearer to a slouched hat thrown
Upon the green, and touched the silver plume,
And felt as if he had touched a sunset-isle
Of feathery palms beyond a crimson sea.

Another stared at the blue rings of smoke
A storm-scarred seaman puffed from a long pipe
Primed with the strange new herb they had lately found
In far Virginia.   But the little ship
Now plunging into Plymouth Bay none saw.
E'en when she had anchored and her straining boat
Had touched the land, and the boat's crew over the quays
Leapt with a shout, scarce was there one to heed.
A seaman, smiling, swaggered out of the inn
Swinging in one brown hand a gleaming cage
Wherein a big green parrot chattered and clung
Fluttering against the wires.   A troop of girls
With arms linked paused to watch the game of bowls;
And now they flocked around the cage, while one
With rosy finger tempted the horny beak
To bite.   Close overhead a sea-mew flashed
Seaward.   Once, from an open window, soft
Through trellised leaves, not far away, a voice
Floated, a voice that flushed the cheek of Drake,
The voice of Bess, bending her glossy head
Over the broidery frame, in a quiet song.

The song ceased.   Still, with rainbows in their eyes,
The schoolboys watched the bowls like cannon-balls
Roll from the hand of gods along the turf.

Suddenly, tow'rds the green, a little cloud
Of seamen, shouting, stumbling, as they ran
Drew all eyes on them.   The game ceased.   A voice
Rough with the storms of many an ocean roared
"Drake!   Cap'en Drake!   The Armada!
They are in the Channel!   We sighted them—
A line of battleships!   We could not see
An end of them.   They stretch from north to south
Like a great storm of clouds, glinting with guns,
From sky to sky!"
                       So, after all his strife,
The wasted weeks had tripped him, the fierce hours
Of pleading for the sea's command, great hours
And golden moments, all were lost.   The fleet
Of Spain had won the Channel without a blow.

All eyes were turned on Drake, as he stood there
A giant against the sunset and the sea
Looming, alone.   Far off, the first white star
Gleamed in a rosy space of heaven.   He tossed
A grim black ball i' the lustrous air and laughed,—
"Come, lads," he said, "we've time to finish the game"

BOOK XI

FEW minutes, and well wasted those, were spent
On that great game of bowls; for well knew Drake
What panic threatened Plymouth, since his fleet
Lay trapped there by the black head-wind that blew
Straight up the Sound, and Plymouth town itself,
Except the ships won seaward ere the dawn,
Lay at the Armada's mercy.   Never a seaman
Of all the sea-dogs clustered on the quays,
And all the captains clamouring round Lord Howard,
Hoped that one ship might win to the open sea:
At dawn, they thought, the Armada's rolling guns
To windward, in an hour, must shatter them,
Huddled in their red slaughter-house like sheep.

Now was the great sun sunken and the night
Dark.   Far to Westward, like the soul of man
Fighting blind nature, a wild flare of red
Upon some windy headland suddenly leapt
And vanished flickering into the clouds.   Again
It leapt and vanished: then all at once it streamed
Steadily as a crimson torch upheld
By Titan hands to heaven.   It was the first
Beacon!   A sudden silence swept along
The seething quays, and in their midst appeared
Drake.
              Then the jubilant thunder of his voice
Rolled, buffeting the sea-wind far and nigh,
And ere they knew what power as of a sea
Surged through them, his immortal battle-ship
Revenge had flung out cables to the quays,

And while the seamen, as he had commanded,
Knotted thick ropes together, he stood apart
(For well he knew what panic threatened still)
Whittling idly at a scrap of wood,
And carved a little boat out for the child
Of some old sea-companion.
So great and calm a master of the world
Seemed Drake that, as he whittled, and the chips
Fluttered into the blackness over the quay,
Men said that in this hour of England's need
Each tiny flake turned to a battle-ship;
For now began the lanthorns, one by one,
To glitter, and half-reveal the shadowy hulks
Before him.—So the huge old legend grew,
Not all unworthy the Homeric age
Of gods and god-like men.
                                    St. Michael's Mount,
Answering the first wild beacon far away,
Rolled crimson thunders to the stormy sky!
The ropes were knotted.   Through the panting dark
Great heaving lines of seamen all together
Hauled with a shout, and all together again
Hauled with a shout against the roaring wind;
And slowly, slowly, onward tow'rds the sea
Moved the *Revenge*, and seaward ever heaved
The brawny backs together, and in their midst,
Suddenly, as they slackened, Drake was there
Hauling like any ten, and with his heart
Doubling the strength of all, giving them joy
Of battle against those odds,—ay, till they found
Delight in the burning tingle of the blood
That even their hardy hands must feel besmear
The harsh, rough, straining ropes.   There as they toiled,
Answering a score of hills, old Beachy Head
Streamed like a furnace to the rolling clouds
Then all around the coast each windy ness
And craggy mountain kindled.   Peak from peak
Caught the tremendous fire, and passed it on
Round the bluff East and the black mouth of Thames,—
Up, northward to the waste wild Yorkshire fells
And gloomy Cumberland, where, like a giant,

Great Skiddaw grasped the red tempestuous brand,
And thrust it up against the reeling heavens.
Then all night long, inland, the wandering winds
Ran wild with clamour and clash of startled bells;
All night the cities seethed with torches, flashed
With twenty thousand flames of burnished steel;
While over the trample and thunder of hooves blazed forth
The lightning of wild trumpets.   Lonely lanes
Of country darkness, lit by cottage doors
Entwined with rose and honeysuckle, roared
Like mountain-torrents now—East, West, and South,
As to the coasts with pike and musket streamed
The trained bands, horse and foot, from every town
And every hamlet.   All the shaggy hills
From Milford Haven to the Downs of Kent,
And up to Humber, gleamed with many a hedge
Of pikes between the beacon's crimson glares;
While in red London forty thousand men,
In case the Invader should prevail, drew swords
Around their Queen.   All night in dark St. Paul's,
While round it rolled a multitudinous roar
As of the Atlantic on a Western beach,
And all the leaning London streets were lit
With fury of torches, rose the passionate prayer
Of England's peril:

O Lord God of Hosts,
Let Thine enemies know that Thou hast taken
England into Thine hands!

                              The mighty sound
Rolled, billowing round the kneeling aisles, then died,
Echoing up the heights.   A voice, far off,
As on the cross of Calvary, caught it up
And poured the prayer o'er that deep hush, alone:
We beseech Thee, O God, to go before our armies,
Bless and prosper them both by land and sea!
Grant unto them Thy victory, O God,
As Thou usedst to do to Thy children when they please Thee!
All power, all strength, all victory come from Thee!
Then from the lips of all those thousands burst
A sound as from the rent heart of an ocean,
One tumult, one great rushing storm of wings

Cleaving the darkness round the Gates of Heaven:
Some put their trust in chariots and some in horses;
But we will remember Thy name, O Lord our God!

So, while at Plymouth Sound her seamen toiled
All through the night, and scarce a ship had won
Seaward, the heart of England cried to God.
All night, while trumpets yelled and blared without,
And signal cannon shook the blazoned panes,
And billowing multitudes went thundering by,
Amid that solemn pillared hush arose
From lips of kneeling thousands one great prayer
Storming the Gates of Heaven!   *O Lord, our God,*
Heavenly Father, have mercy upon our Queen,
To whom Thy far dispersèd flock do fly
In the anguish of their souls.   Behold, behold,
How many princes band themselves against her,
How long Thy servant hath laboured to them for peace,
How proudly they prepare themselves for battle!
Arise, therefore!   Maintain Thine own cause,
Judge Thou between her and her enemies!
She seeketh not her own honour, but Thine,
Not the dominions of others, but Thy truth,
Not bloodshed but the saving of the afflicted!
O rend the heavens, therefore, and come down,
Deliver Thy people!
To vanquish is all one with Thee, by few
Or many, want or wealth, weakness or strength.
The cause is Thine, the enemies Thine, the afflicted
Thine!   The honour, victory, and triumph
Thine!   Grant her people now one heart, one mind,
One strength.   Give unto her councils and her captains
Wisdom and courage strongly to withstand
The forces of her enemies, that the fame
And glory of Thy Kingdom may be spread
Unto the ends of the world.   Father, we crave
This in Thy mercy, for the precious death
Of Thy dear Son, our Saviour, Jesus Christ!
Amen.
And as the dreadful dawn thro' mist-wreaths broke,
And out of Plymouth Sound at last, with cheers

Ringing from many a thousand throats, there struggled
Six little ships, all that the night's long toil
Had warped down to the sea (but leading them
The ship of Drake) there rose one ocean-cry
From all those worshippers—*Let God arise,*
And let His enemies be scattered!

Under the leaden fogs of that new dawn,
Empty and cold, indifferent as death,
The sea heaved strangely to the seamen's eyes,
Seeing all round them only the leaden surge
Wrapped in wet mists or flashing here and there
With crumbling white.   Against the cold wet wind
Westward the little ships of England beat
With short tacks, close inshore, striving to win
The windward station of the threatening battle
That neared behind the veil.   Six little ships,
No more, beat Westward, even as all mankind
Beats up against that universal wind
Whereon like withered leaves all else is blown
Down one wide way to death: the soul alone,
Whether at last it wins, or faints and fails,
Stems the dark tide with its intrepid sails.
Close-hauled, with many a short tack, struggled and strained,
North-west, South-west, the ships; but ever Westward gained
Some little way with every tack; and soon,
While the prows plunged beneath the grey-gold noon,
Lapped by the crackling waves, even as the wind
Died down a little, in the mists behind
Stole out from Plymouth Sound the struggling score
Of ships that might not win last night to sea.
They followed; but the Six went on before,
Not knowing, alone, for God and Liberty.

Now, as they tacked North-west, the sullen roar
    Of reefs crept out, or some strange tinkling sound
Of sheep upon the hills.   South-west once more
    The bo'sun's whistle swung their bowsprits round;

South-west until the long low lapping splash
　　Was all they heard, of keels that still ran out
Seaward, then with one muffled heave and crash
　　Once more the whistles brought their sails about.

And now the noon began to wane; the west
　　With slow rich colours filled and shadowy forms,
Dark curdling wreaths and fogs with crimsoned breast,
　　And tangled zones of dusk like frozen storms,

Motionless, flagged with sunset, hulled with doom!
　　Motionless?　Nay, across the darkening deep
Surely the whole sky moved its gorgeous gloom
　　Onward; and like the curtains of a sleep

The red fogs crumbled, mists dissolved away!
　　There, like death's secret dawning thro' a dream,
Great thrones of thunder dusked the dying day,
　　And, higher, pale towers of cloud began to gleam.

There, in one heaven-wide storm, great masts and clouds
　　Of sail crept slowly forth, the ships of Spain!
From North to South, their tangled spars and shrouds
　　Controlled the slow wind as with bit and rein;
Onward they rode in insolent disdain
　　Sighting the little fleet of England there,
While o'er the sullen splendour of the main
　　Three solemn guns tolled all their host to prayer,
And their great ensign blazoned all the doom-fraught **air**.

The sacred standard of their proud crusade
　　Up to the mast-head of their flag-ship soared:
On one side knelt the Holy Mother-maid,
　　On one the crucified Redeemer poured
His blood, and all their kneeling hosts adored
　　Their saints, and clouds of incense heavenward **streamed**,
While pomp of cannonry and pike and sword
　　Down long sea-lanes of mocking menace gleamed,
And chant of priests rolled out o'er seas that darkly **dreamed**.

Who comes to fight for England? Is it ye,
  Six little straws that dance upon the foam?
Ay, sweeping o'er the sunset-crimsoned sea
  Let the proud pageant in its glory come,
Leaving the sunset like a hecatomb
  Of souls whose bodies yet endure the chain!
Let slaves, by thousands, branded, scarred and dumb,
  In those dark galleys grip their oars again,
And o'er the rolling deep bring on the pomp of Spain;—

Bring on the pomp of royal paladins
  (For all the princedoms of the land are there!)
And for the gorgeous purple of their sins
  The papal pomp bring on with psalm and prayer:
Nearer the splendour heaves; can ye not hear
  The rushing foam, not see the blazoned arms,
And black-faced hosts thro' leagues of golden air
  Crowding the decks, muttering their beads and charms
To where, in furthest heaven, they thicken like locust-swarms?

Bring on the pomp and pride of old Castille,
  Blazon the skies with royal Aragon,
Beneath Oquendo let old Castille reel.
  The purple pomp of priestly Rome bring on;
And let her censers dusk the dying sun,
  The thunder of her banners on the breeze
Following Sidonia's glorious galleon
  Deride the sleeping thunder of the seas,
While twenty thousand warriors chant her litanies.

Lo, all their decks are kneeling!   Sky to sky
  Responds!   It is their solemn evening hour.
SALVE REGINA, though the daylight die,
  SALVE REGINA, though the darkness lour;
Have they not still the kingdom and the power?
  SALVE REGINA, hark, their thousands cry,
From where like clouds to where like mountains tower
  Their crowded galleons looming far or nigh,
SALVE REGINA, hark, what distant seas reply!

What distant seas, what distant ages hear?
  Bring on the pomp! the sun of Spain goes down:
The moon but swells the tide of praise and prayer;
  Bring on the world-wide pomp of her renown;
Let darkness crown her with a starrier crown,
  And let her watch the fierce waves crouch and fawn
Round those huge hulks from which her cannon frown,
  While close inshore the wet sea-mists are drawn
Round England's Drake: then wait, in triumph, for the dawn.

The sun of Rome goes down; the night is dark!
  Still are her thousands praying, still their cry
Ascends from the wide waste of waters, hark!
  AVE MARIA, darker grows the sky!
AVE MARIA, *those about to die*
  Salute thee!   Nay, what wandering winds blaspheme
With random gusts of chilling prophecy
  Against the solemn sounds that heavenward stream!
The night is come at last.   Break not the splendid dream.

        But through the misty darkness, close inshore,
        North-west, South-west, and ever Westward strained
        The little ships of England.   All night long,
        As down the coast the reddening beacons leapt,
        The crackle and lapping splash of tacking keels,
        The bo'suns' low sharp whistles and the whine
        Of ropes, mixing with many a sea-bird's cry
        Disturbed the darkness, waking vague swift fears
        Among the mighty hulks of Spain that lay
        Nearest, then fading through the mists inshore
        North-west, then growing again, but farther down
        Their ranks to Westward with each dark return
        And dark departure, till the rearmost rank
        Of grim sea-castles heard the swish and creak
        Pass plashing seaward thro' the wet sea-mists
        To windward now of all that monstrous host,
        Then heard no more than wandering sea-birds' cries
        Wheeling around their leagues of lanthorn-light,
        Or heave of waters, waiting for the dawn.

Dawn, everlasting and almighty dawn
  Rolled o'er the waters.   The grey mists were fled.
See, in their reeking heaven-wide crescent drawn
  Those masts and spars and cloudy sails, outspread
Like one great sulphurous tempest soaked with red,
  In vain withstand the march of brightening skies:
The dawn sweeps onward and the night is dead,
  And lo, to windward, what bright menace lies,
What glory kindles now in England's wakening eyes?

There, on the glittering plains of open sea,
  To windward now, behind the fleets of Spain,
Two little files of ships are tossing free,
  Free of the winds and of the wind-swept main:
Were they not trapped?   Who brought them forth again,
  Free of the great new fields of England's war,
With sails like blossoms shining after rain,
  And guns that sparkle to the morning star?
Drake!—first upon the deep that rolls to Trafalgar!

And Spain knows well that flag of fiery fame,
  Spain knows who leads those files across the sea;
Implacable, invincible, his name
  El Draque, creeps hissing through her ranks to lee;
But now she holds the rolling heavens in fee,
  His ships are few.   *They surge across the foam,*
The hunt is up!   But need the mountains flee
  Or fear the snarling wolf-pack?   Let them come!
They crouch, but dare not leap upon the flanks of Rome.

Nearer they come and nearer!   Nay, prepare!
  Close your huge ranks that sweep from sky to sky!
Madness itself would shrink; but Drake will dare
  Eternal hell!   Let the great signal fly—
Close up your ranks; El Draque comes down to die!
  El Draque is brave!   The vast sea-cities loom
Thro' heaven: Spain spares one smile of chivalry,
  One wintry smile across her cannons' gloom
As that frail fleet full-sail comes rushing tow'rds its doom.
  26

Suddenly, as the wild change of a dream,
Even as the Spaniards watched those lean sharp prows
Leap straight at their huge hulks, watched well content,
Knowing their foes, once grappled, must be doomed;
Even as they caught the rush and hiss of foam
Across that narrow, dwindling gleam of sea,
And heard, abruptly close, the sharp commands
And steady British answers, caught one glimpse
Of bare-armed seamen waiting by their guns,
The vision changed!   The ships of England swerved
Swiftly—a volley of flame and thunder swept
Blinding the buffeted air, a volley of iron
From four sheer broadsides, crashing thro' a hulk
Of Spain.   She reeled, blind in the fiery surge
And fury of that assault.   So swift it seemed
That as she heeled to leeward, ere her guns
Trained on the foe once more, the sulphurous cloud
That wrapped the sea, once, twice, and thrice again
Split with red thunder-claps that rent and raked
Her huge beams through and through.   Ay, as she heeled
To leeward still, her own grim cannon belched
Their lava skyward, wounding the void air,
And, as by miracle, the ships of Drake
Were gone.   Along the Spanish rear they swept
From North to South, raking them as they went
At close range, hardly a pistol-shot away,
With volley on volley.   Never Spain had seen
Seamen or marksmen like to these who sailed
Two knots against her one.   They came and went,
Suddenly neared or sheered away at will
As if by magic, pouring flame and iron
In four full broadsides thro' some Spanish hulk
Ere one of hers burst blindly at the sky.
Southward, along the Spanish rear they swept,
Then swung about, and volleying sheets of flame,
Iron, and death, along the same fierce road
Littered with spars, reeking with sulphurous fumes,
Returned, triumphantly rushing, all their sails
Alow, aloft, full-bellied with the wind.

Then, then, from sky to sky, one mighty surge
    Of baleful pride, huge wrath, stormy disdain,
With shuddering clouds and towers of sail would urge
    Onward the heaving citadels of Spain,
Which dragged earth's thunders o'er the groaning main,
    And held the panoplies of faith in fee,
Beating against the wind, struggling in vain
    To close with that swift ocean-cavalry:
Spain had all earth in charge!   Had England, then, the sea?

Spain had the mountains—mountains flow like clouds.
    Spain had great kingdoms—kingdoms melt away!
Yet, in that crescent, army on army crowds,
    How shall she fear what seas or winds can say?—
The seas that leap and shine round earth's decay,
    The winds that mount and sing while empires fall,
And mountains pass like waves in the wind's way,
    And dying gods thro' shuddering twilights call.
Had England, then, the sea that sweeps o'er one and all?

See, in gigantic wrath the *Rata* hurls
    Her mighty prows round to the wild sea-wind:
The deep like one black maelstrom round her swirls
    While great Recaldé follows hard behind:
Reeling, like Titans, thunder-blasted, blind,
    They strive to cross the ships of England—yea,
Challenge them to the grapple, and only find
    Red broadsides bursting o'er the bursting spray,
And England surging still along her windward way!

To windward still *Revenge* and *Raleigh* flash
    And thunder, and the sea flames red between:
In vain against the wind the galleons crash
    And plunge and pour blind volleys thro' the screen
Of rolling sulphurous clouds at dimly seen
    Topsails that, to and fro, like sea-birds fly!
Ever to leeward the great hulks careen;
    Their thousand cannon can but wound the sky,
While England's little *Rainbow* foams and flashes by.

Suddenly the flag-ship of Recaldé, stung
To fury it seemed, heeled like an avalanche
To leeward, then reeled out beyond the rest
Against the wind, alone, daring the foe
To grapple her.   At once the little *Revenge*
With Drake's flag flying flashed at her throat,
And hardly a cable's-length away out-belched
Broadside on broadside, under those great cannon,
Crashing through five-foot beams, four shots to one,
While Howard and the rest swept to and fro
Keeping at deadly bay the rolling hulks
That looming like Leviathans now plunged
Desperately against the freshening wind
To rescue the great flag-ship where she lay
Alone, amid the cannonades of Drake,
Alone, like a volcanic island lashed
With crimson hurricanes, dinning the winds
With isolated thunders, flaking the skies
With wrathful lava, while great spars and blocks
Leapt through the cloudy glare and fell, far off,
Like small black stones into the hissing sea.

Oquendo saw her peril far away!
   His rushing prow thro' heaven begins to loom,
Oquendo, first in all that proud array,
   Hath heart the pride of Spain to reassume:
He comes; the rolling seas are dusked with gloom
   Of his great sails!   Now round him once again,
Thrust out your oars, ye mighty hulks of doom;
   Forward, with hiss of whip and clank of chain!
Let twice ten hundred slaves bring on the wrath of Spain!

Sidonia comes!   Toledo comes!—huge ranks
   That rally against the storm from sky to sky,
As down the dark blood-rusted chain-locked planks
   Of labouring galleys the dark slave-guards ply
Their knotted scourges, and the red flakes fly
   From bare scarred backs that quiver and heave once more,
And slaves that heed not if they live or die
   Pull with numb arms at many a red-stained oar,
Nor know the sea's dull crash from cannon's growing roar.

Bring on the wrath!   From heaven to rushing heaven
  The white foam sweeps around their fierce array;
In vain before their shattering crimson levin
  The ships of England flash and dart away:
Not England's heart can hold that host at bay!
  See, a swift signal shoots along her line,
Her ships are scattered, they fly, they fly like spray
  Driven against the wind by wrath divine,
While, round Recaldé now, Sidonia's cannon shine.

The wild sea-winds with golden trumpets blaze!
  One wave will wash away the crimson stain
That blots Recaldé's decks.   Her first amaze
  Is over: down the Channel once again
Turns the triumphant pageantry of Spain
  In battle-order, now.   Behind her, far,
While the broad sun sinks to the Western main,
  Glitter the little ships of England's war,
And over them in heaven glides out the first white star.

The sun goes down: the heart of Spain is proud:
  Her censers fume, her golden trumpets blow!
Into the darkening East with cloud on cloud
  Of broad-flung sail her huge sea-castles go:
Rich under blazoned poops like rose-flushed snow
  Tosses the foam.   Far off the sunset gleams:
Her banners like a thousand sunsets glow,
  As down the darkening East the pageant streams,
Full-fraught with doom for England, rigged with princely
        dreams.

Nay, "rigged with curses dark," as o'er the waves
Drake watched them slowly sweeping into the gloom
That thickened down the Channel, watched them go
In ranks compact, roundels impregnable,
With Biscay's bristling broad-beamed squadron drawn
Behind for rear-guard.   As the sun went down
Drake flew the council-flag.   Across the sea
That gleamed still like a myriad-petalled rose
Up to the little *Revenge* the pinnaces foamed.

There, on Drake's powder-grimed escutcheoned poop
They gathered, Admirals and great flag-captains,
Hawkins, Frobisher, shining names and famous,
And some content to serve and follow and fight
Where duty called unknown, but heroes all.
High on the poop they clustered, gazing East
With faces dark as iron against the flame
Of sunset, eagle-faces, iron lips,
And keen eyes fiercely flashing as they turned
Like sword-flames now, or dark and deep as night
Watching the vast Armada slowly mix
Its broad-flung sails with twilight where it dragged
Thro' thickening heavens its curdled storms of clouds
Down the wide darkening Channel.

                             "My Lord Howard,"
Said Drake, "it seems we have but scarred the skins
Of those huge hulks: the hour grows late for England.
'Twere well to handle them again at once." A growl
Of fierce approval answered; but Lord Howard
Cried out, "Attack we cannot, save at risk
Of our whole fleet. It is not death I fear,
But England's peril. We have fought all day,
Accomplished nothing. Half our powder is spent!
I think it best to hang upon their flanks
Till we be reinforced."

                        "My lord," said Drake,
"Had we that week to spare for which I prayed,
And were we handling them in Spanish seas,
We might delay. There is no choosing now.
Yon hulks of doom are steadfastly resolved
On one tremendous path and solid end—
To join their powers with Parma's thirty thousand
(Not heeding our light horsemen of the sea),
Then in one earthquake of o'erwhelming arms
Roll Europe over England. They've not grasped
The first poor thought which now and evermore
Must be the sceptre of Britain, the steel trident
Of ocean-sovereignty. That mighty fleet
Invincible, impregnable, omnipotent,
Must here and now be shattered, never be joined
With Parma, never abase the wind-swept sea,

With oaken roads for thundering legions
To trample in the splendour of the sun
From Europe to our island.

                As for food,
In yonder enemy's fleet there is food enough
To feed a nation; ay, and powder enough
To split an empire. I will answer for it
Ye shall not lack of either, nor for shot,
Not though ye pluck them out of your own beams
To feed your hungry cannon. Cast your bread
Upon the waters. Think not of the Queen!
She will not send it! For she hath not known
(How could she know?) this wide new realm of hers,
When we ourselves—her seamen—scarce have learnt
What means this kingdom of the ocean-sea
To England and her throne—food, life-blood, life!
She could not understand who, when our ships
Put out from Plymouth, hardly gave them store
Of powder and shot to last three fighting days,
Or rations even for those. Blame not the Queen,
Who hath striven for England as no king hath fought
Since England was a nation. Bear with me,
For I must pour my heart before you now
This one last time. Yon fishing-boats have brought
Tidings how on this very day she rode
Before her mustered pikes at Tilbury.
Methinks I see her riding down their lines
High on her milk-white Barbary charger, hear
Her voice—'My people, though my flesh be woman,
My heart is of your kingly lion's breed:
I come myself to lead you!' I see the sun
Shining upon her armour, hear the voice
Of all her armies roaring like one sea—
God save Elizabeth, our English Queen!
'God save her,' I say, too; but still she dreams,
As all too many of us—bear with me!—dream,
Of Crécy, when our England's war was thus;
When we, too, hurled our hosts across the deep
As now Spain dreams to hurl them on our isle.
But now our war is otherwise. We claim
The sea's command, and Spain shall never land

One swordsman on our island.   Blame her not,
But look not to the Queen.   The people fight
This war of ours, not princes.   In this hour
God maketh us a people.   We have seen
Victories, never victory like to this,
When in our England's darkest hour of need
Her seamen, without wage, powder, or food,
Are yet on fire to fight for her.   Your ships
Tossing in the great sunset of an Empire,
Dawn of a sovereign people, are all manned
By heroes, raggèd, hungry, who will die
Like flies ere long, because they have no food
But turns to fever-breeding carrion
Not fit for dogs.   They are half-naked, hopeless
Living, of any reward; and if they die
They die a dog's death.   We shall reap the fame
While they—great God! and all this cannot quench
The glory in their eyes.   They will be served
Six at the mess of four, eking it out
With what their own rude nets may catch by night,
Silvering the guns and naked arms that haul
Under the stars with silver past all price,
While some small ship-boy in the black crow's nest
Watches across the waters for the foe.
My lord, it is a terrible thing for Spain
When poor men thus go out against her princes;
For so God whispers 'Victory' in our ears,
I cannot dare to doubt it."
                                        Once again
A growl of fierce approval answered him,
And Hawkins cried—"I stand by Francis Drake";
But Howard, clinging to his old-world order,
Yet with such manly strength as dared to rank
Drake's wisdom of the sea above his own,
Sturdily shook his head.   "I dare not risk
A close attack.   Once grappled we are doomed.
We'll follow on their trail no less, with Drake
Leading.   Our oriflamme to-night shall be
His cresset and stern-lanthorn.   Where that shines
We follow."

Drake, still thinking in his heart,—
"And if Spain be not shattered here and now
We are doomed no less," must even rest content
With that good vantage.

                                    As the sunset died
Over the darkling emerald seas that swelled
Before the freshening wind, the pinnaces dashed
To their own ships; and into the mind of Drake
There stole a plot that twitched his lips to a smile.
High on the heaving purple of the poop
Under the glimmer of firm and full-blown sails
He stood, an iron statue, glancing back
Anon at his stern-cresset's crimson flare,
The star of all the shadowy ships that plunged
Like ghosts amid the grey stream of his wake,
And all around him heard the low keen song
Of hidden ropes above the wail and creak
Of blocks and long low swish of cloven foam,
A keen rope-music in the formless night,
A harmony, a strong intent good sound,
Well-strung and taut, singing the will of man.
"Your oriflamme," he muttered,—"so you travail
With sea-speech in the tongue of old Poictiers—
Shall be my own stern-lanthorn.   Watch it well,
My good Lord Howard."

                                    Over the surging seas
The little *Revenge* went swooping on the trail,
Leading the ships of England.   One by one
Out of the gloom before them slowly crept,
Sinister gleam by gleam, like blood-red stars,
The rearmost lanthorns of the Spanish Fleet,
A shaggy purple sky of secret storm
Heaving from north to south upon the black
Breast of the waters.   Once again with lips
Twitched to a smile, Drake suddenly bade them crowd
All sail upon the little *Revenge*.   She leapt
Forward.   Smiling he watched the widening gap
Between the ships that followed and her light,
Then as to those behind, its flicker must seem
Wellnigh confused with those of Spain, he cried,
"Now, master bo'sun, quench their oriflamme,

Dip their damned cresset in the good black Sea!
The rearmost light of Spain shall lead them now,
A little closer, if they think it ours.
Pray God, they come to blows!"

                        Even as he spake
His cresset-flare went out in the thick night:
A fluttering as of blind bewildered moths
A moment seized upon the shadowy ships
Behind him, then with crowded sail they steered
Straight for the rearmost cresset-flare of Spain.

BOOK XII

MEANWHILE, as in the gloom he slipped aside
Along the Spanish ranks, waiting the crash
Of battle, suddenly Drake became aware
Of strange sails bearing up into the wind
Around his right, and thought, "the Armada strives
To weather us in the dark."   Down went his helm,
And all alone the little *Revenge* gave chase,
Till as the moon crept slowly forth, she stood
Beside the ghostly ships, only to see
Bewildered Flemish merchantmen, amazed
With fears of Armageddon—such vast shrouds
Had lately passed them on the rolling seas.
Down went his helm again, with one grim curse
Upon the chance that led him thus astray;
And down the wind the little *Revenge* once more
Swept on the trail.   Fainter and fainter now
Glared the red beacons on the British coasts,
And the wind slackened and the glimmering East
Greyed and reddened, yet Drake had not regained
Sight of the ships.   When the full glory of dawn
Dazzled the sea, he found himself alone,
With one huge galleon helplessly drifting
A cable's-length away.   Around her prow,
Nuestra Señora del Rosario,
Richly emblazoned, gold on red, proclaimed
The flagship of great Valdes, of the fleet
Of Andalusia, captain-general.   She,

Last night, in dark collision with the hulks
Of Spain, had lost her foremast.   Through the night
Her guns, long rank on deadly rank, had kept
All enemies at bay.   Drake summoned her
Instantly to surrender.   She returned
A scornful answer from the glittering poop
Where two-score officers crowned the golden sea
And stained the dawn with blots of richer colour
Loftily clustered in the glowing sky,
Doubleted with cramoisy velvet, wreathed
With golden chains, blazing with jewelled swords
And crusted poignards.   "What proud haste was this?"
They asked, glancing at their huge tiers of cannon
And crowded decks of swarthy soldiery;
"What madman in yon cockle-shell defied
Spain?"
          "Tell them it is El Draque," he said, "who lacks
The time to parley; therefore it will be well
They strike at once, for I am in great haste."
There, at the sound of that renownèd name,
Without a word down came their blazoned flag.
Like a great fragment of the dawn it lay
Crumpled upon their decks. . . .

Into the soft bloom and Italian blue
Of sparkling, ever-beautiful Torbay,
Belted as with warm Mediterranean crags,
The little *Revenge* foamed with her mighty prize,
A prize indeed—not for the casks of gold
Drake split in the rich sunlight and poured out
Like dross amongst his men, but in her hold
Lay many tons of powder, worth their weight
In rubies now to Britain.   Into the hands
Of swarthy Brixham fishermen he gave
Prisoners and prize, then—loaded stem to stern
With powder and shot—their swiftest trawlers flew
Like falcons following a thunder-cloud
Behind him, as with crowded sail he rushed
On England's trail once more.   Like a caged lion
Drake paced his deck, praying he yet might reach
The fight in time; and ever the warm light wind

Slackened.   Not till the sun was half-way fallen
Once more crept out in front those dusky thrones
Of thunder, heaving on the smooth bright sea
From North to South with Howard's clustered fleet
Like tiny clouds, becalmed, not half a mile
Behind the Spaniards.   For the breeze had failed
Their blind midnight pursuit; and now attack
Seemed hopeless.   Even as Drake drew nigh, the last
Breath of the wind sank.   One more day had flown,
Nought was accomplished; and the Armada lay
Some leagues of golden sea-way nearer now
To its great goal.   The sun went down: the moon
Rose glittering.   Hardly a cannon-shot apart
The two fleets lay becalmed upon the silver
Swell of the smooth night-tide.   The hour had come
For Spain to strike.   The ships of England drifted
Helplessly, at the mercy of those great hulks
Oared by their thousand slaves.

                    Onward they came,
Swinging suddenly in tremendous gloom
Over the silver seas.   But even as Drake,
With eyes on fire at last for his last fight,
Measured the distance ere he gave the word
To greet it with his cannon, suddenly
The shining face of the deep began to shiver
With dusky patches: the doomed English sails
Quivered and, filling smart from the North-east,
The little *Revenge* rushed down their broken line
Signalling them to follow, and ere they knew
What miracle had saved them, they all sprang
Their luff and ran large out to sea.   For now
The Armada lay to windward, and to fight
Meant to be grappled and overwhelmed; but dark
Within the mind of Drake, a fiercer plan
Already had shaped itself.

                  "They fly!   They fly!"
Rending the heavens from twice ten thousand throats
A mighty shout rose from the Spanish Fleet.
Over the moonlit waves their galleons came
Towering, crowding, plunging down the wind
In full chase, while the tempter, Drake, laughed low

To watch their solid battle-order break
And straggle. When once more the golden dawn
Dazzled the deep, the labouring galleons lay
Scattered by their unequal speed. The wind
Veered as the sun rose. Once again the ships
Of England lay to windward. Down swooped Drake
Where like a mountain the *San Marcos* heaved
Her giant flanks alone, having out-sailed
Her huge companions. Then the sea-winds blazed
With broadsides. Two long hours the sea flamed red
All round her. One by one the Titan ships
Came surging to her rescue, and met the buffet
Of battle-thunders, belching iron and flame;
Nor could they pluck her forth from that red chaos
Till great Oquendo hurled his mighty prows
Crashing athwart those thunders, and once more
Gathered into unshakeable battle-order
The whole Armada raked the reeking seas.
Then up the wind the ships of England sheered
Once more, and one more day drew to its close,
With little accomplished, half their powder spent,
And all the Armada moving as of old,
From sky to sky one heaven-wide zone of storm,
(Though some three galleons out of all their host
Laboured woundily) down the darkening Channel.
And all night long on England's guardian heights
The beacons reddened, and all the next long day
The impregnable Armada never swerved
From its tremendous path. In vain did Drake,
Frobisher, Hawkins, Howard, greatest names
In all our great sea-history, hover and dart
Like falcons round the mountainous array.
Till now, as night fell and they lay abreast
Of the Isle of Wight, once more the council flag
Flew from the little *Revenge*. With iron face
Thrust close to Howard's, and outstretched iron arm,
Under the stars Drake pointed down the coast
Where the red beacons flared. "The shoals," he hissed,
"The shoals from Owers to Spithead and the net
Of channels yonder in Portsmouth Roads. At dawn
They'll lie to leeward of the Invincible
Fleet!"

Swiftly, in mighty sweeping lines Drake set
Before the council his fierce battle-plan
To drive the Armada down upon the banks
And utterly shatter it—stroke by well-schemed stroke
As he unfolded there his vital plot
And touched their dead cold warfare into life
Where plan before was none, he seemed to tower
Above them, clad with the deep night of stars;
And those that late would rival knew him now,
In all his great simplicity, their king,
One of the gods of battle, England's Drake,
A soul that summoned Cæsar from his grave,
And swept with Alexander o'er the deep.

So when the dawn thro' rolling wreaths of cloud
Struggled, and all the waves were molten gold,
The heart of Spain exulted, for she saw
The little fleet of England cloven in twain
As if by some strange discord.   A light breeze
Blew from the ripening East; and, up against it,
Urged by the very madness of defeat,
Or so it seemed, one half the British fleet
Drew nigh, towed by their boats, to challenge the vast
Tempest-winged heaving citadels of Spain,
At last to the murderous grapple; while far away
Their other half, led by the flag of Drake,
Stood out to sea, as if to escape the doom
Of that sheer madness, for the light wind now
Could lend them no such wings to hover and swoop
As heretofore.   Nearer the mad ships came
Towed by their boats, till now upon their right
To windward loomed the Fleet Invincible
With all its thunder-clouds, and on their left
To leeward, gleamed the perilous white shoals
With their long level lightnings under the cliffs
Of England, from the green glad garden of Wight
To the Owers and Selsea Bill.   Right on they came,
And suddenly the wrench of thundering cannon
Shook the vast hulks that towered above them.   Red
Flamed the blue sea between.   Thunder to thunder
Answered, and still the ships of Drake sped out

To the open sea.   Sidonia saw them go,
Furrowing the deep that like a pale-blue shield
Lay diamond-dazzled now in the full light.
Rich was the omen of that day for Spain,
The feast-day of Sidonia's patron-saint!
And the priests chanted and the trumpets blew
Triumphantly!   A universal shout
Went skyward from the locust-swarming decks,
A shout that rent the golden morning clouds
From heaven to menacing heaven, as castle to castle
Flew the great battle-signal, and like one range
Of moving mountains, those almighty ranks
Swept down upon the small forsaken ships!
The lion's brood was in the imperial nets
Of Spain at last.   Onward the mountains came
With all their golden clouds of sail and flags
Like streaming cataracts; all their glorious chasms
And glittering steeps, echoing, re-echoing,
Calling, answering, as with the herald winds
That blow the golden trumpets of the morning
From Skiddaw to Helvellyn.   In the midst
The great *San Martin* surged with heaven-wide press
Of proudly billowing sail; and yet once more
Slowly, solemnly, like another dawn
Up to her mast-head soared in thunderous gold
The sacred standard of their last crusade;
While round a hundred prows that heaved thro' heaven
Like granite cliffs, their black wet shining flanks,
And swept like moving promontories, rolled
The splendid long-drawn thunders of the foam,
And flashed the untamed white lightnings of the sea
Back to a morn unhalyarded of man,
Back to the unleashed sun and blazoned clouds
And azure sky—the unfettered flag of God.

Like one huge moving coast-line on they came
    Crashing, and closed the ships of England round
With one fierce crescent of thunder and sweeping flame,
    One crimson scythe of Death, whose long sweep drowned
The eternal ocean with its mighty sound,

From heaven to heaven, one roar, one glitter of doom.
While out to the sea-line's blue remotest bound
    The ships of Drake still fled, and the red fume
Of battle thickened and shrouded shoal and sea with gloom.

The distant sea, the close white menacing shoals
    Are shrouded!   And the lion's brood fight on!
And now death's very midnight round them rolls;
    Rent is the flag that late so proudly shone!
The red decks reel and their last hope seems gone!
    Round them they still keep clear one ring of sea:
It narrows; but the lion's brood fight on,
    Ungrappled still, still fearless and still free,
While the white menacing shoals creep slowly out to lee.

Now through the red rents of each fire-cleft cloud,
    High o'er the British blood-greased decks flash out
Thousands of swarthy faces, crowd on crowd
    Surging, with one tremendous hurricane shout
On, to the grapple! and still the grim redoubt
    Of the oaken bulwarks rolls them back again,
As buffeted waves that shatter in the furious bout
    When cannonading cliffs meet the full main
And hurl it back in smoke—so Britain hurls back Spain;

Hurls her back, only to see her return,
    Darkening the heavens with billow on billow of sail:
Round that huge storm the waves like lava burn,
    The daylight withers, and the sea-winds fail!
Seamen of England, what shall now avail
    Your naked arms?   Before those blasts of doom
The sun is quenched, the very sea-waves quail:
    High overhead their triumphing thousands loom,
When hark! what low deep guns to windward suddenly boom?

What low deep strange new thunders far away
    Respond to the triumphant shout of Spain?
Is it the wind that shakes their giant array?
    Is it the deep wrath of the rising main?
Is it—*El Draque?* El Draque! Ay, shout again,
    His thunders burst upon your windward flanks;

The shoals creep out to leeward! Is it plain
  At last, what earthquake heaves your herded ranks
Huddled in huge dismay tow'rds those white foam-swept
      banks?

Plain, it was plain at last, what cunning lured,
What courage held them over the jaws o' the pit,
Till Drake could hurl them down.   The little ships
Of Howard and Frobisher, towed by their boats,
Slipped away in the smoke, while out at sea
Drake, with a gale of wind behind him, crashed
Volley on volley into the helpless rear
Of Spain and drove it down, huddling the whole
Invincible Fleet together upon the verge
Of doom.   One awful surge of stormy wrath
Heaved thro' the struggling citadels of Spain.
From East to West their desperate signal flew,
And like a drove of bullocks, with the foam
Flecking their giant sides, they staggered and swerved,
Careening tow'rds the shallows as they turned,
Then in one wild stampede of sheer dismay
Rushed, tacking seaward, while the grey sea-plain
Smoked round them, and the cannonades of Drake
Raked their wild flight; and the crusading flag,
Tangled in one black maze of crashing spars,
Whirled downward like the pride of Lucifer
From heaven to hell.

             Out tow'rds the coasts of France
They plunged, narrowly weathering the Ower banks;
Then, once again, they formed in ranks compact,
Roundels impregnable, wrathfully bent at last
Never to swerve again from their huge path
And solid end—to join with Parma's host,
And hurl the whole of Europe on our isle.
Another day was gone, much powder spent;
And, while Lord Howard exulted and conferred
Knighthoods on his brave seamen, Drake alone
Knew that his mighty plan, in spite of all,
Had failed, knew that wellnigh his last great chance
Was lost of wrecking the Spaniards ere they joined
Parma.   The night went by, and the next day,

With scarce a visible scar the Invincible Fleet
Drew onwards tow'rds its goal, unshakeable now
In that grim battle-order.   Beacons flared
Along the British coast, and pikes flashed out
All night, and a strange dread began to grip
The heart of England, as it seemed the might
Of seamen most renowned in all the world
Checked not that huge advance.   Yet at the heart
Of Spain no less there clung a vampire fear
And strange foreboding, as the next day passed
Quietly, and behind her all day long
The shadowy ships of Drake stood on her trail
Quietly, patiently, as death or doom,
Unswerving and implacable.

                        While the sun
Sank thro' long crimson fringes on that eve,
The fleets were passing Calais and the wind
Blew fair behind them.   A strange impulse seized
Spain to shake off those bloodhounds from her trail,
And suddenly the whole Invincible Fleet
Anchored, in hope the following wind would bear
The ships of England past and carry them down
To leeward.   But their grim insistent watch
Was ready; and though their van had wellnigh crashed
Into the rear of Spain, in the golden dusk,
They, too, a cannon-shot away, at once
Anchored, to windward still.

                        Quietly heaved
The golden sea in that tremendous hour
Fraught with the fate of Europe and mankind,
As yet once more the flag of council flew,
And Hawkins, Howard, Frobisher, and Drake
Gathered together upon the little *Revenge*,
While like a triumphing fire the news was borne
To Spain, already, that the Invincible Fleet
Had reached its end, ay, and "that great black dog
Sir Francis Drake" was writhing now in chains
Beneath the torturer's hands.

                        High on his poop
He stood, a granite rock, above the throng
Of captains, there amid the breaking waves

Of clashing thought and swift opinion,
Silent, gazing where now the cool fresh wind
Blew steadily up the terrible North Sea
Which rolled under the clouds into a gloom
Unfathomable.   Once only his lips moved
Half-consciously, breathing those mighty words,
The clouds His chariot! Then, suddenly, he turned
And looked upon the little flock of ships
That followed on the fleet of England, sloops
Helpless in fight.   These, manned by the brave zeal
Of many a noble house, from hour to hour
Had plunged out from the coast to join his flag.
"Better if they had brought us powder and food
Than sought to join us thus," he had growled; but now
"Lord God," he cried aloud, "they'll light our road
To victory yet!"   And in great sweeping strokes
Once more he drew his mighty battle-plan
Before the captains.   In the thickening gloom
They stared at his grim face as at a man
Risen from hell, with all the powers of hell
At his command, a face tempered like steel
In the everlasting furnaces, a rock
Of adamant, while with a voice that blent
With the ebb and flow of the everlasting sea
He spake, and at the low deep menacing words
Monotonous with the unconquerable
Passion and level strength of his great soul
They shuddered; for the man seemed more than man,
And from his iron lips resounded doom
As from the lips of cannon, doom to Spain,
Inevitable, unconquerable doom.

And through that mighty host of Spain there crept
    Cold winds of fear, as to the darkening sky
Once more from lips of kneeling thousands swept
    The vespers of an Empire—one vast cry,
SALVE REGINA! God, what wild reply
    Hissed from the clouds in that dark hour of dreams?
AVE MARIA, *those about to die*
    Salute thee! See, what ghostly pageant streams
Above them?   What thin hands point down like pale moon-
          beams?

Thick as the ghosts that Dante saw in hell
  Whirled on the blast thro' boundless leagues of pain,
Thick, thick as wind-blown leaves innumerable,
  In the Inquisition's yellow robes her slain
And tortured thousands, dense as the red rain
  That wellnigh quenched her fires, went hissing by
With twisted shapes, raw from the racks of Spain,
  SALVE REGINA!—rushing thro' the sky,
And pale hands pointing down and lips that mocked her cry.

Ten thousand times ten thousand!—what are these
  That are arrayed in yellow robes and sweep
Between your prayers and God like phantom seas
  Prophesying over your masts?   Could Rome not keep
The keys?   Who loosed these dead to break your sleep?
  SALVE REGINA, cry, yea, cry aloud,
AVE MARIA!   Ye have sown: shall ye not reap?
  SALVE REGINA!   Christ, what fiery cloud
Suddenly rolls to windward, high o'er mast and shroud?

Are hell-gates burst at last?   For the black deep
  To windward burns with streaming crimson fires!
Over the wild strange waves, they shudder and creep
  Nearer—strange smoke-wreathed masts and spars, red
        spires
And blazing hulks, vast roaring blood-red pyres,
  Fierce as the flames ye fed with flesh of men
Amid the imperial pomp and chanting choirs
  Of Alva—from El Draque's red hand again
Sweep the wild fire-ships down upon the Fleet of Spain.

Onward before the freshening wind they come
  Full fraught with all the terrors, all the bale
That flamed so long for the delight of Rome,
  The shrieking fires that struck the sunlight pale,
The avenging fires at last!   Now what avail
  Your thousand ranks of cannon?   Swift, cut free,
Cut your scorched cables!   Cry, reel backward, quail,
  Crash your huge huddled ranks together, flee!
Behind you roars the fire, before—the dark North Sea!

* * * * * * * * * * * *

Dawn, everlasting and omnipotent
Dawn rolled in crimson o'er the spar-strewn waves,
As the last trumpet shall in thunder roll
O'er heaven and earth and ocean.   Far away,
The ships of Spain, great raggèd piles of gloom
And shaggy splendour, leaning to the North
Like sun-shot clouds confused, or rent apart
In scattered squadrons, furiously plunged,
Burying their mighty prows i' the broad grey rush
Of smoking billowy hills, or heaving high
Their giant bowsprits to the wandering heavens,
Labouring in vain to return, struggling to lock
Their far-flung ranks anew, but drifting still
To leeward, driven by the ever-increasing storm
Straight for the dark North Sea.   Hard by there lurched
One gorgeous galleon on the ravening shoals,
Feeding the white maw of the famished waves
With gold and purple webs from kingly looms
And spilth of world-wide empires.   Howard, still
Planning to pluck the Armada plume by plume,
Swooped down upon that prey and swiftly engaged
Her desperate guns; while Drake, our ocean-king,
Knowing the full worth of that doom-fraught hour,
Glanced neither to the left nor right, but stood
High on his poop, with calm implacable face
Gazing as into eternity, and steered
The crowded glory of his dawn-flushed sails
In superb onset, straight for the great fleet
Invincible; and after him the main
Of England's fleet, knowing its captain now,
Followed, and with them rushed—from sky to sky
One glittering charge of wrath—the storm's white waves,
The twenty thousand foaming chariots
Of God.
              None but the everlasting voice
Of him who fought at Salamis might sing
The fight of that dread Sabbath.   Not mankind
Waged it alone.   War raged in heaven that day,
Where Michael and his angels drave once more
The hosts of darkness ruining down the abyss

Of chaos. Light against darkness, Liberty
Against all dark old despotism, unsheathed
The sword in that great hour. Behind the strife
Of men embattled deeps beyond all thought
Moved in their awful panoply, as move
Silent, invisible, swift, under the clash
Of waves and flash of foam, huge ocean-glooms
And vast reserves of inappellable power.
The bowsprits ranked on either fore-front seemed
But spear-heads of those dread antagonists
Invisible: the shuddering sails of Spain
Dusk with the shadow of death, the sunward sails
Of England full-fraught with the breath of God.
Onward the ships of England and God's waves
Triumphantly charged, glittering companions,
And poured their thunders on the extreme right
Of Spain, whose giant galleons as they lurched
Heavily to the roughening sea and wind
With all their grinding, wrenching cannon, worked
On rolling platforms by the helpless hands
Of twenty thousand soldiers, without skill
In stormy seas, rent the indifferent sky
Or tore the black troughs of the swirling deep
In vain, while volley on volley of flame and iron
Burst thro' their four-foot beams, fierce raking blasts
From ships that came and went on wings of the wind
All round their mangled bulk, scarce a pike's thrust
Away, sweeping their decks from stem to stern
(Between the rush and roar of the great green waves)
With crimson death, rending their timbered towns
And populous floating streets into wild squares
Of slaughter and devastation; driving them down,
Huddled on their own centre, cities of shame
And havoc, in fiery forests of tangled wrath,
With hurricanes of huge masts and swarming spars
And multitudinous decks that heaved and sank
Like earthquake-smitten palaces, when doom
Comes, with one stride, across the pomp of kings.
All round them shouted the everlasting sea,
Burst in white thunders on the streaming poops

And blinded fifty thousand eyes with spray.
Once, as a gorgeous galleon, drenched with blood
Began to founder and settle, a British captain
Called from his bulwarks, bidding her fierce crew
Surrender and come aboard.   Straight through the heart
A hundred muskets answered that appeal.
Sink or destroy!   The deadly signal flew
From mast to mast of England.   Once, twice, thrice,
A huge sea-castle heaved her haggled bulk
Heavenward, and with a cry that rent the heavens
From all her crowded decks, and one deep roar
As of a cloven world or the dark surge
Of chaos yawning, sank: the swirling slopes
Of the sweeping billowy hills for a moment swarmed
With struggling insect-men, sprinkling the foam
With tossing arms; then the indifferent sea
Rolled its grey smoking waves across the place
Where they had been.   Here a great galleasse poured
Red rivers through her scuppers and torn flanks,
And there a galleon, wrapped in creeping fire,
Suddenly like a vast volcano split
Asunder, and o'er the vomiting sulphurous clouds
And spouting spread of crimson, flying spars
And heads torn from their trunks and scattered limbs
Leapt, hideous gouts of death, against the glare.
Hardly the thrust of a pike away, the ships
Of England flashed and swerved, till in one mass
Of thunder-blasted splendour and shuddering gloom
Those gorgeous floating citadels huddled and shrank
Their towers, and all the glory of dawn that rolled
And burned along the tempest of their banners
Withered, as on a murderer's face the light
Withers before the accuser.   All their proud
Castles and towers and heaven-wide clouds of sail
Shrank to a darkening horror, like the heart
Of Evil, plucked from midnight's fiercest gloom,
With all its curses quivering and alive;
A horror of wild masts and tangled spars,
Like some great kraken with a thousand arms
Torn from the filthiest cavern of the deep,

Writhing, and spewing forth its venomous fumes
On every side. *Sink or destroy!*—all day
The deadly signal flew; and ever the sea
Swelled higher, and the flashes of the foam
Broadened and leapt and spread as a wild white fire
That flourishes with the wind; and ever the storm
Drave the grim battle onward to the wild
Menace of the dark North Sea. At set of sun,
Even as below the sea-line the broad disc
Sank like a red-hot cannon-ball through scurf
Of seething molten lead, the *Santa Maria*
Uttering one cry that split the heart of heaven
Went down with all hands, roaring into the dark.
Hardly five rounds of shot were left to Drake!
Gun after gun fell silent, as the night
Deepened—"Yet we must follow them to the North,"
He cried, "or they'll return yet to shake hands
With Parma! Come, we'll put a brag upon it,
And hunt them onward as we lacked for nought!"
So, when across the swinging smoking seas,
Grey and splendid and terrible broke the day
Once more, the flying Invincible fleet beheld
Upon their weather-beam, and dogging them
Like their own shadow, the dark ships of Drake,
Unswerving and implacable. Ever the wind
And sea increased; till now the heaving deep
Swelled all around them into sulky hills
And rolling mountains, whose majestic crests,
Like wild white flames far blown and savagely flickering
Swept thro' the clouds; and, on their vanishing slopes,
Past the pursuing fleet began to swirl
Scores of horses and mules, drowning or drowned,
Cast overboard to lighten the wild flight
Of Spain, and save her water-casks, a trail
Telling of utmost fear. And ever the storm
Roared louder across the leagues of rioting sea,
Driving her onward like a mighty stag
Chased by the wolves. Off the dark Firth of Forth
At last, Drake signalled and lay head to wind,
Watching. "The chariots of God are twenty thousand,"

He muttered, as, for a moment close at hand,
Caught in some league-wide whirlpool of the sea,
The mighty galleons crowded and towered and plunged
Above him on the huge o'erhanging billows,
As if to crash down on his decks; the next,
A mile of ravening sea had swept between
Each of those wind-whipt straws and they were gone,
With all their tiny shrivelling scrolls of sail,
Through roaring deserts of embattled death,
Where like a hundred thousand chariots charged
With lightnings and with thunders, the great deep
Hurled them away to the North.   From sky to sky
One blanching bursting storm of infinite seas
Followed them, broad white cataracts, hills that grasped
With struggling Titan hands at reeling heavens,
And roared their doom-fraught greetings from Cape Wrath
Round to the Bloody Foreland.
                              There should the yeast
Of foam receive the purple of many kings,
And the grim gulfs devour the blood-bought gold
Of Aztecs and of Incas, and the reefs,
League after league, bristle with mangled spars,
And all along their coasts the murderous kerns
Of Catholic Ireland strip the gorgeous silks
And chains and jewel-encrusted crucifixes
From thousands dead, and slaughter thousands more
With gallow-glass axes as they blindly crept
Forth from the surf and jagged rocks to seek
Pity of their own creed.
                         To meet that doom
Drake watched their sails go shrivelling, till the last
Flicker of spars vanished as a skeleton leaf
Upon the blasts of winter, and there was nought
But one wide wilderness of splendour and gloom
Under the northern clouds.
                           "Not unto us,"
Cried Drake, "not unto us—but unto Him
Who made the sea, belongs our England now!
Pray God that heart and mind and soul we prove
Worthy among the nations of this hour

And this great victory, whose ocean fame
Shall wash the world with thunder till that day
When there is no more sea, and the strong cliffs
Pass like a smoke, and the last peal of it
Sounds thro' the trumpet."
                                    So, with close-hauled sails,
Over the rolling triumph of the deep,
Lifting their hearts to heaven, they turned back home.

990